Komm mit!®

Testing Program

HOLT, RINEHART AND WINSTON

A Harcourt Classroom Education Company

Austin · New York · Orlando · Atlanta · San Francisco · Boston · Dallas · Toronto · London

Contributing Writers

Helen Becker
Phyllis Manning
Renate Wise

Cover Photo/Illustration Credits
Group of students: George Winkler/HRW Photo
KOMM MIT! is a trademark licensed to Holt, Rinehart and Winston, registered in the United States of America and/or other jurisdictions.

Printed in the United States of America

ISBN 0-03-065581-1

2 3 4 5 6 7   066   05 04 03

Contents

Chapter Quizzes and Tests

Speaking Tests

To the Teacher

The *Komm mit! Testing Program* contains the following assessment materials: quizzes, Chapter Tests, and Speaking Tests. For other assessment options, such as performance assessment or portfolio suggestions, see the *Alternative Assessment Guide*. The *Testing Program* is organized by chapter, and each chapter contains these components:

- **Quizzes (Prüfungen)** Six quizzes accompany each chapter, two quizzes for each **Stufe**. Each is short enough to be administered within approximately 20 minutes, leaving ample time for other activities. The first quiz for each **Stufe** (Quiz A) focuses on the grammar and vocabulary for that section of the chapter. These Grammar and Vocabulary quizzes principally test writing and reading skills, and feature more discrete-point, closed-ended assessment. They may be used for evaluation, or as review in preparation for the second quiz in each **Stufe** and the Chapter Tests. The second **Stufe** quiz (Quiz B) assesses listening, reading, and writing skills as well as culture, using a combination of closed and open-ended formats. Listening and reading sections evaluate comprehension of the **Stufe** material, while the writing portion asks students to express themselves in real-life situations. You will find the listening section of each **Stufe** quiz (Quiz B) recorded on the *Audio Compact Discs* for the corresponding chapter. The scripts and answers to all the quizzes are also included in the *Testing Program.* For ease in grading, the total point value for three quizzes, one from each **Stufe**, equals 100. The Grammar and Vocabulary quiz for each **Stufe** usually has the same point value as its Quiz B counterpart, allowing you to choose to administer either of the two quizzes in any given **Stufe**.

- **Chapter Tests (Klassenarbeiten)** The Chapter Tests for Chapters 1–12 include listening, reading, writing, and culture segments. They are designed to be completed in one class period. Score sheets are provided with the tests, as well as listening scripts and answer keys. With the exception of the writing and some culture segments, the Chapter Tests are designed to facilitate mechanical or electronic scoring. You will find the listening segments of the Chapter Tests recorded on the *Audio Compact Discs* for the corresponding chapter.

- **Midterm and Final Exams (längere Klassenarbeiten)** The Midterm Exam is a comprehensive exam covering material from Chapters 1–6, while the Final Exam focuses on material from Chapters 7–12. These exams evaluate listening, reading, writing, and culture. As in the Chapter Tests, the listening, reading, and some of the culture sections are designed to facilitate mechanical or electronic scoring. Score sheets, scripts, and answers are provided for both exams. You will find the listening portions of these exams on *Audio Compact Discs* 6 and 12, respectively.

- **Speaking Tests (mündliche Prüfungen)** There is one Speaking Test for each chapter. For more detailed suggestions on administering and grading these tests, see "To the Teacher" and the rubrics on pages 341 and 342 of this book.

Name _____ Klasse _____ Datum _____

Bei den Baumanns

Quiz 1-1A

■ Erste Stufe

Maximum Score: 35

Grammar and Vocabulary

A. Respond to the following questions and commands, using the English words as cues. (9 points)

Beschreibe deinen Bruder! (17 years old, slender, has blond hair and green eyes)

1. _____

Wie charakterisierst du deine Schwester? (intelligent, hard-working, funny)

2. _____

Was machst du gern? (cooking and fencing, but not sledding)

3. _____

SCORE _____

B. A friend of yours is writing to a pen pal in Germany, and needs your help with vocabulary. Complete the following paragraph, using the words in the box below. (8 points)

| Langstreckenlauf | 100-Meter-Lauf | Weitsprung | Leichtathletik |
| Speerwerfen | Hürdenlauf | Stabhochsprung | Kugelstoßen |

Meine Kusine ist sehr sportlich, und macht 4. _____ (track and field)

sehr gern. Sie hat den 5. _____ (long-distance run) am liebsten, und

ist auch sehr gut im 6. _____ (hurdling). Sie findet aber das

7. _____ (javelin throw) und den 8. _____

(long jump) gar nicht so einfach. Ich mag den 9. _____ (pole vault)

am liebsten, aber dabei habe ich oft Pech. Mein Cousin ist der beste Läufer in seiner

Mannschaft; im 10. _____ (100-yard dash) hat er den Rekord. Er hat

auch Erfolg beim 11. _____ (shot put).

SCORE _____

C. Complete the following statements and questions, using the verbs in parentheses as prompts. (10 points)

(sprechen) Meine Schwester 12. _____ jetzt über ihre Lieblingsfächer.

(geben) 13. _____ du ihm ein Poster zum Geburtstag?

(nehmen) Sein Bruder 14. _____ ein Stück Kuchen.

(wissen) Meine Kusine 15. _____ nicht, wo das Rathaus ist.

(fahren) Nach der Schule 16. _____ mein Cousin nach Salzburg.

(essen) Was 17. _____ du da? Pralinen?

(sehen) Mein Opa 18. _____ nicht mehr gut.

(lesen) Eure Tante 19. _____ sehr gern, nicht wahr?

(einladen) Der Hans 20. _____ uns alle 21. _____ .

SCORE [   ]

D. Express the following sentences in German, using the English statements as cues. (8 points)

Jürgen was in a bad mood yesterday, but today he is in a good mood.

22. _____

_____

Read the book! It's really good. (Use the **du**-form of the command.)

23. _____

_____

Is he talking about his grandmother?

24. _____

_____

She is pleasant, but lazy.

25. _____

_____

SCORE [   ]

TOTAL SCORE [   ]

Bei den Baumanns

■ Erste Stufe

Quiz 1-1B

Maximum Score: 30

I. Listening

A. Alex is showing his classmate, Jutta, some of his family photos. As you listen to a description of Alex's sister Kati, write any key words you hear in each of the categories below. The first category has been done for you as an example. (8 points)

Kati:

1. Aussehen: *hübsch; schlank*

2. Haare: _____

3. Augen: _____

4. Eigenschaft(en): _____

SCORE ☐

II. Reading

B. Read the following ad that Bernd wrote for a pen pal. He heard from three students and chose one of them based on interests they had in common. Which one did he choose? Give two reasons in English for your choice, based directly on evidence from these readings. (6 points)

> Gesucht: BRIEFFREUND/IN
> für Realschüler, 15 Jahre, vollschlank, mittellange Haare, trägt Kontaktlinsen. Lustiger, neugieriger Typ, Umweltfreund, tierlieb aber unsportlich.
> Interessen: fotografieren, malen, Musik hören (besonders Jazz).
> Adresse: Bernd Steiner, D-70192 Stuttgart, Rafelweg 16

Responses:

Andrea: Ein sehr hübsches sechzehnjähriges Mädchen, das in einem Vorort von Seattle wohnt. Sie ist in der Schule sehr fleißig und sammelt in der Freizeit gern Briefmarken und Münzen. Sie ist Mitglied in einem Briefmarkenverein.

Guy: Ein siebzehnjähriger Junge aus Denver. Er hat kurze Haare, ist groß und schlank und ein super Basketballspieler. Er spielt in einer Schulmannschaft. Er macht auch gerne Leichtathletik. Seine Lieblingsmusik ist Rock 'n Roll.

Bea: Ein vierzehnjähriges Mädchen aus Boston. Sie ist groß und vollschlank und trägt eine Brille. In Musik und Kunst hat sie sehr gute Noten. Sie spielt ganz gut Klarinette und auch Saxophon. Sie sammelt Poster von Reitpferden und ist Mitglied im „World Wildlife Fund".

KAPITEL 1

Quiz 1-1B

5. For Bernd's pen pal, I chose _____ because:

6. _____

_____

7. _____

_____

SCORE ☐

III. Writing

C. You are an exchange student in Germany, and you are going over to your friend Jochen's house for the first time. Write a connected, friendly conversation using the following lines. (16 points)

8.   DU _____

JOCHEN   Ich wohne in Roxel, das ist ein Vorort von Münster. Komm, ich nehme dich auf

meinem Moped mit!

[Zu Hause bei Jochen]

9.   DU _____

JOCHEN   Das Mädchen auf dem Foto? Das ist meine Schwester Simone.

10.   DU _____

JOCHEN   Ja, ich hab sogar zwei Brüder, Hannes und Norbert.

11.   DU _____

JOCHEN   Hannes ist schon neunzehn und studiert an der Uni, und Norbert ist siebzehn.

SCORE ☐

TOTAL SCORE ☐

Bei den Baumanns

Quiz 1-2A

Maximum Score: 35

■ Zweite Stufe

Grammar and Vocabulary

A. For each word listed below, supply the German equivalent. Don't forget to include the articles and plural forms! (8 points)

earring   **1.** _____   headband   **5.** _____

scarf   **2.** _____   cap   **6.** _____

bracelet   **3.** _____   handbag   **7.** _____

hat   **4.** _____   necklace   **8.** _____

SCORE ☐

B. For each sentence below, replace the underlined word with the appropriate pronoun. (6 points)

Der Gürtel ist schick.   **9.** _____

Er braucht die Kugelschreiber für die Schule.   **10.** _____

Ich meine, dass das Hemd preiswert ist.   **11.** _____

Sie möchte diese Jacke nicht.   **12.** _____

Wir brauchen das Geschenk für unsere Oma.   **13.** _____

Ja, ich suche den Taschenrechner.   **14.** _____

SCORE ☐

C. Rearrange the following words to form logical questions and statements. Be sure to use the correct forms of the verbs and the appropriate articles. (12 points)

(der) Pulli / stark / finden / er

15. _____

am Nachmittag / ihr / (die) Wörterbücher / kaufen

16. _____

   Testing Program   **5**

Quiz 1-2A

zu teuer / sein / (das) Kleid / mir

17. _____

du / möchten / (der) Bleistift / ?

18. _____

SCORE _____

D. Complete the following conversation by filling in each blank with the appropriate word or phrase from the box. Note: each word and phrase may be used more than once or not at all. (9 points)

brauche	besonders	Farbe	viel zu lang	kostet
Wunsch	heißt	fesch	passt	Größe	gefällt	Grün

VERKÄUFER Was möchten Sie, bitte?

DU Ich **19.** _____ einen Pulli.

VERKÄUFER Und welche **20.** _____ haben Sie?

DU **21.** _____ 40.

VERKÄUFER Hier haben wir einen. **22.** _____ Ihnen der Pulli?

DU Nicht **23.** _____ . Ich habe Blau nicht gern. Haben Sie

diesen Pulli auch in **24.** _____ ?

VERKÄUFER Sicher!

DU Ah, diesen Pulli finde ich schön. Ich probiere ihn an.

(*Später*)

VERKÄUFER Und wie **25.** _____ der Pulli?

DU Prima! Er sieht wirklich **26.** _____ aus. Ich nehme ihn.

VERKÄUFER Sehr gut! Er **27.** _____ € 49.

SCORE _____

TOTAL SCORE _____

1 Bei den Baumanns

■ Zweite Stufe

Maximum Score: 40

I. Listening

A. Reiman's department store has had a sale going on for several days. What can you still buy? First read over the list of items you want to buy. Then listen as the salesclerk tells you what's available. For each item write either **yes** if you can still buy it or **no** if it is sold out. (8 points)

Liste von Sachen, die du kaufen willst:

1. _____ rotes Polohemd, Größe S

2. _____ Polyacryl-Pulli in Blau, Größe 40, für Damen

3. _____ Polyacryl-Pullover in Blau für Herren

4. _____ Sweatshirt mit Rockermotiv, Größe L

SCORE _____

II. Reading

B. Read the article about fashion and then decide if the statements that follow are true (T) or false (F). (12 points)

Kleider machen Leute

Ist deine Jacke aus echtem Leder oder ist sie aus Vinyl? Ziehst du am liebsten Markenwaren wie Adidas® und Calvin Klein® an, oder suchst du lieber etwas Preiswertes, wenn du Sportkleidung oder Klamotten für die Schule kaufst?

Früher, in der Renaissance, zum Beispiel, hatten Frauen und Männer Kleider aus Seide und Brokat. Sie schmückten sich mit Halsketten und Ohrringen aus Perlen und Juwelen und Brillanten. Sie waren auch parfümiert. So was war ein Zeichen (sign) von Erhabenheit (high social standing).

Heute ziehen Millionäre Levis® Jeans an. Und heute gibt es wieder einen Trend zu natürlichen Stoffen (fabrics). Echte Baumwolle, reine Wolle und Leinen sind bei Umweltfreunden Mode. Ungefärbte (undyed) Baumwolle und natürliche Stoffe sind jetzt ziemlich teuer, denn sie sind wieder „in". Schick sind jetzt auch Flohmärkte und Secondhandläden, wo junge Leute einen individuellen Look suchen.

Gibt es heute Demokratie in der Welt der Mode (world of fashion)? Oder sehen wir eine neue Art (kind) von Kleidungssnobismus?

_____ 5. During the Renaissance both men and women of social standing wore expensive fabrics.

_____ 6. During the Renaissance men were not allowed to wear perfume.

_____ 7. Today, rich as well as poor people wear jeans.

_____ 8. Environmentally conscious people wear clothes made of silk and leather.

SCORE _____

Quiz 1-2B

III. Writing

C. You just ran into a friend at school. Write a connected, friendly conversation using the following lines. (12 points)

URSEL   Mensch, siehst du aber fesch aus! Neues T-Shirt, was? Wo hast du es gekauft?

9.   DU   _____

URSEL   War es denn teuer?

10.   DU   _____

URSEL   Der Aufdruck gefällt mir besonders. Ist das T-Shirt aus Baumwolle?

11.   DU   _____

URSEL   Meinst du, sie haben noch so ein T-Shirt in Größe M?

12.   DU   _____

D. You want to compliment your friend on his new shirt, but he thinks it is a bit too short. Create a brief exchange with an appropriate compliment and appropriate responses. (4 points)

13.   DU   _____

FREUND   Nicht zu kurz?

14.   DU   _____

SCORE ☐

IV. Culture

E. The three German teens interviewed for the **Landeskunde** in this chapter are all active in sports. How do you think they would react to the idea of introducing American-style varsity football into their schools? Write a short paragraph in English giving reasons based on the information in the textbook. (4 points)

15.   _____

_____

_____

SCORE ☐

TOTAL SCORE ☐

Bei den Baumanns

■ Dritte Stufe

Maximum Score: 30

Grammar and Vocabulary

A. Answer the following questions, using the words in parentheses as cues. (10 points)

> Was willst du heute Abend machen? (ins Konzert gehen)

1. _____

> Wohin möchten sie nach der Schule gehen? (in den Zoo)

2. _____

> Will er mit uns Tennis spielen? (Nein, Fußball)

3. _____

> Was wollen Sie am Sonntag machen? (reiten)

4. _____

> Möchtet ihr um neun Uhr die Stadt besichtigen? (Nein, wandern gehen)

5. _____

SCORE [   ]

B. Answer the following questions according to your own schedule. (4 points)

> Was möchtest du heute nach der Schule machen?

6. _____

> Was willst du am Wochenende machen?

7. _____

SCORE [   ]

Quiz 1-3A

C. Write a conversation that takes place in a café, using the English phrases as prompts. The box below contains the verbs you will need. Use each verb only once. (8 points)

| essen   möchten   nehmen   bekommen |

The waitperson asks what you would like:

8. _____

You tell the waitperson that you would like soup:

9. _____

You ask your friend what he wants:

10. _____

Your friend responds that he wants a cheese sandwich:

11. _____

SCORE [   ]

D. As you and your friends eat, the waitperson returns to the table to ask you how everything tastes. Use the English phrases as prompts to compose the conversation below. (8 points)

The waitperson asks you how it (the food) tastes:

12. _____

You say it is excellent:

13. _____

Your friend says her bologna sandwich doesn't taste good:

14. _____

Your friend explains that the sandwich is too salty:

15. _____

SCORE [   ]

TOTAL SCORE [   ]

Holt German 2 Komm mit!, Chapter 1

KAPITEL 1

Name _____ Klasse _____ Datum _____

Bei den Baumanns

■ Dritte Stufe

Maximum Score: 30

I. Listening

A. Klaus and his sister, Susa, have invited their cousin Dieter to a café. Listen as the waiter takes their order and write down what each person orders to eat and drink. (12 points)

	Speisen	Getränke
1. Klaus		
2. Susa		
3. Dieter		

SCORE

II. Reading

B. Read the following conversation and indicate whether the statements that follow are true (T) or false (F). (8 points)

KEMAL Möchtest du meine Kartoffelsuppe essen?
GERD Schmeckt sie dir nicht?
KEMAL Nein, sie ist zu salzig.
GERD Dann will ich sie auch nicht. Bestell dir doch etwas anderes!
KEMAL Ich hab keinen Hunger mehr. Was willst du heute Abend machen? Willst du Tennis spielen?
GERD Wir haben doch gestern Tennis gespielt! Eigentlich will ich heute Abend keinen Sport machen. Gehen wir doch ins Kino! Oder wir können bei mir zu Hause Musik hören oder Fernsehen schauen.
KEMAL Du weißt doch, dass ich nicht gern ins Kino gehe oder Fernsehen schaue. Ich geh vielleicht heute Abend joggen und du kannst faulenzen.
GERD Eine ausgezeichnete Idee!

_____ 4. Kemal schmeckt die Kartoffelsuppe nicht, weil sie zu salzig ist.

_____ 5. Kemal und Gerd sind bei Gerd zu Hause.

_____ 6. Gerd spielt heute Abend Tennis.

_____ 7. Kemal will heute Abend faulenzen.

SCORE

KAPITEL 1

Quiz 1-3B

III. Writing

C. Answer the following letter. Be sure to answer all the questions asked and to include an appropriate salutation and closing. (8 points)

München, den 26. September

Liebe(r)_____!

Es freut mich unheimlich, dass du nächstes Wochenende zu uns kommst! Kommst du denn am Freitag oder erst am Samstagmorgen? Wir wollen am Samstag mit der Clique an den Starnberger See fahren. Segelst du gern? Am Abend können wir dann in eine Diskothek. Gehst du oft in Diskos tanzen?

Am Sonntag gehen meine Großeltern vormittags in die Kirche. Sollen wir mitgehen oder lieber zu Hause faulenzen?

Schreib mir schnell wieder.

Mit herzlichem Gruß
von deiner *Marianne*

_____

_____

_____

_____

_____

_____

_____

SCORE [ ]

IV. Culture

D. Based on the **Landeskunde** in **Kapitel 1**, do you think German teenagers are interested in or like the same types of things as teenagers in the United States? Support your answer with two examples from the **Landeskunde** interviews. (2 points)

8. _____

_____

SCORE [ ]

TOTAL SCORE [ ]

Name _____ Klasse _____ Datum _____

Bei den Baumanns

Chapter Test

I. Listening

Maximum Score: 30 points

A. Listen as Vivian describes her family. Choose the best answer from the alternatives given. (10 points)

1. Vivian looks like
   a. her father.
   b. her mother.
   c. her brother.
   d. her sister.

2. She has
   a. dark brown hair.
   b. light eyes.
   c. a slender build.
   d. perfect teeth.

3. Vivian likes to... in her free time.
   a. work with computers
   b. swim and play tennis
   c. play football and frisbee®
   d. play handball and tennis

4. In this family, the parents and children
   a. give school music lessons.
   b. play six different instruments.
   c. play six different sports.
   d. don't have much in common.

5. Vivian seems to
   a. want more friends.
   b. be unhappy about her appearance.
   c. wish she were like her mother.
   d. be pretty satisfied with herself and family life.

SCORE [ ]

B. Erika and Martin are at a party with other students as their acquaintance, Sabine, arrives. Listen to their conversation and choose the best alternative to describe Sabine's clothes. (10 points)

6. Erika thinks Sabine's jacket is made of
   a. cotton.
   b. natural leather.
   c. imitation leather.
   d. synthetics.

7. Erika guesses that the jacket costs
   a. 100 euros.
   b. 150 euros.
   c. 200-300 euros.
   d. 300-400 euros.

Chapter Test

8. Sabine's necklace is
   a. an antique.
   b. made of pure gold.
   c. from a secondhand shop.
   d. a family heirloom.

9. Sabine's jacket is
   a. from her Oma.
   b. from a secondhand shop.
   c. real leather.
   d. made of silk.

10. Erika believes Sabine's jeans were at least 100 euros, but Sabine paid
    a. 7 euros.
    b. 15 euros.
    c. 18 euros.
    d. 22 euros.

SCORE [   ]

C. Listen to Erika, Martin, and Sabine's conversation again and choose the best answers from among the alternatives given. (10 points)

11. Martin's first impression of Sabine is that she
    a. is very intelligent.
    b. has wealthy parents.
    c. looks very chic.
    d. collects antiques.

12. Erika's first reaction to Sabine is probably
    a. envy or jealousy of Sabine.
    b. appreciation of Sabine's ability to look nice on a small budget.
    c. pity for Sabine's poor taste in clothes.
    d. anger at Martin's lack of sense about money matters.

13. Sabine admires
    a. Erika's pretty hair.
    b. Erika's taste in headbands.
    c. Erika's new outfit.
    d. Martin's taste in antique jewelry.

14. Sabine is especially pleased with her handbag because
    a. it looks like synthetic.
    b. it's made of genuine suede leather.
    c. it was expensive.
    d. it looks just like real leather.

15. Sabine's attitude toward clothes is:
    a. She only buys well-known brand names.
    b. She won't buy anything that has been used.
    c. She isn't really very interested in clothes.
    d. She's proud of being a bargain hunter.

SCORE [   ]

Chapter Test

II. Reading

Maximum Score: 30 points

D. For each set, identify the one response that is NOT appropriate. (10 points)

16. Ich möchte eine Tasse Tee. Was trinkst du?
    a. Bestellst du mir bitte eine Limo?
    b. Ich nehme lieber eine Limo.
    c. Ich möchte unbedingt eine Limo.
    d. Das schmeckt nicht!

17. Guten Tag! Haben Sie einen Wunsch?
    a. Ja, danke. Ich brauche eine Mütze.
    b. Ich ziehe Jeans zu der Fete an.
    c. Eigentlich suche ich einen Wollschal.
    d. Haben Sie dieses Armband in Silber?

18. Welche Größe brauchen Sie?
    a. Ich brauche im Moment gar nichts.
    b. Lieber XL. Das ist bequemer.
    c. Ich weiß nicht. Kann ich's erst anprobieren?
    d. Gewöhnlich nehme ich XL.

19. Wie schmeckt's dir denn?
    a. Ausgezeichnet!
    b. Nicht besonders. Und dir?
    c. Ehrlich? Nicht zu süß?
    d. Mir ist's zu sauer.

20. Toller Taschenrechner! War er teuer?
    a. Meinst du? ... fünfzwanzig Mark, also nicht so teuer.
    b. Ja, mir gefällt er auch. Er war schon ein bisschen teuer — dreißig Euro.
    c. Wirklich? ... Nein, den habe ich schon lange.
    d. Keine Ahnung, du. Den Rechner habe ich von meinem Onkel bekommen.

SCORE [   ]

E. On the first day of school, Ursula wrote a note to Jens asking about his morning. Unscramble Jens' reply by putting his sentences in chronological order. (10 points)

a. Um Viertel nach zehn hab ich Deutsch.
b. Danach hab ich Mathe, um halb zwölf.
c. Und zuletzt Erdkunde.
d. Montag ist ein ganz schlechter Tag für mich. Zuerst hab ich um acht Uhr Bio — zwei Stunden!
e. Um zwölf habe ich Musik.

_____ 21.

_____ 22.

_____ 23.

_____ 24.

_____ 25.

SCORE [   ]

Chapter Test

F. Later, Martin wanted to know what Jens would be doing after school. Unscramble Jens' reply by putting his sentences in chronological order. (10 points)

    a. Dann um 4.00 Uhr gehen Uli und ich schwimmen.
    b. Am Abend können wir vielleicht noch ins Café gehen.
    c. Nach der Schule ist eine Menge los. Zuerst hab ich mit Uli Fußballtraining.
    d. Komm doch mit! Wir sind bis sechs in der Badehalle.
    e. Aber spätestens um acht muss ich zu Hause sein.

_____ 26.

_____ 27.

_____ 28.

_____ 29.

_____ 30.   SCORE [   ]

III. Culture

Maximum Score: 14 points

G. Answer the following three questions based on what you learned about German teenagers' interests and tastes from the **Landeskunde** section of this chapter. (14 points)

    31. If you invited three German teenagers to dinner, it would be best to serve
      a. chef salads.
      b. pizza or spaghetti.
      c. bratwurst with sauerkraut.

    32. If you're talking with German teens about books, you could expect that
      a. they know many German authors, but no American authors.
      b. they know Twain, Faulkner, and Hemingway, but no popular current authors.
      c. they know nearly as many US authors as most Americans their age do.

    33. If you're talking about music, you could expect that
      a. they know mostly German classical music.
      b. they know mostly German popular music and rock.
      c. they know about as much about the Beatles and Tina Turner as most American teens do.

    34. If you order a **Limo** in a German café, you will get
      a. fresh homemade lemonade.
      b. soda pop.
      c. tea with lemon.

    35. If you go shopping for clothes in Germany, you will need to know your German size (38, 40, etc.) in order to ask for
      a. a dress shirt or blouse.
      b. a T-shirt.
      c. a sweat shirt.

Chapter Test

36. If you stay with a middle-class German family, you can expect that
    a. they will have their own house (single-family dwelling).
    b. the school-age sons or daughters will all share one bedroom.
    c. the school-age children will each have a bicycle.

37. If you stay with a middle-class German family, you can expect that
    a. you will need to ride a bike in order to get around with your host siblings and friends.
    b. since you have a driver's license, you will be allowed to drive one of their cars.
    c. your host family will take you everywhere in the family car.

SCORE [   ]

IV. Writing

Maximum Score: 26 points

H. You are very curious about a new member of your club. You ask one of your friends all about her. Use the following question words to complete each sentence. (6 points)

a. wo   b. was   c. wie   d. welche   e. wer

_____ 38. DU: _____ ist das Mädchen da?

ER: Das ist meine Kusine.

_____ 39. DU: Und _____ heißt sie?

ER: Annette.

_____ 40. DU: _____ wohnt sie denn?

ER: In einem Vorort von Hamburg.

_____ 41. DU: _____ macht sie gern?

ER: Sie malt gern und zeichnet auch.

_____ 42. DU: _____ Schulfächer hat sie gern? Bestimmt Kunst.

ER: Nein, eigentlich Biologie und Mathe — und Sport.

_____ 43. DU: _____ alt ist sie? So alt wie du?

ER: Nein, sie ist ein bisschen älter, schon sechzehn.

SCORE [   ]

Chapter Test

KAPITEL 1

I. Write a paragraph of at least five sentences introducing yourself to Sebastian. Include information from each of the following categories: **Name, Aussehen, Haare, Augen, Eigenschaften, Sport,** and **andere Interessen oder Hobbys.** (10 points)

_____

_____

_____

_____

_____

_____

SCORE [   ]

J. Write a second paragraph of at least five sentences to Sebastian explaining what you do in your free time. Comment on at least two things you like to do and one thing you don't like to do. Also mention what you like to do in the evenings and on weekends. Be sure to use the following phrases in your paragraph: **gern, nicht gern, am Abend,** and **am Wochenende.** (10 points)

_____

_____

_____

_____

_____

_____

SCORE [   ]

TOTAL SCORE [   ]

KAPITEL 1 Chapter Test Score Sheet

Circle the letter that matches the most appropriate response.

I. Listening

Maximum Score: 30 points

A. (10 points)

1. a b c d
2. a b c d
3. a b c d
4. a b c d
5. a b c d

SCORE [   ]

B. (10 points)

6. a b c d
7. a b c d
8. a b c d
9. a b c d
10. a b c d

SCORE [   ]

C. (10 points)

11. a b c d
12. a b c d
13. a b c d
14. a b c d
15. a b c d

SCORE [   ]

II. Reading

Maximum Score: 30 points

D. (10 points)

16. a b c d
17. a b c d
18. a b c d
19. a b c d
20. a b c d

SCORE [   ]

E. (10 points)

21. a b c d e
22. a b c d e
23. a b c d e
24. a b c d e
25. a b c d e

SCORE [   ]

F. (10 points)

26. a b c d e
27. a b c d e
28. a b c d e
29. a b c d e
30. a b c d e

SCORE [   ]

III. Culture

Maximum Score: 14 points

G. (14 points)

31. a b c
32. a b c
33. a b c
34. a b c
35. a b c
36. a b c
37. a b c   SCORE [   ]

IV. Writing

Maximum Score: 26 points

H. (6 points)

38. a b c d e

39. a b c d e

40. a b c d e

41. a b c d e

42. a b c d e

43. a b c d e

SCORE [   ]

I. (10 points)

_____

_____

_____

_____

_____

_____

_____

_____

_____

_____

SCORE [   ]

J. (10 points)

_____

_____

_____

_____

_____

_____

_____

_____

_____

_____

SCORE [   ]

TOTAL SCORE [   ]

Quiz 1-1B Kapitel 1 Erste Stufe

I. Listening

A.

JUTTA Wer ist das mit dem Tennisschläger? Ist das deine Schwester Kati?

ALEX Die mit dem Tennisschläger? Ach, nein! Kati spielt nicht Tennis — sie ist überhaupt nicht sportlich. Das ist meine Kusine Hannelore. Kati ist schlank und hat lange, blonde Haare wie Hannelore, aber Hannelore hat grüne Augen, und Katis Augen sind blau. Beide Mädchen sind natürlich sehr hübsch.

JUTTA Also, Kati ist nicht sportlich. Was macht sie denn gern?

ALEX Meistens liest sie Sciencefictionbücher oder bastelt an Modellen. Sie ist auch sehr fleißig in der Schule.

Quiz 1-2B Kapitel 1 Zweite Stufe

I. Listening

A.

Verkäuferin:

Viele Sachen sind schon ausverkauft, aber weiße Polohemden haben wir noch in allen Größen. Rote Hemden haben wir aber nur noch in S und XL. Blaue Polohemden haben wir nicht mehr in XL.

Polyacryl-Pullover für Damen gibt es noch in Blau, Weiß und Rot in Größen 36, 38 und 42; Größe 40 haben wir leider nicht mehr. Für Herren gibt es keine Pullis mehr. Sie sind leider alle ausverkauft.

Die Sweatshirts mit Aufdruck sind auch fast alle. Wir haben nur noch die mit Rockermotiven in allen Größen — S, M, L, XL und XXL.

Quiz 1-3B Kapitel 1 Dritte Stufe

I. Listening

A.

BEDIENUNG Was bekommen Sie?

SUSA Na, Klaus, du hast großen Hunger, nicht? Was bekommst du?

KLAUS Ich möchte die Tagessuppe, ein Wurstbrot und eine Limo, bitte. Und du, Susa?

SUSA Für mich einen Eisbecher.

BEDIENUNG Es gibt verschiedene Eisbecher. Möchten Sie lieber einen mit Südfrüchten oder mit Schokoladensoße und Schlagsahne, oder mit ...

SUSA *[lacht]* Am besten einen mit ganz viel Kalorien! Also den mit Schokoladensoße und Sahne, bitte. Und eine Tasse Kaffee. Und du, Dieter?

DIETER Im Moment will ich gar nichts.

KLAUS Komm, Dieter, wir laden dich doch ein!

DIETER Also, schön. Dann nehme ich eben ein Stück Himbeertorte.

BEDIENUNG Und etwas zu trinken?

DIETER Nein, danke!

Answers to Quizzes 1-1A, 1-1B

ANSWERS Quiz 1-1A

A. (9 points; 3 points per item)
Answers will vary. Possible answers:
1. Er ist siebzehn Jahre alt und schlank und hat blonde Haare und grüne Augen.
2. Meine Schwester ist intelligent, fleißig und lustig.
3. Ich koche und fechte gern, aber ich rodle nicht gern.

B. (8 points; 1 point per item)
4. Leichtathletik
5. Langstreckenlauf
6. Hürdenlauf
7. Speerwerfen
8. Weitsprung
9. Stabhochsprung
10. 100-Meter-Lauf
11. Kugelstoßen

C. (10 points; 1 point per item)
12. spricht
13. Gibst
14. nimmt
15. weiß
16. fährt
17. isst
18. sieht
19. liest
20. lädt
21. ein

D. (8 points; 2 points per item)
Answers will vary. Possible answers:
22. Jürgen war gestern schlecht gelaunt, aber heute ist er gut gelaunt.
23. Lies das Buch! Es ist wirklich toll.
24. Spricht er über seine Oma (Groß-mutter)?
25. Sie ist sympathisch, aber faul.

ANSWERS Quiz 1-1B

I. Listening

A. (8 points: 2 points per item)
1. Aussehen: hübsch; schlank *(given)*
2. Haare: lang, blond
3. Augen: blau
4. Eigenschaft(en): unsportlich; fleißig

II. Reading

B. (6 points: 2 points per item)
5. Best pen pal: Bea.
Answers will vary. Possible answers:
6. Bea is good at art and music, two of Bernd's interests.
7. She seems to like animals, as does Bernd, because she collects horse posters.

III. Writing

C. (16 points: 4 points per item)
Answers will vary. Possible answers:
8. Wo wohnst du denn?
9. Wer ist das da?
10. Und hast du auch Brüder?
11. Und wie alt sind sie?

Answers to Quizzes 1-2A, 1-2B

ANSWERS Quiz 1-2A

A. (8 points; 1 point per item)
1. der Ohrring, –e
2. der Schal, –s; das Tuch, –¨er
3. das Armband, –¨er
4. der Hut, –¨e
5. der Stirnband, –¨er
6. die Mütze, –n
7. die Handtasche, –n
8. die Halskette, –n

B. (6 points; 1 point per item)
9. Er
10. sie
11. es
12. sie
13. es
14. ihn

C. (12 points; 3 points per item)
Answers will vary. Possible answers:
15. Er findet den Pulli stark.
16. Am Nachmittag kauft ihr die Wörterbücher.
17. Das Kleid ist mir zu teuer.
18. Möchtest du den Bleistift?

D. (9 points; 1 point per item)
19. brauche
20. Größe
21. Größe
22. Gefällt
23. besonders
24. Grün
25. passt
26. fesch
27. kostet

ANSWERS Quiz 1-2B

I. Listening
A. (8 points: 2 points per item)
1. yes
2. no
3. no
4. yes

II. Reading
B. (12 points: 3 points per item)
5. T
6. F
7. T
8. F

III. Writing
C. (12 points: 3 points per item)
Possible answers:
9. Meinst du? Ich habe es bei ... gekauft.
10. Nein, es war nicht teuer.
11. Ja, klar! / Nein, leider nicht. Es ist aus ...
12. Ja, sie haben noch Größe M.

D. (4 points: 2 points per item)
Answers will vary. Possible answers:
13. Dein Hemd sieht toll aus. Es gefällt mir.
14. Nein, überhaupt nicht zu kurz.

IV. Culture
E. (4 points)
15. Answers will vary.

KAPITEL 1

ANSWERS Quiz 1-3A

A. (10 points; 2 points per item)
Answers will vary. Possible answers:
1. Ich will heute Abend ins Konzert gehen.
2. Sie möchten nach der Schule in den Zoo gehen.
3. Nein, er will mit uns Fußball spielen.
4. Ich will am Sonntag reiten.
5. Nein, wir möchten um neun Uhr wandern gehen.

B. (4 points; 2 points per item)
Answers will vary. Possible answers:
6. Heute nach der Schule möchte ich ins Kino gehen.
7. Am Wochenende will ich nach Fredericksburg fahren.

C. (8 points; 2 points per item)
Answers will vary. Possible answers:
8. Was bekommen Sie, bitte?
9. Ich möchte eine Suppe, bitte!
10. Was nimmst du?
11. Ich esse ein Käsebrot.

D. (8 points; 2 points per item)
Answers will vary. Possible answers:
12. Wie schmeckt's?
13. Ausgezeichnet!
14. Das Wurstbrot schmeckt nicht.
15. Es ist zu salzig.

ANSWERS Quiz 1-3B

I. Listening

A. (12 points: 4 points per item)
1. Klaus: Suppe, Wurstbrot; Limo
2. Susa: Eisbecher [mit Schokoladensoße und Sahne]; Kaffee
3. Dieter: Himbeertorte; nichts

II. Reading

B. (8 points: 2 points per item)
4. T 5. F 6. F 7. F

III. Writing

C. (8 points: 2 points per item)
Answers will vary. Possible answer:
Liebe Marianne!
Ich komme am Freitag, am Abend. Ich segle sehr gern. Ich gehe auch oft in die Disko. Am Sonntag aber möchte ich faulenzen!
Bis dann!

IV. Culture

D. (2 points)
8. Answers will vary. Possible answer: German students like many of the same things as students here. For example, they like to read Stephen King and eat pizza.

Scripts for Chapter Test Kapitel 1

I. Listening

A.   In meiner Familie ist es eigentlich so: ich sehe mehr wie mein Vater aus, und mein Bruder sieht meiner Mutter ganz ähnlich.

Hier — das kannst du auf diesem Familienfoto sehen. Vater und ich, wir haben dunkelbraune Haare und braune Augen, aber mein Bruder Klaus und Mutti sind ganz blond. Von meinem Vater habe ich den breiten Mund und das schöne Lächeln. *[Laughs]* Der Klaus ist ein Meter neunzig, also viel größer als Vati, und hat zudem sehr breite Schultern. Vati und ich, wir sind kleiner, und ich bin leider nicht so schlank wie die Mutti.

Aber das macht doch nichts. In Sport bin ich gar nicht schlecht. Ich spiele ganz gut Tennis und Handball. Manchmal spielen Vati und ich zusammen. Klaus schwimmt ganz gern und spielt ab und zu ein bisschen Frisbee®, ist aber nicht sehr sportlich. Er interessiert sich mehr für Computer und Musik.

Wir sind alle ziemlich musikalisch. Unsere Eltern haben sich ja auf der Musikhochschule kennen gelernt. Mutti spielt Klavier und Gitarre. Vati spielt Geige und Saxophon. Ich spiele Cello, und Klaus spielt prima Trompete und Kontrabass. Wenn wir sonntags alle zu Hause sind, machen wir zusammen Musik. Das finde ich echt schön!

B. and C.

MARTIN Guck mal, das ist die Sabine! Sieht doch schick aus, nicht wahr?

ERIKA Soll sie auch! Hast du eine Ahnung, wie viel Geld die für Klamotten ausgibt?

MARTIN Wie meinst du das?

ERIKA Na, schau dir die Jacke an — echt Wildleder! Wie viel kostet wohl so was?

MARTIN Keine Ahnung. 100 Euro? 150?

ERIKA Du träumst, Mensch! Sag lieber zwei- oder dreihundert! Und ihre Jeans ist von Calvin Klein, also mindestens hundert Euro.

MARTIN Ja, ich sehe schon, was du meinst. So eine antike, goldene Halskette ist bestimmt auch nicht billig, oder?

ERIKA Pass auf! Sie kommt zu uns. Abend, Sabine!

SABINE Na, grüß dich, Erika! Abend, Martin! Ihr seht aber toll aus, ihr beiden. Du, Erika, dein Stirnband ist echt Klasse. Passt genau richtig zu den Haaren.

ERIKA Meinst du? Wir bewundern gerade dein Outfit.

MARTIN Die antike Halskette ist doch elegant.

SABINE Gefällt sie dir? Na, sie ist natürlich nicht echt. Ich habe sie für 20 Euro in dem Secondhandladen in der Ritterstraße gekauft.

MARTIN 20 Euro! Ich glaubte vielleicht 100.

SABINE Martin, altes Haus, du meinst doch nicht, ich bin das Fräulein Neureich! Diese Jacke kommt auch aus einem Secondhand Shop — 40 Euro hat sie gekostet. Die Ärmel waren mir allerdings ein wenig zu lang, da habe ich sie zu Hause geändert und etwas kürzer gemacht. Für die Jeans habe ich nur 18 Euro bezahlt — schon bleich gewaschen. Nur die Handtasche ist neu. Die habe ich von der Omi zum Geburtstag bekommen. Schaut mal! Die ist aus Kunststoff, sieht aber genau wie Leder aus, nicht wahr?

Answers to Chapter Test Kapitel 1

I. Listening Maximum Score: 30 points

A. (10 points: 2 points per item)   **B.** (10 points: 2 points per item)   **C.** (10 points: 2 points per item)

1. a	6. b	11. c
2. a	7. c	12. a
3. d	8. c	13. b
4. b	9. b	14. d
5. d	10. c	15. d

II. Reading Maximum Score: 30 points

D. (10 points: 2 points per item)   **E.** (10 points: 2 points per item)   **F.** (10 points: 2 points per item)

16. d	21. d	26. c
17. b	22. a	27. a
18. a	23. b	28. d
19. c	24. e	29. b
20. c	25. c	30. e

III. Culture Maximum Score: 14 points

G. (14 points: 2 points per item)

31. b
32. c
33. c
34. b
35. a
36. c
37. a

IV. Writing Maximum Score: 26 points

H. (6 points: 1 point per item)

38. e
39. c
40. a
41. b
42. d
43. c

I. (10 points: 2 points per item)
    Answers will vary.

J. (10 points: 2 points per item)
    Answers will vary.

KAPITEL 1

2 Bastis Plan

■ Erste Stufe

Maximum Score: 35

Grammar and Vocabulary

A. You're describing the chores various people have to do. Fill in the blanks below with the correct forms of **müssen** and the German equivalents of the English phrases in parentheses. (14 points)

Morgen **1.** _____ ich **2.** _____ (dry the clothes).

Nach der Schule **3.** _____ ihr **4.** _____ (clean the garage).

Am Montag **5.** _____ du **6.** _____ (dust).

Einmal in der Woche **7.** _____ meine Schwester

8. _____ (polish the car).

Mittwochs **9.** _____ wir meiner Mutter

10. _____ (help in the kitchen).

Sein Bruder **11.** _____ heute Nachmittag

12. _____ (take out the garbage).

Die Schüler **13.** _____ manchmal **14.** _____ (iron the clothes).

SCORE [   ]

B. Respond to the following invitations, using the German phrases in parentheses as prompts for the first two, and supplying your own reason for the third. (9 points)

Wir gehen jetzt in die Stadt, Klamotten kaufen. Kommst du mit? — Ich kann leider nicht,

weil **15.** _____ .

(zu viele Hausaufgaben haben)

Ich möchte am Sonntag nach Graz fahren. Wollt ihr mitkommen? — Das geht leider nicht, denn

16. _____ .

(unsere Oma besuchen müssen)

Quiz 2-1A

Mein Bruder und ich gehen am Donnerstag ins Kino. Kommst du mit? — Das geht leider nicht,

17. _____ .

(supply your own reason)

SCORE ⬚

C. Fill in the blanks below with the correct forms of **können** and the appropriate forms of the pronouns and nouns given in parentheses. [12 points]

18. _____ wir etwas für 19. _____ (du) tun?

Du 20. _____ für 21. _____ (die Oma) Geschirr spülen.

Ihr 22. _____ für 23. _____ (ich) die Fenster putzen.

Ich 24. _____ für 25. _____ (ihr) den Tisch decken.

Für 26. _____ (wer) 27. _____ er einkaufen gehen?

Ingrids Kinder 28. _____ für 29. _____ (der Opa) den Rasen

mähen.

SCORE ⬚

TOTAL SCORE ⬚

Name _____ Klasse _____ Datum _____

2 Bastis Plan

■ Erste Stufe

Maximum Score: 30

I. Listening

A. It's Saturday afternoon, and Dieter and Regina are talking on the phone. As you listen to their conversation, put a check mark in the appropriate columns to indicate when Regina is going to do each of the chores she mentions. Then answer the multiple choice question below. (10 points)

	Samstagnachmittag	Samstagabend	Sonntag
Geschirr spülen			
Betten machen			
die Küche aufräumen			
Staub saugen			
Hausaufgaben machen			
Rasen mähen			
einkaufen gehen			
Fenster putzen			

1. Who did NOT invite whom?
   a. Regina's parents did not invite Aunt Irmgard.
   b. Regina did not invite Beatrice.
   c. Dieter did not invite Regina.
   d. Regina did not invite Dieter.

SCORE [ ]

II. Reading

B. Read the following ad in the classifieds and then decide if the statements that follow are true (T) or false (F). (8 points)

> Haben Sie keine Zeit für Haus- und Gartenarbeiten? Wir, die PUTZMEISTER, putzen Ihr Haus von oben bis unten. Wir waschen, trocknen und bügeln Ihre Wäsche. Wir mähen Ihren Rasen und machen andere Gartenarbeiten. Sie geben eine Party und brauchen Hilfe in der Küche? Kein Problem! Wir kochen für Ihre Gäste und räumen dann auch Ihre Küche auf. Wir tragen sogar den Müll weg. Wir wollen Ihnen das Leben leichter machen! Wir geben Ihnen einen ganz nach Ihren Wünschen abgestimmten Service. Rufen Sie uns an, um ein individuelles, kostenloses *(free of charge)* Angebot zu erhalten. Unsere Geschäftszeiten sind Mo-Fr 8.00-17.00. ☎ 08442-916319. Am Wochenende und in Notfällen *(emergencies)* erreichen Sie uns auch: ☎ 08442-916318.

_____ 2. The company specializes in house and garden work.

Quiz 2-1B

_____ 3. The company's goal is to make life easier for the customer.

_____ 4. The company cleans and polishes cars, if the customer is willing to pay.

_____ 5. The company is open Monday through Saturday.

SCORE [   ]

III. Writing

C. Write a connected, friendly conversation using the following lines. Be sure to use the verb **müssen** and the sequencing words **zuerst** and **dann** in your conversation. (12 points)

MANFRED Du, wir gehen heute ins Kino. Möchtest du mitkommen?

6. DU _____

MANFRED Warum denn nicht?

7. DU _____

8. [und] _____

MANFRED Na, schade. Also, vielleicht nächstes Mal.

SCORE [   ]

TOTAL SCORE [   ]

KAPITEL 2

Bastis Plan

■ Zweite Stufe

Grammar and Vocabulary

A. Give the German names of the fruits and vegetables described below. (6 points)

a vegetable, they're green and long   1. _____

a fruit, they're egg-shaped and purple   2. _____

a vegetable, they're small, green, and round 3. _____

a fruit, they're long and yellow   4. _____

a fruit, they're round and orange   5. _____

a green, leafy vegetable   6. _____

SCORE [   ]

B. Complete the following questions and statements with the correct forms of **sollen**. (6 points)

Was **7.** _____ wir denn tun?

Frau Meier, Sie **8.** _____ die Erdbeeren im Obst- und Gemüseladen kaufen.

Ich **9.** _____ jetzt zur Bäckerei gehen.

10. _____ Renate die Trauben essen? Sie sehen gar nicht frisch aus.

Du **11.** _____ heute Zwiebeln kaufen, denn sie sind jetzt im Angebot.

Ihr **12.** _____ euren Großeltern helfen.

SCORE [   ]

C. Transform the following phrases into **du**-commands. (6 points)

zur Metzgerei fahren   **13.** _____

das Zimmer aufräumen   **14.** _____

ein Stück Kuchen nehmen   **15.** _____

für mich einkaufen gehen   **16.** _____

Quiz 2-2A

den Tisch decken   17. _____

das Brot essen   18. _____

SCORE ☐

D. Complete the following questions and statements with the correct past tense forms of sein. (6 points)

Ihr **19.** _____ heute Morgen im Supermarkt, nicht wahr?

Ich **20.** _____ gestern bei meiner Oma.

21. _____ Sie letzte Woche in Prag, Frau Wiese?

Er **22.** _____ letzten Sommer in den Vereinigten Staaten.

23. _____ du in den Ferien in Dresden?

Wir **24.** _____ letzten Monat am Bodensee.

SCORE ☐

E. Complete the following conversation, using the words in the box below. (6 points)

> Liter   noch   alles   Kilo   Äpfel
>   sonst

VERKÄUFER   Guten Tag! Wie kann ich Ihnen helfen?

DU   Ich brauche bitte ein **25.** _____ Kartoffeln und zwei Gurken.

VERKÄUFER   Und was bekommen Sie **26.** _____ ?

DU   Hmm. Ich glaube, ich will fünf **27.** _____ .

VERKÄUFER   **28.** _____ noch etwas?

DU   Zwei **29.** _____ Milch.

VERKÄUFER   Haben Sie noch einen Wunsch?

DU   Nein, danke, das ist **30.** _____ .

SCORE ☐

TOTAL SCORE ☐

Bastis Plan

Quiz 2-2B

Maximum Score: 40

■ Zweite Stufe

I. Listening

A. Michael and Mandy are organizing a party for tonight. Their mother wants to go shopping with them. Listen to their conversation twice and write the quantity needed beside each item, using the vocabulary in the box for quantities. Then answer question 5 below. (10 points)

1. _____ Aufschnitt

2. _____ Tomaten

3. _____ Pfirsiche oder Aprikosen

4. _____ Cola

5. How many people are coming to the party? _____

Gramm Pfund Kilo Liter kein/e/en etwas viel/e

SCORE [ ]

II. Reading

B. Read Heike's e-mail message to her friend Marion and answer the questions that follow. (8 points)

Liebe Marion:

Wie geht es dir? Es geht mir gut, aber ich habe zur Zeit so viel zu tun. Meine Freundin Erika wird morgen 17 und sie hat mich zu ihrer Geburtstagsparty eingeladen. Ich will für sie einen Zwetschgendatschi backen. Ich weiß, wie gern sie Zwetschgendatschi isst! Ich war heute schon im Obstladen „Fruchthof" und hab drei Kilo Zwetschgen gekauft. Die sind vielleicht teuer! Das Kilo hat fast 3 Euro gekostet. Jetzt muss ich noch in den Supermarkt, um Hefe *(yeast)*, Zucker, Milch, Mehl, Eier und Zimt *(cinnamon)* zu kaufen. Morgen Vormittag will ich dann den Zwetschgendatschi machen, denn die Party beginnt schon am frühen Nachmittag. Meinst du, dass ich sonst noch etwas zur Party mitbringen soll? Soll ich noch einen Bohnensalat oder einen Gurkensalat machen? Oder vielleicht einen Obstsalat mit Pfirsichen und Bananen? Bitte schreib bald zurück und sag mir, was ich machen soll.

Deine Heike

6. Was ist ein Zwetschgendatschi?
   a. ein Obstsalat   b. ein Kuchen   c. ein Fleischgericht   d. eine Torte

7. Warum muss Heike noch in den Supermarkt gehen?
   a. Sie will Obst kaufen, um eine Obstsalat zu machen.
   b. Sie will noch ein Geschenk für Erika kaufen.
   c. Sie braucht Zutaten *(ingredients)* für den Zwetschgendatschi.
   d. Sie will die Zwetschgen im Supermarkt kaufen, weil sie dort billiger sind.

8. Wann ist Erikas Geburtstagsparty?
   a. am späten Nachmittag   c. am frühen Nachmittag
   b. am Abend   d. am frühen Morgen

Quiz 2-2B

9. Mit welchen Früchten will Heike einen Obstsalat machen?
   a. mit Zwetschgen
   b. mit Bohnen
   c. mit Gurken
   d. mit Bananen und Pfirsichen

SCORE _____

III. Writing

C. Frau Müller just went shopping and is on her way home. On the way, she meets her neighbor, Frau Lehmann. Write a connected, polite conversation, using the lines below. (16 points)

FRAU LEHMANN   Guten Tag, Frau Müller! Die Einkaufstasche sieht ganz schön schwer aus! Was haben Sie denn gekauft?

10.   FRAU MÜLLER _____

FRAU MÜLLER   Mmm. Schönes, frisches Obst! Haben Sie das im Supermarkt gekauft?

11.   FRAU MÜLLER   Nein, _____

FRAU LEHMANN   Ja, dort sind die Lebensmittel bestimmt frischer als im Supermarkt, kosten aber auch mehr, nicht wahr?

12.   FRAU MÜLLER   Nein, _____

FRAU LEHMANN   Wirklich? Und diese schönen Brötchen! Wo haben Sie die her?

13.   FRAU MÜLLER _____

SCORE _____

IV. Culture

D. According to the **Landeskunde** in this chapter, if you are invited to a German home, for which occasion would the items below be most suitable? (6 points)

a. as a present for an older host/hostess
b. for a friend your own age having a **Fete**
c. as a present for someone's birthday or saint's day

_____ 14. a small bouquet of fresh flowers

_____ 15. a book

_____ 16. a package of chips or nuts

_____ 17. a box of candy

_____ 18. an article of clothing

_____ 19. something to snack on

SCORE _____

TOTAL SCORE _____

KAPITEL 2

Name _____ Klasse _____ Datum _____

Bastis Plan

▇ Dritte Stufe

Maximum Score: 35

Grammar and Vocabulary

A. Give the German equivalents of the following English words and phrases. Don't forget to include the articles and plural forms of nouns, where applicable. (7 points)

chocolate   1. _____

alarm clock   2. _____

ring   3. _____

radio   4. _____

painting   5. _____

tennis racket   6. _____

made of silver   7. _____

SCORE [   ]

B. Complete the following statements and questions by filling in the correct dative forms of the pronouns and nouns in parentheses. (8 points)

Ich gebe **8.** _____ (mein Vater) ein Buch zu Weihnachten.

9. _____ (wer) schenkst du die Armbanduhr?

Meine Schwester hat bald Namenstag. Was soll ich **10.** _____ (sie) kaufen?

Was schenkst du **11.** _____ (deine Kusine) zum Geburtstag?

Anke möchte **12.** _____(er) CDs geben.

Soll ich **13.** _____ (du) Schmuck kaufen?

Ihr gebt **14.** _____ (die Lehrerin) einen Blumenstrauß.

Ich glaube, meine Mutter schenkt **15.** _____ (ich) Klamotten zu Weihnachten.

SCORE [   ]

Quiz 2-3A

C. Complete the following questions and statements with the correct forms of **mögen**. (6 points)

Was für Filme 16. _____ ihr? Horrorfilme?

17. _____ Sie Fantasyromane, Herr Gärtner?

Du 18. _____ sicher eine Tasse Kaffee.

Hannelore 19. _____ Sportartikel.

Wir 20. _____ deutsches Essen.

Thomas und Birgit 21. _____ Blumen.

SCORE _____

D. Answer the following questions in German, according to your own preferences. (8 points)

What do you like?

22. _____

What do you prefer?

23. _____

What do you like best?

24. _____

What do you not like?

25. _____

SCORE _____

E. Complete the following sentences, using the English in parentheses as prompts. (6 points)

Möchtest du 26. _____ (another) Saft?

Nein, 27. _____ (no more juice).

Ja, bitte! Ich möchte 28. _____ (another) Banane.

SCORE _____

TOTAL SCORE _____

KAPITEL 2

Name _____ Klasse _____ Datum _____

2 Bastis Plan

■ Dritte Stufe

I. Listening

A. Listen to the following conversation and choose the best answer from the alternatives given. (6 points)

1. Where is this conversation taking place?
   a. at Anneliese's grandmother's house
   b. at a café
   c. at Anneliese's house
   d. at Mark's house

2. What is the general topic of conversation?
   a. Oma's coffee and cake
   b. gifts to buy for Mark's mother
   c. chores that Anneliese has to do today
   d. Anneliese's weekend plans

3. Which of the following statements is true?
   a. Anneliese would like more cake.
   b. Mark would NOT like more cake.
   c. The grandmother would NOT like another piece of cake.
   d. Anneliese had three pieces of cake, and Mark had four.

SCORE _____

II. Reading

B. Read an excerpt from the website of an online gift shop and answer the questions that follow. (8 points)

In unserem maritimen Geschenk-Shop finden Sie Geschenke für alle, die die See (*sea*) gern mögen. Segelt (*sail*) Ihr Vater oder Opa gern? Dann kaufen Sie ihm doch eine Kapitänsmütze. Unsere Mützen sind aus weißer Baumwolle und haben vorne einen Anker aus echtem Gold. Für den Sohn oder die Tochter haben wir tolle Modelle. Basteln Sie doch mit den Kindern ein Ruderboot, ein Kanu oder ein Rennboot. Für die maritimen Experten in der Familie haben wir Navigationskompasse, Knotentafeln mit Instrumenten und Globen. Unsere Schiffslampen mit Silberständer und unsere Steuerräder aus Holz bringen die See in Ihr Wohnzimmer (*living room*). Besucht Ihre Frau gern Leuchttürme? Dann schenken Sie ihr doch ein Radio oder einen Wecker, der die Form eines Leuchtturms hat.

Kaufen Sie doch ein Geschenk, das vom Herzen kommt! Sie können alle Artikel bequem per Online-Shop bestellen.

4. In what items does this gift shop specialize?
   a. in gifts that are associated with the sea   c. in gifts for children
   b. in gifts that are made out of gold   d. in gifts that the whole family can use

Quiz 2-3B

5. What is a **Leuchtturm**?
   a. a lamp   **b.** a boat   **c.** a lighthouse   **d.** an anchor

6. What item does this gift shop NOT carry?
   a. model canoes   **b.** alarm clocks   **c.** compasses   **d.** fishing nets

7. According to the text, what items bring the sea into the living room?
   a. lamps and steering wheels   **c.** anchors made of gold
   b. items that are made of wood   **d.** instruments for navigation

SCORE [＿＿＿]

III. Writing

C. Write a paragraph about your favorite things. You can write about food, books, movies, activities, or clothes. Be sure to include the following phrases in your description: **am liebsten, überhaupt nicht gern,** and **lieber,** and be sure to give a reason explaining why something is your favorite using a **weil-** or **denn-**clause. (12 points)

_____

_____

_____

_____

_____

SCORE [＿＿＿]

IV. Culture

D. Assume that you are an exchange student in Germany this year. (4 points)

8. If someone says **du** to your teacher (and your teacher doesn't mind), then that person may be
   a. the teacher's pupil.
   b. a close relative.
   c. a student of hers from last year.
   d. the parent of one of her students.

9. You're at a grill party hosted by one of your host mother's friends. You've stuffed yourself on **Wurst** and potato salad and can't eat another thing. The hostess would like to know if you want more **Wurst**. How would you reply?

   DU _____

SCORE [＿＿＿]

TOTAL SCORE [＿＿＿]

KAPITEL 2

Bastis Plan

Chapter Test

I. Listening

Maximum Score: 30 points

A. Max, Karl, and Tina are trying to decide on a gift for their grandfather. Read the questions below and then listen to their conversation twice. As you listen, answer the following questions. (20 points)

1. Their grandfather will be. . . years old.
   a. sixty   **b.** sixty-five   **c.** seventy   **d.** seventy-five

2. The three siblings decide against flowers because they are
   a. unsuitable for a man.   **c.** boring.
   b. not very personal.   **d.** too expensive.

3. What second suggestion do the siblings discuss?
   a. a watch   **b.** a painting   **c.** a gift certificate   **d.** food

4. They decide against clothes because they are
   a. unsuitable for a man.   **c.** boring, and he already has too many.
   b. not very personal.   **d.** too expensive.

5. Tina suggests a certain book because their grandfather
   a. has a lot of books.
   b. is interested in sailing as a hobby.
   c. reads best sellers.
   d. is interested in tourism.

6. What is the reaction of the two brothers to Tina's suggestion?
   a. It sounds very boring.
   b. It's not nice enough for a special birthday.
   c. It's very expensive.
   d. They are not into buying books.

7. The grandchildren decide on
   a. flowers.   **b.** food.   **c.** clothes.   **d.** a book.

8. Tina has
   a. no money.   **b.** 10 euros.   **c.** 15 euros.   **d.** 68 euros.

9. The main question that remains at the end of the conversation is
   a. whether their grandfather already has it.
   b. how much money they have between the three of them.
   c. whether their father will help them out with the money.
   d. which one has enough money to buy the gift.

10. What could you infer from the conversation about the siblings' relationship to their grandfather?
    a. They don't spend much time with him.
    b. They spend quite a bit of time with him and know a lot about him.
    c. They don't know much about his interests, because they are not very close to him.
    d. They have not seen him since they were young children.

SCORE [ ]

Chapter Test

B. Kati and Jürgen are trying to think of ways to earn money, and decide to look in the newspaper for ideas. Read the questions below and then listen to their conversation twice. As you listen, answer the following questions. (10 points)

11. In the newspaper, the base price for a car wash is
   a. 3 euros. **c.** 8 euros and 90 cents.
   b. 10 euros. **d.** 5 euros.

12. Hand drying and polishing usually cost
   a. 3 euros 50 per hour.
   b. nothing (it's always included in the base price).
   c. 10 euros extra per car.
   d. 3 euros extra per car.

13. Kati figures
   a. they will each get 10 euros per car.
   b. they will each get 6 euros per car.
   c. they will each get exactly 5 euros per hour.
   d. they will each get exactly 10 euros per hour.

14. Jürgen figures they will earn less because they have to pay for all of the following things EXCEPT
   a. a vacuum cleaner. **c.** soap.
   b. wax for polishing. **d.** water.

15. Kati mentions that her friend Monika used to earn money by
   a. cleaning garages. **c.** polishing floors.
   b. washing cars. **d.** washing and ironing clothes.

SCORE _____

II. Reading

Maximum Score: 30 points

C. Skim the partial conversation between Erika and Nicole. Then insert into the blanks the letter of the most appropriate response from the choices below. Use each lettered item only once. (10 points)

   a. Was für Musik hört er am liebsten?
   b. Was für Hobbys und Interessen hat er?
   c. Du sollst ihm doch das geben, was er will, nicht, was du gerne hörst.
   d. Dann schenk ihm eine besondere Briefmarke! Oder ein Album aus Leder. Das ist doch etwas Persönliches.
   e. Willst du ihm nicht einfach eine Geburtstagskarte machen? Selbst gemachte Sachen sind oft die allerbesten Geschenke.

   ERIKA   Du, mein Bruder hat bald Geburtstag, und ich weiß überhaupt nicht, was ich ihm schenken soll.

16. NICOLE   _____

   ERIKA   Na, er sammelt Briefmarken, hauptsächlich die älteren deutschen von vor 1940 und macht Freiluftballonfahrten in einem Ballon-Club.

17. NICOLE   _____

Holt German 2 Komm mit!, Chapter 2

ERIKA Das geht nicht. So viel Geld habe ich doch nicht. Beides ist ziemlich teuer.

18. NICOLE _____

ERIKA Geht leider auch nicht. Beim Zeichnen und Basteln und so was habe ich zwei linke Hände. Selbst gemachte Sachen mache ich nicht so gern.

19. NICOLE _____

ERIKA Ganz doofe! Elvis Presley und Rolling Stones und blödes Zeug. Die Musik gefällt mir gar nicht.

20. NICOLE _____

ERIKA Ja, eigentlich hast du schon Recht. Ich gebe ihm also eine CD seiner Lieblingsgruppe. Ich gehe morgen ins Musikgeschäft. Kommst du mit?

SCORE [ ]

D. Read the following short essay written by Jörg, a Gymnasium student in Germany, and answer the questions below. (12 points)

Manchmal will ich nicht zu Hause helfen, und dann sagt mein Opa immer, dass ich es zu gut habe. Als er in meinem Alter war – ich bin jetzt fünfzehn – musste er viel zu Hause helfen. Im Winter musste er immer Kohle *(coal)* aus dem Keller holen und sie die vielen Treppen *(flights of stairs)* hochtragen *(carry)*. Letzte Woche wollte ich nicht Staub saugen, und mein Opa sagte: „Du hast einen elektrischen Staubsauger, mit dem du leicht und bequem Staub saugen kannst. Als ich so alt war wie du, da gab es keine elektrischen Staubsauger. Ich musste alle zwei Wochen die Teppiche nach draußen *(outside)* bringen und den Staub mit einem Teppichklopfer *(carpet beater)* herausklopfen. Das war vielleicht anstrengend *(exhausting)*."

Manchmal, wenn ich wieder nicht zu Hause helfen will, denke ich an *(think about)* die Worte meines Opas. Dann räume ich mein Zimmer auf, decke den Tisch und sortiere den Müll. Natürlich sauge ich auch Staub.

21. In general, what is Jörg's essay about?
   a. his favorite family member: his grandfather
   b. what life was like when his father was young
   c. a description of different carpet-cleaning methods
   d. how he feels about his chores around the house

22. What does Jörg's grandfather do when Jörg does not want to do his chores?
   a. He gives advice on how to do the chores faster and better.
   b. He does the chores for him.
   c. He shows Jörg the old way of doing chores.
   d. He tells Jörg stories about the way things were done when he was young.

23. One thing the grandfather did when he was young was
   a. vacuum.
   b. clean rugs by beating them.
   c. set the table for his own mother.
   d. go shopping and carry the heavy bags.

Chapter Test

24. When Jörg doesn't want to do housework, what does the grandfather tell him?
    a. Jörg's chores are easy compared to those he had to do when he was young.
    b. When he was young, men did not help at home.
    c. Vacuuming was easy because there was electricity.
    d. Only girls were expected to help.

25. What effect do the grandfather's words have on Jörg?
    a. They make Jörg think that his chores are really not that bad.
    b. They annoy Jörg and he refuses to do any chores.
    c. Jörg tells his grandfather that his friends don't have to do chores.
    d. Jörg doesn't listen to his grandfather.

26. Which of the following chores does Jörg NOT mention?
    a. cleaning his room   c. vacuuming
    b. clearing the table after meals   d. setting the table

SCORE [   ]

E. Read the following interview responses to this question: What do you like and not like about school? After you have read each interview response, match each English statement with the interview it best summarizes. (8 points)

_____ 27. | *Das Beste ist ein Wandertag. Die Klasse lernt sich besser kennen. Die Lehrer sind nicht mehr so verschlossen wie im Unterricht.* **Realschülerin, 13 Jahre**

_____ 28. | *Doof ist, wenn ich mich blamiere. Wenn meine Mitschüler mich kaltherzig ausjohlen. Dann bekomme ich Herzklopfen. Ich schäme mich bis in die Zehenspitzen.* **Gymnasiastin, 12 Jahre**

_____ 29. | *Ich finde es furchtbar, wenn ein Lehrer oder eine Lehrerin weggeht, an die man sich gewöhnt hat und die man gern hatte. Immer der blöde Lehrerwechsel!* **Realschüler, 14 Jahre**

_____ 30. | *Ich glaube, das allerbeste an der Schule ist, daß wir etwas lernen für unser späteres Leben.* **Gymnasiastin, 16 Jahre**

Excerpts from "Das Pausenklingeln ist die schönste Musik!" from *Eltern*, October 1990, pp. 208-209. Copyright © 1990 by Gruner+Jahr AG & Co. Reprinted by permission of the publisher.

a. Taking a hiking trip with classmates is the best, because you get to know them better.
b. Learning something for the future is the best thing about school.
c. It's terrible when teachers you like leave.
d. It's awful when other students tease you coldheartedly.

SCORE [   ]

III. Culture

Maximum Score: 10 points

F. Based on what you have learned in the **Landeskunde** and **Zum Lesen** sections so far, choose the best answers from among the alternatives given. (10 points)

31. If you live in a small German town or suburb, you will probably see all of the following EXCEPT
    a. a farm produce truck going door to door.   c. school buses.
    b. an underground subway.   d. people going grocery shopping by bicycle.

KAPITEL 2

Chapter Test

32. In German families today,
    a. boys never help in the kitchen.
    b. girls never do yardwork.
    c. teens aren't expected to do any housework.
    d. it's usual for teens to help around the house.

33. You're invited to Sunday afternoon coffee and cake at an older German couple's home. The best thing to take would be
    a. a small bouquet of flowers.
    b. a permanent arrangement of plastic flowers.
    c. a couple of bags of chips.
    d. just bring yourself (that is, no gift for the hostess).

34. You're invited to your friend's party. You had better NOT take
    a. a dozen red roses.   c. a homemade salad.
    b. a couple of bags of chips. d. some music to listen to.

35. If it is a Saturday you could expect that
    a. you will only have time in the morning to shop.
    b. the stores will close around two in the afternoon.
    c. the stores will close around four in the afternoon.
    d. stores will have regular weekday hours, but afterward there will be a fest in the downtown area.

SCORE [＿＿＿＿]

KAPITEL 2

IV. Writing

Maximum Score: 30 points

G. Write the responses indicated in the blanks below. (10 points)

36. Möchtest du noch etwas Saft?

   [*accept politely*] _____

37. Und wie schmeckt der Saft?

   [*say it tastes very good*] _____

38. Noch ein Brot? Es gibt Wurstbrote und Käsebrote.

   [*accept and say which you prefer*] _____

   _____

39. Du sollst noch etwas Kartoffelsalat essen. Bitte, nimm dir doch noch etwas!

   [*refuse politely but praise the salad*] _____

   _____

40. Sonst noch etwas? Oliven? Chips? Ein bisschen Dip?

   [*refuse politely and give a reason*] _____

   _____

SCORE [＿＿＿＿]

Chapter Test

H. Write a note to a classmate inviting him or her to do something with you this afternoon. Use the cues and all the information below in your note. (10 points)

    – invite your classmate   – you have already seen *Dracula* once
    – where: to a café   – but you really like horror films
    – afterward: to the movies, to see *Dracula*   – meet at café: 3 pm

_____

_____

_____

_____

_____

_____

_____

_____

_____

SCORE _____

I. Write a short paragraph about what you do to help other people and how often.
Mention four things you do and one thing you never do for someone. Use the following phrases in your paragraph: **manchmal, oft, einmal/zweimal in der Woche,
einmal/zweimal im Monat**, and **nie**. (10 points)

_____

_____

_____

_____

_____

_____

_____

_____

SCORE _____

TOTAL SCORE _____

Holt German 2 Komm mit!, Chapter 2

KAPITEL 2

KAPITEL 2 Chapter Test Score Sheet

Circle the letter that matches the most appropriate response.

I. Listening
Maximum Score: 30 points

A. (20 points)

1. a b c d
2. a b c d
3. a b c d
4. a b c d
5. a b c d

6. a b c d
7. a b c d
8. a b c d
9. a b c d
10. a b c d

SCORE [ ]

B. (10 points)

11. a b c d
12. a b c d
13. a b c d
14. a b c d
15. a b c d

SCORE [ ]

II. Reading
Maximum Score: 30 points

C. (10 points)

16. a b c d e
17. a b c d e
18. a b c d e
19. a b c d e
20. a b c d e

SCORE [ ]

D. (12 points)

21. a b c d
22. a b c d
23. a b c d
24. a b c d
25. a b c d
26. a b c d

SCORE [ ]

E. (8 points)

27. a b c d
28. a b c d
29. a b c d
30. a b c d

SCORE [ ]

III. Culture
Maximum Score: 10 points

F. (10 points)

31. a b c d
32. a b c d
33. a b c d
34. a b c d
35. a b c d

SCORE [ ]

KAPITEL 2

IV. **Writing**   Maximum Score: 30 points

G. (10 points)

36. _____

_____

37. _____

_____

38. _____

_____

39. _____

_____

40. _____

_____

H. (10 points)   SCORE [   ]

_____
_____
_____
_____
_____
_____
_____
_____
_____

I. (10 points)   SCORE [   ]

_____
_____
_____
_____
_____
_____
_____
_____
_____
_____

SCORE [   ]   TOTAL SCORE [   ]

KAPITEL 2

Listening Scripts for Quizzes 2-1B, 2-2B, 2-3B

Quiz 2-1B Kapitel 2 Erste Stufe

I. Listening

A. *[sound of phone ringing]*

REGINA Hier Kleinert.

DIETER Tag, Regina. Ich bin's — der Dieter. Wie geht's dir denn?

REGINA Ganz gut, danke! Und dir?

DIETER Es geht schon. Hör mal, Regina! Ich habe gerade eine neue CD gekauft. Willst du nicht gleich zu mir kommen und sie mit mir anhören?

REGINA Jetzt gleich? Nun, das geht leider nicht. Ich muss heute Nachmittag zu Hause helfen.

DIETER Was musst du denn machen?

REGINA Ja, … zuerst muss ich das Geschirr vom Mittagessen spülen und danach die Küche aufräumen. Wir bekommen am Sonntag Besuch.

DIETER Wer kommt denn?

REGINA Meine Mutter hat die Tante Irmgard und ihre Familie eingeladen. Also am Sonntag muss ich noch Staub saugen.

DIETER Na ja. Wie sieht's denn mit heute Abend aus?

REGINA Für den Abend habe ich schon die Beatrice eingeladen. Wir müssen Hausaufgaben machen.

DIETER Prima! Dann bringe ich heute Abend meine CD, und wir hören sie bei dir.

REGINA Aber Dieter! Nein … *[click of telephone being hung up as Regina protests]*

Quiz 2-2B Kapitel 2 Zweite Stufe

I. Listening

A. MUTTER Was brauchen wir denn für die Fete? Sollen wir einen Einkaufszettel zusammenstellen?

MICHAEL Ja, wie viele sind wir denn? Neun?

MANDY Wenn die Beate ihre Kusine mitbringt, sind wir zehn.

MUTTER Na schön. Also, Aufschnitt für zehn Personen. Rechnen wir rund hundert Gramm pro Person, so macht das genau ein Kilo.

MICHAEL Und dann noch ein paar Tomaten … ein Pfund Tomaten reicht schon. Wir schneiden sie dann in Scheiben für die Brote.

MUTTER Ist mir recht. Und heute Nachmittag will ich euch eine Obsttorte backen. Wir können im Laden schauen, was es heute Frisches gibt.

MANDY Vielleicht Pfirsiche oder Aprikosen?

MUTTER Schön. Ich brauche so ungefähr 600 Gramm davon. So teuer ist das ja nicht.

MICHAEL Die anderen Leute wollen alle verschiedene Dips und Chips mitbringen.

MUTTER Gut! Dann kaufen wir noch vier Flaschen Cola, die Einliterflaschen. Vier Liter Cola — das ist bestimmt genug. Also, da haben wir's. Jetzt los in den Supermarkt!

Quiz 2-3B Kapitel 2 Dritte Stufe

I. Listening

A. OMA Noch eine Tasse Kaffee, Anneliese?

ANNELIESE Bitte!

OMA Und du, Mark, noch etwas Kaffee?

MARK Danke, Omi. Aber der war doch prima. Dein Kaffee duftet immer so schön kräftig.

OMA Ich mahle den immer frisch, hier in der Küche, weißt du. Sonst habe ich Kaffee nicht so furchtbar gern. So, wollt ihr keinen Pflaumenkuchen mehr?

MARK Ich kann wirklich nicht mehr. Leider!

ANNELIESE Kein Wunder. Du hast schon drei Stück gegessen!

MARK Und du hast schon zwei Stück Kuchen gegessen, Mädchen.

OMA Das schadet doch nichts. Die Anneliese ist doch so schlank.

MARK Nun, sie passt auf ihre schlanke Linie auf. Zu Hause isst sie keinen Kuchen und keine Torte und nichts, wo Schokolade drin ist.

ANNELIESE Wir backen sowieso zu Hause keinen Kuchen, weil Mutti keine Zeit hat, weißt du, und die Sachen von der Bäckerei schmecken mir nicht besonders.

OMA Selbstverständlich. Hausgemacht ist natürlich das Beste. Ich nehme auch noch ein Stück. Den Rest könnt ihr dann nachher mit nach Hause nehmen.

KAPITEL 2

ANSWERS Quiz 2-1A

A. (14 points; 1 point per item)
1. muss
2. die Wäsche trocknen
3. müsst
4. die Garage aufräumen
5. musst
6. Staub wischen
7. muss
8. das Auto polieren
9. müssen
10. in der Küche helfen
11. muss
12. den Müll wegtragen
13. müssen
14. die Wäsche bügeln

B. (9 points; 3 points per item)
Answers will vary. Possible answers:
15. ich zu viele Hausaufgaben habe
16. wir müssen unsere Oma besuchen
17. weil ich am Donnerstag zu Hause helfen muss.

C. (12 points; 1 point per item)
18. Können
19. dich
20. kannst
21. die Oma
22. könnt
23. mich
24. kann
25. euch
26. wen
27. kann
28. können
29. den Opa

ANSWERS Quiz 2-1B

I. Listening

A. (10 points: 2 points per item)

	Samstagnachmittag	Samstagabend	Sonntag
Geschirr spülen	✔		
Betten machen			
die Küche aufräumen	✔		
Staub saugen			✔
Hausaufgaben machen		✔	
Rasen mähen			
einkaufen gehen			
Fenster putzen			

1. d

II. Reading

B. (8 points: 2 points per item)
2. T
3. T
4. F
5. F

III. Writing

C. (12 points: 4 points per item)
Answers will vary. Possible answers:
6. Das geht leider nicht. / Ich kann leider nicht.
7.-8. Student should give 2 reasons why not, using **müssen** correctly and the sequencing words **zuerst** and **dann**.

ANSWERS Quiz 2-2A

A. (6 points; 1 point per item)
1. grüne Bohnen
2. Zwetschgen
3. Erbsen
4. Bananen
5. Pfirsiche
6. Spinat

B. (6 points; 1 point per item)
7. sollen
8. sollen
9. soll
10. Soll
11. sollst
12. sollt

C. (6 points; 1 point per item)
13. Fahr zur Metzgerei!
14. Räum das Zimmer auf!
15. Nimm ein Stück Kuchen!
16. Geh für mich einkaufen!
17. Deck den Tisch!
18. Iss das Brot!

D. (6 points; 1 point per item)
19. wart
20. war
21. Waren
22. war
23. Warst
24. waren

E. (6 points; 1 point per item)
25. Kilo
26. noch
27. Äpfel
28. Sonst
29. Liter
30. alles

ANSWERS Quiz 2-2B

I. Listening

A. (10 points: 2 points per item)
1. 1 Kilo
2. 1 Pfund
3. 600 Gramm
4. 4 Liter
5. 10

II. Reading

B. (8 points: 2 points per item)
6. b
7. c
8. c
9. d

III. Writing

C. (16 points: 4 points per item)
Answers will vary. Possible answers:
10. Ich habe nur Obst und Gemüse gekauft und Milch fürs Wochenende.
11. Nein, Obst und Gemüse kaufe ich immer im Obst- und Gemüseladen in der ...straße.
12. Nein, nicht immer. Ein Pfund Tomaten kostet nur 50 Cent heute.
13. Die habe ich in der Bäckerei Kupp gekauft.

IV. Culture

D. (6 points: 1 point per item)
14. a
15. c
16. b
17. a
18. c
19. b

KAPITEL 2

KAPITEL 2

ANSWERS Quiz 2-3A

A. (7 points; 1 point per item)
1. die Schokolade
2. der Wecker, –
3. der Ring, –e
4. das Radio, –s
5. das Gemälde, –
6. der Tennisschläger, –
7. aus Silber

B. (8 points; 1 point per item)
8. meinem Vater
9. Wem
10. ihr
11. deiner Kusine
12. ihm
13. dir
14. der Lehrerin
15. mir

C. (6 points; 1 point per item)
16. mögt
17. Mögen
18. magst
19. mag
20. mögen
21. mögen

D. (8 points; 2 points per item)
Answers will vary. Possible answers:
22. Ich lese Bücher von Dürrenmatt gern.
23. Ich habe Sciencefictionfilme lieber.
24. Am liebsten höre ich Musik.
25. Ich habe Spinat nicht gern.

E. (6 points; 2 points per item)
26. noch einen
27. keinen Saft mehr
28. noch eine

ANSWERS Quiz 2-3B

I. Listening

A. (6 points: 2 points per item)
1. a
2. a
3. b

II. Reading

B. (8 points: 2 points per item)
4. a
5. c
6. d
7. a

III. Writing

C. (12 points: 3 points per item)
Ich esse am liebsten Hamburger, weil sie sehr gut schmecken. Aber Hot Dogs esse ich überhaupt nicht gern. Dann esse ich lieber Wurst.

IV. Culture

D. (4 points: 2 points per item)
8. b
9. Nein, danke! Ich möchte keine Wurst mehr.

Scripts for Chapter Test Kapitel 2

I. Listening

A.

KARL Opa hat nächste Woche den siebzigsten Geburtstag. Was schenken wir ihm?

TINA Vielleicht einen ganz großen Blumenstrauß?

MAX Na, Mensch, Blumen schenkt ihm doch jeder. Von uns Enkelkindern soll er doch was Besonderes bekommen, etwas ganz Persönliches, was zu ihm passt. Blumen sind doch zu unpersönlich.

KARL Ja, stimmt. Aber was? Etwas zum Essen? Zum Anziehen?

MAX Lieber nichts zum Essen. Der ist doch zuckerkrank. Es gibt eine Menge Sachen, die er gar nicht essen darf.

KARL Na, aber mit Klamotten ist's auch nicht so gut. Krawatten sind langweilig. Er hat schon 'nen ganzen Schrank voll Sporthemden und Jacken und so was.

TINA Ja, und die Oma strickt ihm doch das ganze Jahr über Pullis und Wollschals.

MAX Ich bin dafür, dass wir ihm ein schönes Buch geben. Er liest ganz gerne über Segelfahrten und große Entdeckungsreisen und so was mit möglichst vielen See- und Landkarten drin.

TINA Ich weiß was! Bei Bertelsmann im Schaufenster haben sie ein großes Bilder-buch über Magellan, das ist doch der, der die Weltumsegelung gemacht hat, nicht wahr?

MAX Über Magellan? Und illustriert?

TINA Ja, ganz toll — 68 Euro.

KARL Ach, das ist aber wirklich teuer!

MAX Ja, das finde ich auch. Aber Opas siebzigster Geburtstag ist doch was ganz Besonderes.

KARL Haben wir denn genug Geld? Bei mir sind bestimmt nicht mehr als 25 Euro in der Sparbüchse.

TINA Ich habe vielleicht 15.

MAX Und ich bin beinahe bankrott. Meint ihr, der Papa gibt uns vielleicht 30 Euro?

TINA Möglich ist's schon.

B.

JÜRGEN Hier ist eine Möglichkeit — Auto waschen.

KATI Was kostet das? Wie viel kann man dafür bekommen?

JÜRGEN Für einfaches Waschen acht Euro neunzig und für Handtrocknen und Polieren noch drei Euro dazu.

KATI Schön. Können wir machen. Sagen wir, wir machen das alles: waschen, trocknen und polieren, und bekommen 12 Euro dafür. Dann bekommt jeder von uns brutto sechs Euro.

JÜRGEN Jeder sechs Euro — nicht schlecht. Und wo machen wir das?

KATI Hier bei uns. Im Garten. Dann kostet das nichts, nur ein paar Euro für Flug-blätter — die müssen wir natürlich in der Gegend verteilen.

JÜRGEN Aber Vati bezahlt das Wasser bestimmt nicht. Das kostet was. Und Waschmittel müssen wir kaufen und auch Wachs zum Polieren. Was meinst du, sollen wir das machen?

KATI Besser als Wäsche waschen und bügeln. Die Monika hat das eine Zeitlang gemacht — sie bekommt so einen Euro fünfzig für ein Hemd und einen Euro für ein Betttuch. Das ist gar nicht viel Geld.

Answers to Chapter Test Kapitel 2

I. Listening Maximum Score: 30 points

A. (20 points: 2 points per item)

1. c	6. c
2. b	7. d
3. d	8. c
4. c	9. c
5. b	10. b

B. (10 points: 2 points per item)

11. c
12. d
13. b
14. a
15. d

II. Reading Maximum Score: 30 points

C. (10 points: 2 points per item)

16. b
17. d
18. e
19. a
20. c

D. (12 points: 2 points per item)

21. d
22. d
23. b
24. a
25. a
26. b

E. (8 points: 2 points per item)

27. a
28. d
29. c
30. b

III. Culture Maximum Score: 10 points

F. (10 points: 2 points per item)

31. b
32. d
33. a
34. a
35. c

IV. Writing Maximum Score: 30 points

G. (10 points: 2 points per item)
Answers will vary. Possible answers:
36. Ja, bitte! Noch einen Saft, bitte!
37. Der Saft schmeckt prima!
38. Ja, bitte! Ich nehme noch ein Wurstbrot.
39. Nein, danke! Keinen Salat mehr. Aber der Salat war sehr gut.
40. Nein, danke! Ich habe keinen Hunger mehr.

H. (10 points: 2 points per item)
Answers will vary. Possible answer:
Nach der Schule gehe ich ins Café und danach ins Kino. Kommst du mit? Heute läuft *Dracula* im Kino. Ich habe ihn schon einmal gesehen, aber ich finde Horrorfilme ganz toll! Ich bin um drei Uhr im Café.

I. (10 points: 2 points per item)
Answers will vary. Possible answer:
Sehr oft mache ich für meine Mutter Einkäufe. Und manchmal sauge ich auch für sie Staub. Einmal in der Woche gehe ich für meine Oma einkaufen, und einmal im Monat mähe ich den Rasen. Aber Wäsche waschen tue ich nie.

KAPITEL 2

Wo warst du in den Ferien?

Erste Stufe

Maximum Score: 30

Grammar and Vocabulary

A. Fill in the blanks below, using the prompts in parentheses, to find out how you and your family are preparing for an upcoming vacation. (10 points)

In den **1.** _____ (vacation) will meine Familie die Innenstadt von München

2. _____ (to visit a place, sightsee). Wir möchten in Dresden viel

3. _____ (to take photographs). Deswegen brauchen wir eine

4. _____ (camera). Weil wir auch **5.** _____ (to film,

videotape) wollen, nehmen wir unsere **6.** _____ (video camera) mit. Ich

und meine Schwester können sie **7.** _____ (to use [a camera]). Natürlich

bringen wir auch viele **8.** _____ (rolls of film) mit. Wenn wir wieder zu

Hause sind, werden wir schöne **9.** _____ (slides) und

10. _____ (color photographs) von unserer Reise haben. Ich freue mich,

dass wir bald wegfahren!

SCORE ____

B. Answer the questions below by asserting that you have already done the activity mentioned. You will need to use the conversational past in order to do this. Pay close attention to those verbs taking **haben** and those taking **sein** as helping verbs. (10 points)

Wohnst du in Dresden?	**11.** _____
Fährst du in die Schweiz?	**12.** _____
Hilfst du dem Opa?	**13.** _____
Kaufst du der Petra ein Poster?	**14.** _____
Bleibst du in Österreich?	**15.** _____
Hörst du Musik?	**16.** _____
Besichtigst du Berlin?	**17.** _____
Gehst du nach Hause?	**18.** _____

Quiz 3-1A

Trinkst du eine Limo?   19. _____

Kommst du mit?   20. _____

SCORE [   ]

C. Using the words below, write sentences in the conversational past tense.
(10 points)

ihr / wandern / letzte Woche

21. _____

Sie (formal) / aussehen / toll / gestern

22. _____

ich / spielen / Klavier

23. _____

wir / machen / eine Reise in die Schweiz

24. _____

du / laufen / 5 Kilometer

25. _____

Ulrike und Jörg / essen / Semmeln

26. _____

Birgit / lesen / den Fantasyroman

27. _____

ich / schenken / meiner Tante / Parfüm

28. _____

ihr / schwimmen / im Meer

29. _____

wir / fahren / nach Bayern

30. _____

SCORE [   ]

TOTAL SCORE [   ]

KAPITEL 3

Name _____ Klasse _____ Datum _____

Wo warst du in den Ferien?

■ Erste Stufe

Maximum Score: 30

I. Listening

A. Ulrich and Tina, like many high school students in former West Germany, are very curious about students their own age in former East Germany. Listen to their conversation twice and as you listen, mark the statements below true (T) or false (F). (12 points)

_____ 1. Ulrich visited his cousin in Dresden.

_____ 2. Ulrich stayed at his cousin's house all day and did nothing.

_____ 3. Ulrich spent his evenings visiting churches, museums, and monuments.

_____ 4. He interviewed a lot of people on the street.

_____ 5. Among other things, he was interested in what they bought or didn't buy.

_____ 6. All the people in Dresden were very happy about German reunification.

SCORE _____

II. Reading

B. Read the description of Nuremberg and then decide if the statements that follow are true (T) or false (F). (10 points)

Nürnberg - Eine Weltstadt des Mittelalters

Nürnberg ist eine Weltstadt des Mittelalters. Die Stadt wurde im Jahre 1050 gegründet und hat heute ungefähr eine halbe Million Einwohner. Die Altstadt mit der Burg, die schönen Stadtkirchen und die fünf Kilometer lange Stadtmauer erinnern an die Blütezeit der Stadt im 15. und 16. Jahrhundert. Der Dichter Hans Sachs, der Maler Albrecht Dürer und der Schnitzer Veit Stoß prägten einst das künstlerische Stadtbild Nürnbergs. Martin Behaim entwarf den ersten Erdglobus. Peter Henlein baute die erste Taschenuhr. Im Jahre 1835 fuhr die erste deutsche Eisenbahn zwischen Nürnberg und Führt. Nach der totalen Zerstörung im Zweiten Weltkrieg wurde Nürnberg langsam wieder aufgebaut. Der Wiederaufbau der Altstadt wurde 1966 größtenteils abgeschlossen. Heute besichtigen Besucher die Kaiserburg, Kirchen, Brunnen und Fachwerkhäuser. Bedeutende Einrichtungen wie das Germanische Nationalmuseum und das Dürerhaus und kulturelle Veranstaltungen bringen jedes Jahr Besucher aus aller Welt nach Nürnberg. Besucher sind auch herzlich eingeladen Spezialitäten wie Nürnberger Bratwürste und Lebkuchen zu probieren.

_____ 7. Peter Henlein invented the globe.

_____ 8. The old part of Nuremberg was not at all damaged in World War II.

_____ 9. Nuremberg is home to about 500,000 people.

_____ 10. Nuremberg's time of prosperity was in the fifteenth and sixteenth centuries.

_____ 11. Nuremberg's castle is located in a suburb of Nuremberg.

SCORE [　　　]

III. Writing

C. Write a connected, friendly conversation about your last vacation which includes the following lines. (8 points)

SCHULKAMERADIN Wo warst du in den Ferien?

12.　　　　　　DU _____

SCHULKAMERADIN Was hast du denn dort gemacht?

13.　　　　　　DU _____

14.　　　　　　[und] _____

SCHULKAMERADIN Und was noch?

15.　　　　　　DU _____

SCORE [　　　]

TOTAL SCORE [　　　]

KAPITEL 3

Wo warst du in den Ferien?

■ Zweite Stufe

Grammar and Vocabulary

A. Fill in the blanks below to complete the report describing what you and your family saw and did while visiting Frankfurt. Don't forget to include articles where appropriate. (9 points)

Letzten Monat haben wir Frankfurt **1.** _____ (visited). Eine tolle

Stadt! Zuerst haben wir **2.** _____ (the cathedral) und ein paar

3. _____ (museums) besichtigt, und dann haben wir

4. _____ (the cross-timbered houses) gesehen. Mein Bruder Björn

und ich sind die **5.** _____ (Frankfurt's main shopping street) entlang

spaziert, aber wir haben nichts gekauft. Später am Tag haben wir auch

6. _____ (the house where Goethe was born) und

7. _____ (the city hall of Frankfurt) besichtigt. Am Abend haben

meine Eltern **8.** _____ (the opera house) besucht. Björn und ich sind

nicht mit ihnen gegangen; wir haben nur **9.** _____ (lazed around).

SCORE [＿＿＿＿]

B. Fill in each blank below with the correct simple past tense form of **haben** or **sein**. (8 points)

Frau Stieglitz, **10.** _____ Sie etwas zum Essen?

Ihr **11.** _____ gestern in der Innenstadt, nicht wahr?

Der Thomas **12.** _____ keine Briefmarken.

Ich **13.** _____ viele Hausaufgaben.

Ich bin sicher, dass Christa froh **14.** _____ .

15. _____ du letzten Monat in Hamburg?

Wir **16.** _____ in Kansas bei unserer Tante.

Timo und Nina, wann **17.** _____ ihr Biologie?

SCORE [＿＿＿＿]

Quiz 3-2A

C. Restate the following two sentences, using the conversational past. (2 points)

Ich war heute Nachmittag zu Hause.

18. _____

Du hattest keinen Kuchen.

19. _____

SCORE [   ]

D. Several of your friends are on vacation, and are calling you from their vacation spots. Complete the following sentences with the appropriate prepositions and articles, using contractions whenever possible. (8 points)

Tag, Martin! Wo bist du? **20.** _____ Nordsee? — Nein, ich bin jetzt

21. _____ Italien.

Grüß dich, Monika! Seid ihr **22.** _____ Gebirge? — Nein. Wir sind weiter gefahren,

und sind heute **23.** _____ Türkei.

Du bist **24.** _____ Restaurant? Und wo liegt das Restaurant? — Es liegt

25. _____ Main.

Ihr seid **26.** _____ Elbe? Toll! — Nein, nein. Wir sind **27.** _____ New York.

SCORE [   ]

D. Express the following sentences in German. (8 points)

We were already at the lake.

28. _____

Was Wilhelm at school yesterday?

29. _____

They were in the café, but they had no money.

30. _____

I have never been in London.

31. _____

SCORE [   ]

TOTAL SCORE [   ]

KAPITEL 3

3 Wo warst du in den Ferien?

■ Zweite Stufe

Maximum Score: 40

I. Listening

A. Listen as three students talk about where they were over **Pfingstferien**. Match each description with the correct lettered choice. Note: you will not use all of the choices. (12 points)

_____ 1. Rolf

_____ 2. Peter

_____ 3. Gabi

    a. in the United States
    b. in Frankfurt
    c. in Switzerland
    d. at the sea
    e. in the mountains

Match these three statements with the correct students.

_____ 4. ...wants to go to Switzerland during summer vacation.

_____ 5. ...didn't have enough money to take a trip.

_____ 6. ...didn't have a great vacation because of rain.

SCORE [＿＿＿]

II. Reading

B. Read the following letter and choose the best answers from the choices below. (8 points)

Liebe Elfriede!   2. Juli 2001

Wir – mein Mann und ich – haben gerade tolle Ferien gemacht. Wir waren fünf Tage lang auf einem Rhein-Dampfer *(steamship)*, der von Basel in der Schweiz bis Wangeningen in den Niederlanden *(Netherlands)* gefahren ist. Während des Tages hat der Dampfer angelegt *(docked)*, und wir sind an Land gegangen. Wir sind viel in den Weinbergen *(vineyards)* gewandert. Wir haben sehr interessante römische Ruinen und einige mittelalterliche Burgen *(fortresses)* besichtigt. Die waren sehr malerisch. Einfach wunderbar! Mein Mann hat den ganzen Tag fotografiert. Abends haben wir dann mit den anderen Gästen Karten gespielt oder in unserer Kabine gelesen. So sind wir ganz erfrischt und erholt *(rested)* nach Hause gekommen.

      Sie müssen unbedingt so eine Fahrt machen! Ich schicke Ihnen gerne Bilder und Broschüren ...

    7. What is most likely the writer's relationship to Elfriede?
       a. They are sisters.
       b. They have been close friends since childhood.
       c. They are acquaintances.
       d. They are mother and daughter.

Quiz 3-2B

8. The writer of this letter has just returned from
   a. a cruise of the Greek isles.
   b. a trip down the Rhine by boat.
   c. a hiking trip through the Netherlands.
   d. a five-day tour of Switzerland.

9. The writer was especially pleased with
   a. the number of photos her husband took.
   b. the number of cities they visited.
   c. the picturesque ruins and fortresses.
   d. the number of shows they saw.

10. One thing she did NOT mention doing was
    a. visiting medieval fortresses.
    b. hiking through vineyards.
    c. visiting the ruins of Roman buildings.
    d. swimming in the Rhine river.

SCORE _____

III. Writing

C. Write **complete sentences** in the past tense as directed. (16 points)

11. *Say that you were in Switzerland on your vacation.*

_____

12. *Say that you saw/visited the following places in Frankfurt:* **Dom, Goethehaus**

_____

[und] _____

13. *Say that your family was at the following place on vacation: in France, at the ocean*

_____

14. *Say that you did not visit your aunt because you didn't have time.*

_____

SCORE _____

IV. Culture

D. Based on the **Landeskunde** from **Kapitel 3**, answer the following question. (4 points)

15. What is the difference between **Urlaub** and **Ferien**?

_____

SCORE _____

TOTAL SCORE _____

KAPITEL 3

Wo warst du in den Ferien?

■ Dritte Stufe

Grammar and Vocabulary

A. Respond to the following prompts in German. (8 points)

A friend of yours asks you how well you liked a trip you recently took. If you enjoyed it, you would say:

1. _____

If you did not enjoy it, you would say:

2. _____

If someone tells you that he or she liked something, you might respond with:

3. _____

If someone tells you that he or she did not like something, you might respond with:

4. _____

SCORE [   ]

B. For each statement below, describing where various people spent their summer vacations, you need to ask how well they liked it using the verb **gefallen**. Be sure to use the correct forms of all pronouns and articles. (8 points)

Die Heidi war im Schwarzwald.

5. _____

Die Schüler waren an der Ostküste.

6. _____

Ihr wart in den Vereinigten Staaten.

7. _____

Frau Teuber, ich habe gehört, Sie waren in Marokko.

8. _____

Du warst sicher bei deinem Onkel in den Bergen.

9. _____

Die Kinder waren auf der Insel Sylt.

10. _____

Quiz 3-3A

Er war in der Sahara.

11. _____

Am Rhein waren sie.

12. _____

SCORE ____

C. Give the German equivalents of the following English phrases. Remember to use the correct forms of **ein** in your answers. (7 points)

Wo kann man übernachten?

in a youth hostel   13. _____

in a private home   14. _____

in a bed and breakfast   15. _____

in a hotel   16. _____

Wo kann man essen?

in a small restaurant   17. _____

at a snack stand   18. _____

in a restaurant   19. _____

SCORE ____

D. Express the following in German. (12 points)

After lunch we drove to Dresden.

20. _____

He spent the night in a youth hostel, because he didn't have much money.

21. _____

_____

Every morning Günther and Thomas ate at the lake.

22. _____

On the last day I saw the city hall.

23. _____

SCORE ____

TOTAL SCORE ____

KAPITEL 3

Wo warst du in den Ferien?

Quiz 3-3B

■ Dritte Stufe

Maximum Score: 30

I. Listening

A. Katrina just returned from vacation in Tirol and is discussing the trip with her friend Max. Katrina mentions that there were several things her family members did NOT like. Listen to the conversation twice and match each aspect of the trip listed below with the person who did NOT like it. (6 points)

_____ 1. the inn where they stayed

_____ 2. the food prices at the **Gasthof**

_____ 3. hiking

a. Katrina
b. her brother Günther
c. her mother
d. her father

SCORE _____

II. Reading

B. Read Manuela's e-mail message and decide if the statements that follow are true (T) or false (F). (8 points)

Liebe Leila!

Unsere Klassenfahrt nach Österreich war echt super! Wir sind fast jeden Tag Ski gelaufen. Wir sind auch viel gewandert. Unsere Unterkunft war ganz toll. Meine Freundinnen und ich haben in einer kleinen Pension an einem See gewohnt. Der Blick auf den See war phantastisch! Die anderen Schüler haben in der Jugendherberge in Innsbruck übernachtet. Es hat ihnen dort nicht so besonders gefallen, weil sie zu zehnt in einem kleinen Zimmer übernachten mussten. Wir haben jeden Abend in einem Gasthof in Innsbruck gegessen. Das österreichische Essen hat mir echt gut geschmeckt, vor allem das Wiener Schnitzel. Nach dem Abendessen sind wir gewöhnlich mit dem Bus in unsere Pension gefahren. Dort haben wir dann Karten oder Schach gespielt oder haben einfach nur gefaulenzt. Leider war die Klassenfahrt viel zu kurz, nur eine Woche. Und morgen muss ich leider wieder in die Schule gehen. Ich habe viel mit meiner neuen Digitalkamera fotografiert. Ich füge (*attach*) ein paar Fotos bei.

Bis bald,

Manuela

_____ 4. Manuela's trip to Austria lasted a week.

_____ 5. Manuela spent the night with ten other girls in the youth hostel.

_____ 6. Manuela's class ate dinner in the youth hostel's snack bar.

_____ 7. Manuela writes that she will attach pictures of her trip to her e-mail message.

SCORE _____

Quiz 3-3B

III. Writing

C. Write a short letter back to your friend Gerd. Pretend that you spent your vacation at a resort (in the mountains, at the coast, or in some other beautiful area) in a German-speaking country. Describe the following:

 a) where you were and where you stayed overnight

 b) where you usually ate

 c) one thing you really liked

Remember to use the past tense. (12 points)

_____

_____

_____

_____

_____

_____

_____

SCORE _____

IV. Culture

D. Use the following lettered items as many times as needed to fill in the blanks for the two questions below. (4 points)

 a. in einer Jugendherberge   c. in einer Imbissstube
 b. in einem Restaurant   d. in einem Gasthof

 8. In which of the places above could you both eat and stay overnight? _____

 9. In which of the places above could you eat, but not stay overnight? _____

SCORE _____

TOTAL SCORE _____

KAPITEL 3

KAPITEL 3

Wo warst du in den Ferien?

I. Listening

Maximum Score: 28 points

A. Gerd is calling his friend Christa on the phone on Sunday morning. Listen to their conversation twice and as you listen, choose the best answers from among the alternatives below. (10 points)

1. Gerd called Christa because
   a. he didn't see her at work.
   b. he usually sees her at the opera but she didn't go last night.
   c. he heard from someone that she was sick.
   d. he didn't find her at home last night.

2. Christa was not where Gerd expected because
   a. she had to work late.
   b. she went out.
   c. she didn't feel well.
   d. she didn't have money for the tickets.

3. Christa did all of the following last night EXCEPT
   a. wash her hair.
   b. listen to relaxation music.
   c. read a novel.
   d. eat chocolate.

4. Christa suggested that she and Gerd
   a. take a walk in the country.
   b. take a drive in the country.
   c. look at new cars.
   d. go out to breakfast together.

5. Christa didn't have money for the opera because
   a. she didn't get paid last week.
   b. she bought a car last week.
   c. she went on a trip last week.
   d. she spent her money on the new novel they had talked about.

SCORE [ ]

B. Elena was in Switzerland during summer vacation. Ahmet has never been there, but he has some ideas about it. Listen to their conversation twice and then mark the statements below either true (**a**) or false (**b**). (8 points)

_____ 6. Elena went to visit her father's cousin.

_____ 7. Ahmet thought Zürich would be boring.

_____ 8. Elena said there wasn't much to do there.

KAPITEL 3

Chapter Test

_____ 9. Elena visited two churches.

_____ 10. Elena is not interested in art.

_____ 11. One cannot participate in water sports in Zürich.

_____ 12. Elena thought the food was very good.

_____ 13. Overall, Elena did not enjoy the trip.   SCORE ☐

C. Frank was in five different places on his whirlwind trip through southern Europe. Listen to a description of his trip and put the locations below in the order in which he visited them. (10 points)

_____ 14.   **a.** Atlantic Ocean

_____ 15.   **b.** Black Sea

_____ 16.   **c.** Turkey

_____ 17.   **d.** the Pyrenees (mountains)

_____ 18.   **e.** Spanish coast   SCORE ☐

II. Reading   Maximum Score: 30 points

D. As you read the first paragraph of the reading selection below, decide which of the following nouns are place names and which refer to people. Mark a) for a place and b) for a person or group of people. (12 points)

_____ 19. Berlinerin

_____ 20. Rheinland

_____ 21. Engländer

_____ 22. Normandie

_____ 23. Sibirien

_____ 24. Russen

Eine Berlinerin erzählt

Eigentlich bin ich keine „echte" Berlinerin. Ich wurde in einer kleinen Stadt im Rheinland geboren. Als *(when)* im Jahre 1944 die Amerikaner und die Engländer in der Normandie gelandet sind, haben meine Mutter und Großmutter Angst bekommen *(got afraid)*. Mein Vater war in Gefangenschaft *(imprisoned)* in Sibirien, aber das haben wir nicht gewusst. Also sind wir nach Berlin geflohen *(to flee)*. Das war natürlich dumm, denn in Berlin waren schon die Russen.

SCORE ☐

KAPITEL 3

Chapter Test

E. Now read the paragraph on p. 66 again and the next two paragraphs of *Eine Berlinerin erzählt,* and choose the best answers from among the alternatives given. (8 points)

Als der Krieg *(war)* zu Ende war, haben meine Mutter und meine Oma keine Arbeit gefunden *(found)*. Morgens und abends haben wir Suppe und Brot von der Heilsarmee *(Salvation Army)* bekommen.

1947 ist mein Vater dann zurückgekommen. Er ist zu Fuß von Sibirien nach Deutschland marschiert. Er hat uns im Rheinland gesucht. Mit Hilfe des Roten Kreuzes *(Red Cross)* hat er uns dann in Berlin gefunden. Er wollte mit uns wieder zurück ins Rheinland gehen. Aber unser Haus dort war abgebrannt *(burned down)* und die Fabrik, wo er gearbeitet hatte, existierte nicht mehr. Also sind wir in Berlin geblieben.

25. In the woman's memory, 1944 was the year that
   a. her mother and grandmother went to a Red Cross center for refugees.
   b. her father was released from prison.
   c. her mother and grandmother fled from the Russians.
   d. her mother and grandmother fled from the Americans and the British.

26. At the end of the war, the woman, her mother, and her grandmother survived by
   a. selling soup and bread.
   b. working on heavy construction.
   c. working in a kind of field kitchen.
   d. getting food from the Salvation Army.

27. 1947 was the year that
   a. the factory where her father worked was rebuilt.
   b. her father took them back to the **Rheinland.**
   c. her father returned on foot from Siberia.
   d. her father did not return as expected.

28. At the end of the narrative, the family decided to live in
   a. the **Rheinland.**
   b. Berlin.
   c. the USA.
   d. Normandy.

SCORE [   ]

F. The following statements form a brief biography when organized chronologically. Put the lettered statements in the correct order. The first one has been done for you. (10 points)

a. Danach ist er in die USA gegangen und hat dort an einer Universität studiert.

b. Er hat eine Amerikanerin geheiratet *(married)* und ist in den USA geblieben.

c. Direkt nach dem Universitätsstudium hat er als Lehrer gearbeitet.

d. Er hat fünfunddreißig Jahre lang in Seattle gewohnt.

e. Er hat das Hildesheimer Gymnasium besucht und sein Abitur dort gemacht.

f. August Schmidt wurde 1940 in Hildesheim geboren.

__f__ 0.

_____ 29.

_____ 30.

_____ 31.

_____ 32.

_____ 33.

SCORE [   ]

KAPITEL 3

Chapter Test

III. Culture

Maximum Score: 12 points

G. Which of the following are associated with Frankfurt, which with Dresden, and which with St. Ulrich? Mark **a)** for Frankfurt, **b)** for Dresden, and **c)** for St. Ulrich. (8 points)

_____ 34. the Elbe River

_____ 35. **der Zwinger**

_____ 36. **die Alpen**

_____ 37. the Main River

_____ 38. **der Römer**

_____ 39. Goethe's birthplace

40. A **Pension** is most similar to
   a. an American luxury hotel.
   b. a retirement plan.
   c. a bed and breakfast.
   d. a retirement home.

41. **Fachwerk** is a style of
   a. older German architecture.
   b. traditional German cooking.
   c. traditional German embroidery.
   d. modern German architecture.

SCORE [   ]

H. Label the German-speaking countries on the map. Mark **a)** for Austria, **b)** for Switzerland, **c)** for Germany, and **d)** for Liechtenstein. (4 points)

_____ 42.

_____ 43.

_____ 44.

_____ 45.

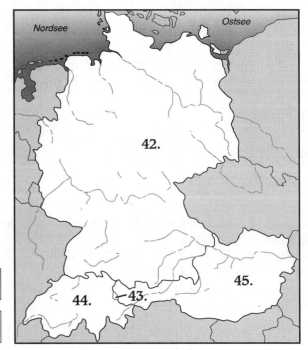

SCORE [   ]

TOTAL SCORE [   ]

KAPITEL 3

IV. Writing
Maximum Score: 30 points

I. Complete the conversation between your friend Monika and yourself by writing appropriate questions for each of Monika's answers. (10 points)

46. DU _____

MONIKA Wir waren am Weißensee in Österreich.

47. DU _____

MONIKA Wir sind gewandert, geschwommen und mit Booten auf dem See gefahren.

48. DU _____

MONIKA Ja, es hat mir sehr gefallen. Es war sehr schön dort.

49. DU _____

MONIKA Also, ich hab keine Kirchen oder Museen besichtigt, aber mein Vater hat sich viel angesehen.

50. DU _____

MONIKA Ja, wir waren auch in den Bergen und sind berggestiegen.

SCORE [   ]

J. On the next page is the **Fragebogen** filled out by the Stegmüllers, whose children Melissa (7) and Jochen (9) accompanied them to St. Ulrich in Tirol. Look at the **Fragebogen,** and then write a postcard from Jochen to his grandmother, telling her about his vacation. Mention where you are and include points 1, 2, 3, and 5 in your postcard. (10 points)

_____

_____

_____

_____

_____

_____

SCORE [   ]

KAPITEL 3

Name _____ Klasse _____ Datum _____

 Chapter Test

FRAGEBOGEN
Fremdenverkehrsverein St. Ulrich
Liebe Gäste!
Im Interesse aller Gäste bei uns möchten wir von Ihnen
erfahren, welche Quartiere und
Unterhaltungsmöglichkeiten Sie am meisten benutzt
haben und was Ihnen bei uns am besten gefallen hat.

1. Wo haben Sie gewohnt?
☐ Hotel   ☐ Gasthof   ☑ Pension   ☐ Privatquartier

2. Wie hat Ihnen die Unterkunft gefallen?
☐ ausgezeichnet   ☑ sehr gut   ☐ gut
☐ nicht besonders   ☐ nicht gut

3. Wo haben Sie gewöhnlich gegessen?
☐ Hotel   ☑ Gasthaus   ☐ Café   ☐ Restaurant   ☐ selbst gekocht

4. Wie war die Qualität des Essens in unseren Lokalen?
☐ ausgezeichnet   ☑ sehr gut   ☐ gut   ☐ nicht gut

5. Wie haben Sie Ihren Urlaub verbracht? Kreuzen Sie bitte die Dinge an, die Sie
am meisten gemacht haben!
☑ wandern   ☐ angeln   ☑ Minigolf
☐ bergsteigen   ☑ Boot fahren   ☐ Tennis
☐ spazierengehen   ☐ radfahren   ☑ Tischtennis
☑ baden gehen   ☐ reiten   ☐ kegeln

6. Was hat den Kindern am meisten Spaß gemacht?
a. _____Ponyreiten_____
b. _____Grillparty_____
c. _____

7. Welche Unterhaltungsprogramme haben Ihnen am besten gefallen? Kreuzen
Sie bitte nur drei Programme an!
☑ Musikabende   ☐ Tanzveranstaltungen   ☐ Vorträge
☑ Theateraufführungen   ☐ Dia-Vorführungen

8. Wie lange waren Sie bei uns?
☐ eine Woche   ☑ zwei Wochen   _____

Vielen Dank! Ihr Fremdenverkehrsverein A-6393 St. Ulrich am Pillersee in Tirol Telefon 05354-88176

K. Using the same data, write a short letter to your former German teacher, Frau
Gertzen. You just got home from Tirol, so tell her about the vacation using the past
tense. Mention where you were und include points 1, 5 (mention two activities),
and 8 in your letter. Also tell your teacher how you liked the trip in general.
(Remember to use the polite form of address.) (10 points)

_____

_____

_____

_____

_____

SCORE ☐

TOTAL SCORE ☐

KAPITEL 3

Name _____ Klasse _____ Datum _____

Circle the letter that matches the most appropriate response.

I. Listening
Maximum Score: 28 points

A. (10 points)

1. a b c d
2. a b c d
3. a b c d
4. a b c d
5. a b c d

SCORE [   ]

B. (8 points)

6. a b
7. a b
8. a b
9. a b
10. a b
11. a b
12. a b
13. a b

SCORE [   ]

C. (10 points)

14. a b c d e
15. a b c d e
16. a b c d e
17. a b c d e
18. a b c d e

SCORE [   ]

II. Reading
Maximum Score: 30 points

D. (12 points)

19. a b
20. a b
21. a b
22. a b
23. a b
24. a b

SCORE [   ]

E. (8 points)

25. a b c d
26. a b c d
27. a b c d
28. a b c d

SCORE [   ]

F. (10 points)

29. a b c d e
30. a b c d e
31. a b c d e
32. a b c d e
33. a b c d e

SCORE [   ]

III. Culture
Maximum Score: 12 points

G. (8 points)

34. a b c
35. a b c
36. a b c
37. a b c
38. a b c
39. a b c

40. a b c d
41. a b c d

SCORE [   ]

H. (4 points)

42. a b c d
43. a b c d
44. a b c d
45. a b c d

SCORE [   ]

KAPITEL 3

IV. Writing   Maximum Score: 30 points

I. (10 points)

46. _____

47. _____

48. _____

49. _____

50. _____

SCORE [   ]

J. (10 points)

_____

_____

_____

_____

_____

_____

_____

_____

_____

_____

SCORE [   ]

K. (10 points)

_____

_____

_____

_____

_____

_____

_____

_____

_____

SCORE [   ]

TOTAL SCORE [   ]

KAPITEL 3

Listening Scripts for Quizzes 3-1B, 3-2B, 3-3B

Quiz 3-1B Kapitel 3 Erste Stufe

I. Listening

A. TINA Was hast du in den Ferien gemacht?

ULRICH Ich war in Dresden. Ich habe meinen Cousin besucht.

TINA Dresden? Was hast du denn alles gesehen? Hast du die Stadt besichtigt?

ULRICH Nein, eigentlich nicht.

TINA Du hast gefaulenzt, was?

ULRICH Nein, überhaupt nicht. Ich habe in Dresden einen Film gedreht — ein Video über die Stadt und die Leute.

TINA Und was hast du alles gefilmt?

ULRICH Na, ich bin einfach so mit der Videokamera losgelaufen und habe versucht, die Menschen in der Stadt zu filmen — ihre Klamotten, ihre Autos, was sie gekauft haben oder nicht gekauft haben und so was. Ich habe auch kurze Interviews mit ihnen gefilmt.

TINA Dein Film muss echt interessant sein. Die Leute in Dresden sind doch froh, dass sie jetzt alles kaufen können, was sie wollen, oder?

ULRICH Nicht immer! Ein Student, zum Beispiel, ist ganz traurig gewesen. Er hat gesagt, die Bücher sind nicht mehr so billig wie früher in der DDR. Sie sind jetzt ziemlich teuer. Als Student hat er natürlich nicht viel Geld. Die Wiedervereinigung hat manche Sachen einfach teurer gemacht.

Quiz 3-2B Kapitel 3 Zweite Stufe

I. Listening

A. 1. MARTINA Wo warst du denn in den Ferien, Rolf?

ROLF Ich hatte leider kein Geld, um wegzufahren. Also bin ich zu Hause geblieben und hab mir die Stadt angesehen. Ich war auf der Zeil, im Dom und im Goethehaus. Ach ja, und eine Bootstour auf dem Main habe ich auch noch gemacht. Und du, Peter, was hast du gemacht?

2. PETER Wir waren ein paar Tage lang an der Nordsee, in Cuxhaven. Aber leider hatten wir nur Regen. Und die See war ganz stürmisch und dunkel. Das waren leider keine schönen Ferien.

3. MARTINA Ach Gabi! Da bist du auch! Hast du schöne Ferien gehabt?

GABI Oh ja! Ich war in der Schweiz. Es war echt toll! In den Sommerferien wollen Andrea und ich wieder in die Schweiz fahren. Hättet ihr keine Lust mitzufahren?

Quiz 3-3B Kapitel 3 Dritte Stufe

I. Listening

A. MAX Ihr wart also doch in den Bergen! Du siehst ja ganz braun aus.

KATRINA Ja, wir sind dorthin gefahren. Aber außer Sonne hat es nichts gegeben.

MAX Wie meinst du das? Hat es dir nicht gefallen?

KATRINA Es geht so.

MAX Wieso denn? Was hat dir nicht gefallen?

KATRINA Nun, unser Gasthof hat mir nicht so gut gefallen. Es war ein bisschen langweilig. Da waren fast keine jungen Leute, nur Familien mit kleinen Kindern. Aber das Essen im Gasthof hat mir gut geschmeckt. Und mein Vater hat immer gesagt, das Essen war viel zu teuer. Das hat ihm natürlich nicht gefallen.

MAX Na ja. Erzähl weiter. Seid ihr wenigstens gewandert?

KATRINA Oh ja. Die Wanderwege waren sehr schön. Das hat mir gut gefallen, aber mein Bruder Günther findet Wandern immer langweilig, zu bequem, sagt er. Er geht lieber bergsteigen.

MAX Und deine Mutter?

KATRINA Sie wandert auch gern. Wir waren auch oft am See und sind geschwommen. Das war toll, aber das Wasser war eiskalt!

Answers to Quizzes 3-1A, 3-1B

ANSWERS Quiz 3-1A

A. (10 points; 1 point per item)
1. Ferien
2. besichtigen
3. fotografieren
4. Kamera
5. filmen
6. Videokamera
7. bedienen
8. Filme
9. Dias
10. Farbbilder

B. (10 points; 1 point per item)
11. Ich habe in Dresden gewohnt.
12. Ich bin in die Schweiz gefahren.
13. Ich habe dem Opa geholfen.
14. Ich habe der Petra ein Poster gekauft.
15. Ich bin in Österreich geblieben.
16. Ich habe Musik gehört.
17. Ich habe Berlin besichtigt.
18. Ich bin nach Hause gegangen.
19. Ich habe eine Limo getrunken.
20. Ich bin mitgekommen.

C. (10 points; 1 point per item)
Answers will vary. Possible answers:
21. Ihr seid letzte Woche gewandert.
22. Sie haben gestern toll ausgesehen.
23. Ich habe Klavier gespielt.
24. Wir haben eine Reise in die Schweiz gemacht.
25. Du bist 5 Kilometer gelaufen.
26. Ulrike und Jörg haben Semmeln gegessen.
27. Birgit hat den Fantasyroman gelesen.
28. Ich habe meiner Tante Parfüm geschenkt.
29. Ihr seid im Meer geschwommen.
30. Wir sind nach Bayern gefahren.

ANSWERS Quiz 3-1B

I. Listening

A. (12 points: 2 points per item)
1. T
2. F
3. F
4. T
5. T
6. F

II. Reading

B. (10 points: 2 points per item)
7. F
8. F
9. T
10. T
11. F

III. Writing

C. (8 points: 2 points per item)
Answers will vary. Possible answers:
12. Ich bin in X gewesen. / Ich bin nach X gefahren.
13.-15. Answers should include three activities expressed in the conversational past.

KAPITEL 3

ANSWERS Quiz 3-2A

A. (9 points; 1 point per item)
1. besucht
2. den Dom
3. Museen
4. die Fachwerkhäuser
5. Zeil
6. das Goethehaus
7. den Römer
8. die Oper
9. gefaulenzt

B. (8 points; 1 point per item)
10. hatten
11. wart
12. hatte
13. hatte
14. war
15. Warst
16. waren
17. hattet

C. (2 points; 1 point per item)
18. Ich bin heute Nachmittag zu Hause gewesen.
19. Du hast keinen Kuchen gehabt.

D. (8 points; 1 point per item)
20. An der
21. in
22. im
23. in der
24. im
25. am
26. an der
27. in

E. (8 points; 2 points per item)
Answers will vary. Possible answers:
28. Wir waren schon am See.
29. War Wilhelm gestern in der Schule?
30. Sie waren im Café, aber sie hatten kein Geld.
31. Ich war noch nie in London.

ANSWERS Quiz 3-2B

I. Listening

A. (12 points: 2 points per item)
1. b   4. Gabi
2. d   5. Rolf
3. c   6. Peter

II. Reading

B. (8 points: 2 points per item)
7. c
8. b
9. c
10. d

III. Writing

C. (16 points: 4 points per item)
Answers will vary. Possible answers:
11. Ich war in den Ferien in der Schweiz.
12. In Frankfurt war ich im Dom und im Goethehaus.
13. Meine Familie war in Frankreich am Meer.
14. Ich habe meine Tante nicht besucht, weil ich keine Zeit hatte.

IV. Culture

D. (4 points)
15. **Urlaub** refers to time off work for vacation, and **Ferien** refers to vacation from school.

ANSWERS Quiz 3-3A

A. (8 points; 2 points per item)
   Answers will vary. Possible answers:
   1. Phantastisch!; Es war echt super!
   2. Nicht besonders.; Es war furchtbar!
   3. Na, prima!; Das freut mich!
   4. Schade!; Das tut mir aber Leid!

B. (8 points; 1 point per item)
   Answers will vary. Possible answers:
   5. Wie hat es der Heidi gefallen?
   6. Wie hat es den Schülern gefallen?
   7. Wie hat es euch gefallen?
   8. Wie hat es Ihnen gefallen?
   9. Wie hat es dir gefallen?
   10. Wie hat es den Kindern gefallen?
   11. Wie hat es ihm gefallen?
   12. Wie hat es ihnen gefallen?

C. (7 points; 1 point per item)
   13. in einer Jugendherberge
   14. in einem Privathaus
   15. in einer Pension
   16. in einem Hotel
   17. in einem Lokal
   18. in einer Imbissstube
   19. in einem Restaurant; in einem Gasthof

D. (12 points; 3 points per item)
   Answers will vary. Possible answers:
   20. Nach dem Mittagessen sind wir nach Dresden gefahren.
   21. Er hat in einer Jugendherberge übernachtet, weil er nicht viel Geld hatte.
   22. Jeden Morgen haben Günther und Thomas am See gegessen.
   23. Am letzten Tag habe ich das Rathaus besichtigt.

ANSWERS Quiz 3-3B

I. Listening

A. (6 points: 2 points per item)
   1. a
   2. d
   3. b

II. Reading

B. (8 points: 2 points per item)
   4. T
   5. F
   6. F
   7. T

III. Writing

C. (12 points: 4 points per item)
   Answers will vary. Possible answer:
   Lieber Gerd!
   In den Ferien war ich in Schwangau. Ich habe in einer Jugendherberge über-nachtet und meistens in einem Lokal oder im Gasthof gegessen. Die Berge haben mir sehr gefallen, aber das Wetter war furchtbar! Na ja!
   Dein(e) ...

IV. Culture

D. (4 points: 2 points per item)
   8. a, d
   9. b, c

Holt German 2 Komm mit!, Chapter 3

Scripts for Chapter Test Kapitel 3

I. Listening

A.

GERD Wo warst du gestern Abend? Ich habe dich natürlich in der Oper gesucht, aber ich konnte dich nicht finden.

CHRISTA Ich bin nicht in die Oper gegangen, weil ich kein Geld hatte. Die Karten sind nicht gerade billig.

GERD Stimmt. Aber was hast du denn den ganzen Abend gemacht?

CHRISTA Ich habe mir gestern einen ganz tollen Roman von Heinrich Böll gekauft. Also dann habe ich eine Kassette mit Entspannungsmusik eingelegt und habe den ganzen Abend gelesen. Und eine Tafel Schokolade habe ich gegessen. Stell dir mal vor, ich habe bis zwei Uhr morgens gelesen, so spannend war der Roman!

GERD Also dann, willst du heute was machen?

CHRISTA Wenn du willst, können wir heute Nachmittag eine kleine Spazierfahrt machen — irgendwohin aufs Land fahren. Gefällt dir das?

GERD Eine Spazierfahrt?

CHRISTA Ja. Ich habe letzte Woche doch endlich das Auto gekauft, den Sportwagen von Audi.

GERD Mensch! Also du hast das Auto wirklich gekauft? Es hat bestimmt einen Haufen Geld gekostet!

CHRISTA Das stimmt. Und jetzt weißt du auch, warum ich kein Geld für die Oper hatte.

B.

AHMET Wo warst du in den Ferien?

ELENA In Zürich, in der Schweiz. Wir haben dort eine Kusine von meinem Vater besucht.

AHMET Wie war's denn? Langweilig?

ELENA Nein, gar nicht. Meine Verwandten sind wirklich nette Leute.

AHMET Und die Stadt? In Zürich gibt es doch nichts zu sehen, nur Banken, oder?

ELENA Das stimmt nicht ganz. Es gibt viel zu sehen. Wir haben die beiden großen Kirchen besichtigt. Und das Rathaus haben wir uns angesehen, und wir sind auch ins Schweizer Nationalmuseum gegangen und in eine Menge Galerien.

AHMET Du findest Kunst interessant?

ELENA Ja schon. Aber das Schönste war, die Stadt liegt direkt am See, und die Kusine von meinem Vater hat ein ganz tolles Segelboot. Wir waren dreimal auf dem See.

AHMET Wie war der Schweizer Käse? Hast du genug davon gegessen?

ELENA Schweizer Käse gibt es genug in der Schweiz und natürlich auch Schokolade. Das Essen war sonst auch wahnsinnig gut. Zweimal haben wir auch in einem sehr gemütlichen Lokal Käsefondue gegessen — das schmeckte sagenhaft!

AHMET Also hat dir Zürich dann sehr gut gefallen.

ELENA Ja, sehr gut. Aber ich freue mich auch, wieder in Hamburg zu sein.

C.

KARIN Hallo, Frank! Wie geht's denn?

FRANK Ganz prima. Ich bin gerade aus den Ferien zurückgekommen. Ich war fünf Wochen unterwegs.

KARIN Wo warst du denn?

FRANK Ich hab eine lange Reise durch Südeuropa gemacht. Ich war überall.

KARIN Wo denn?

FRANK Zuerst war ich in der Türkei, drei Tage in Istanbul. Das war wunderschön. Dann war ich vier Tage am Schwarzen Meer.

KARIN Und dann?

FRANK Dann bin ich nach Spanien geflogen und bin an die Mittelmeerküste gefahren. Ich hab meinen Freund Jochen dort getroffen, und wir haben zwei Wochen am Strand einfach gefaulenzt. Danach waren wir in den Bergen, in den Pyrenäen, und sind berggestiegen und haben kleine Dörfer besichtigt. Ich hab auch mein Spanisch geübt. Und zuletzt war ich am Atlantischen Ozean in Frankreich — noch zwei Wochen. Dort haben wir am Strand gezeltet. Dort ist das Wasser nicht so warm wie in Spanien, aber dafür ist es tagsüber auch nicht so heiß am Strand.

KARIN Mensch, das war bestimmt eine tolle Reise!

KAPITEL 3

Answers to Chapter Test Kapitel 3

I. Listening Maximum Score: 28 points

A. (10 points: 2 points per item)
1. b
2. d
3. a
4. b
5. b

B. (8 points: 1 point per item)
6. a
7. a
8. b
9. a
10. b
11. b
12. a
13. b

C. (10 points: 2 points per item)
14. c
15. b
16. e
17. d
18. a

II. Reading Maximum Score: 30 points

D. (12 points: 2 points per item)
19. b
20. a
21. b
22. a
23. a
24. b

E. (8 points: 2 points per item)
25. d
26. d
27. c
28. b

F. (10 points: 2 points per item)
29. e
30. a
31. c
32. b
33. d

III. Culture Maximum Score: 12 points

G. (8 points: 1 point per item)
34. b
35. b
36. c
37. a
38. a
39. a
40. c
41. a

H. (4 points: 1 point per item)
42. c
43. d
44. b
45. a

IV. Writing Maximum Score: 30 points

I. (10 points: 2 points per item)
46. Wo warst du [in den Ferien]?
47. Was habt ihr denn gemacht?
48. Hat es dir gefallen?
49. Hast du auch Kirchen oder Museen besichtigt?
50. Warst du auch in den Bergen?

J. (10 points: 2 points per item)
Answers will vary. Possible answers:
Liebe Oma!
Wir sind jetzt in Österreich. Wir wohnen in einer Pension. Sie gefällt mir sehr. Meistens essen wir im Gasthof. Wir wandern, schwimmen, fahren Boot and spielen oft Minigolf und Tennis.
    Dein
    Jochen

K. (10 points: 2 points per item)
Answers will vary. Possible answers:
Liebe Frau Gertzen!
Meine Familie und ich waren in den Ferien in Österreich. Dort haben wir in einer Pension gewohnt. Wir sind viel gewandert. Wir sind auch oft auf dem See Boot gefahren. Wir sind zwei Wochen geblieben. Es hat mir sehr gut gefallen!
    Herzliche Grüße,
    [student's name]

Holt German 2 Komm mit!, Chapter 3

KAPITEL **4**

Gesund leben

Quiz 4-1A

Maximum Score: 35

■ Erste Stufe

Grammar and Vocabulary

A. Express the following statements and questions in German. (14 points)

Gisela, do you do a lot for your health?

1. _____

Herr Becker jogs every morning.

2. _____

Anke and Jens, do you eat healthily?

3. _____

I live in a very healthy way.

4. _____

Does he get enough sleep?

5. _____

They don't drink alcohol.

6. _____

Renate exercises every evening.

7. _____

SCORE [   ]

B. Complete the following sentences, expressing approval or disapproval of your friend's health habits. (8 points)

8. _____ , dass du nicht rauchst.

9. _____ , dass du nicht sehr viel Obst isst.

10. _____ , dass du jeden Tag Rad fährst.

11. _____ , dass du die Sonne nicht vermeidest.

SCORE [   ]

KAPITEL 4

Quiz 4-1A

C. Complete the following statements and questions, filling in the first blank with the proper reflexive pronoun, and the second blank with the German equivalent of the words in parentheses. [13 points]

Wir fühlen 12. _____ hier 13. _____ (in the clique) sehr wohl.

Herr Troger, fühlen Sie 14. _____ hier 15. _____ (in this city) nicht sehr wohl?

Fühlst du 16. _____ hier in der Schule 17. _____ (not at all well)?

Ich fühle 18. _____ hier 19. _____ (in the class) ganz wohl.

Ahmet fühlt 20. _____ hier 21. _____ (in the soccer team) supertoll.

Ihr fühlt 22. _____ hier in München 23. _____ (wonderful), nicht?

Fühlen sie 24. _____ hier wohl?

SCORE _____

TOTAL SCORE _____

Name _____ Klasse _____ Datum _____

Gesund leben

Quiz 4-1B

■ Erste Stufe

Maximum Score: 40

I. Listening

A. Ulrike is reading a health magazine as her father comes home from work. Listen to Ulrike and her father's conversation twice. Of the eight **Gesundheitstipps** listed below, put a check mark next to the five Ulrike mentions. (10 points)

Gesundheitstipps	
☐ Rad fahren	☐ Sport machen
☐ die Sonne vermeiden	☐ nicht rauchen
☐ viel Obst und Gemüse essen	☐ genügend schlafen
☐ fettes Essen vermeiden	☐ wenig Alkohol trinken

SCORE _____

II. Reading

B. Read the lettered English statements below and then read the three paragraphs on health-related topics. Decide which of the lettered statements fits best with each paragraph. Note: you will not use all of the choices. (12 points)

a. We now know the probable causes of high blood pressure and other diseases, such as gout, rickets, and scurvy.
b. Using preservatives in foods is not a new invention. (People preserved foods with various substances 200 years ago.)
c. One can now get fresh produce anywhere in Europe at any time of the year.
d. Some of our fresh foods may contain harmful chemicals.

_____ 1. Heute ist es sehr leicht, gesund zu essen. Wissenschaftler *(scientists)* haben uns gesagt, wie viel und welche Nährstoffe *(nutrients),* besonders Vitamine und Miner-alien, wir brauchen. Durch den modernen Transport können wir zu jeder Jahreszeit und überall in Europa frisches Obst und Gemüse bekommen.

_____ 2. Wir wissen auch, dass zu viel Fett nicht gut ist für das Herz (heart). Zu viel Salz erhöht den Blutdruck *(blood pressure).* Leute, die zu viel Fleisch essen, bekommen die Gicht *(gout).* Rachitis *(rickets)* und Skorbut *(scurvy)* kommen von zu wenig Vitamin D und C. Das alles hat man vor 200 Jahren noch nicht gewusst.

_____ 3. Der moderne Mensch hat aber auch neue Probleme geschaffen *(created).* Wir spritzen *(spray)* das Obst und Gemüse oft mit schädlichen *(harmful)* Chemikalien gegen Insekten und Pflanzenkrankheiten *(plant diseases).*

SCORE _____

Quiz 4-1B

III. Writing

C. A friend of yours did not show up at school today and you went to his house to find out what was wrong. Complete the conversation by writing sentences as indicated. (12 points)

4. *You ask your friend how he feels.*

   DU _____

   ER Nicht sehr wohl, aber besser als gestern.

5. *You ask him if he's been eating right.*

   DU _____

   ER Ich habe auf der Fete ein bisschen Heringssalat gegessen — nur ganz wenig. Aber ich bin allergisch gegen Fisch.

6. *You advise him to avoid fish.*

   DU _____

   ER Das tue ich auch meistens.

SCORE ☐

IV. Culture

D. Do Germans do the same kinds of things to stay fit and healthy as Americans do? State your own opinion and support it with at least two pieces of evidence from the **Landeskunde** section of **Kapitel 4**. (6 points)

7. _____

   _____

   _____

   _____

SCORE ☐

TOTAL SCORE ☐

KAPITEL 4

Gesund leben

Quiz 4-2A

Maximum Score: 30

Zweite Stufe

Grammar and Vocabulary

A. Fill in the blanks below with the appropriate forms of the determiner **jeder**. (10 points)

Wir möchten **1.** _____ Museum in der Stadt besichtigen.

2. _____ Sciencefictionfilm gefällt mir.

In **3.** _____ Gasthof sieht man Blumen.

Die Kinder haben **4.** _____ Semmeln gegessen.

Ich schenke **5.** _____ Kusine einen Blumenstrauß.

6. _____ Donnerstag muss ich die Fenster putzen.

Ich möchte **7.** _____ Park besuchen.

8. _____ Schülerin hat um 8 Uhr 30 Deutsch.

Ich gebe **9.** _____ Klassenkameraden ein Stück Kuchen.

In **10.** _____ Hotel gibt es viele Zimmer.

SCORE [   ]

B. You are curious about your friend's health habits, and are peppering him with questions on the subject. Fill in the blanks below, using words from the box. Note: words may be used more than once or not at all. (6 points)

eigentlich	steht's	klar	natürlich	Frage
etwas	mit	darf	sag	

11. _____ mal, joggst du nur einmal am Tag?

Ich habe eine **12.** _____ : Ernährst du dich richtig?

Wie **13.** _____ mit Obst? Isst du **14.** _____ viel Obst?

15. _____ ich dich **16.** _____ fragen? Bist du in einer

Mannschaft?

SCORE [   ]

Quiz 4-2A

KAPITEL 4

C. A friend of yours is making assertions about your health habits. You agree with her, but with reservations. Rearrange the words provided to form logical sentences. Don't forget to use the correct forms of the verbs! (6 points)

Du isst nicht viel Obst!

    stimmen / das /   aber / oft / ich / Gemüse / essen

17. _____

Trinkst du viel Kaffee?

    schon / eigentlich /   trinken / viel / ich / aber / Saft / auch

18. _____

Du schläfst zu wenig!

    können / ja / sein / das /   mich / ernähren / ich / richtig / aber

19. _____

SCORE [   ]

D. Give the German equivalents of the following English sentences. (8 points)

Sara and Uwe, do you seldom eat fruit and vegetables?

20. _____

_____

Usually Herr Bauer drinks milk every day.

21. _____

_____

I'm happy that they normally keep themselves fit.

22. _____

_____

Mostly we eat healthy foods, but every weekend we eat meat or sausage.

23. _____

_____

SCORE [   ]

TOTAL SCORE [   ]

4 Gesund leben

■ Zweite Stufe

I. Listening

A. Michael and his sister, Cornelia, are at home when this conversation takes place. First read the questions below and then listen to the conversation twice. Choose the best answers from among the alternatives given. (8 points)

1. What happened to the drawing pencils?
   a. Michael stole them from Cornelia.
   b. Michael borrowed them WITH Cornelia's permission.
   c. Michael borrowed them WITHOUT Cornelia's permission.
   d. Michael is hiding them from Cornelia.

2. Michael agrees he should buy his own, but he says
   a. he has no money.
   b. he's too lazy.
   c. the stores are already closed.
   d. the stationery store was out of drawing pencils the last time he tried to buy them.

3. Michael agrees with Cornelia that he should save part of his allowance for the end of the month, but he has reservations because
   a. he likes to spend money all at once.
   b. he only gets three euros a month.
   c. things are so expensive it's impossible to save.
   d. his girlfriend just had a birthday and he spent his entire allowance on her.

4. At the end of their discussion, Michael tells Cornelia that
   a. he wants her to loan him money for his own pencils.
   b. he plans to buy his own erasers.
   c. her suggestions are not very practical.
   d. he wants to borrow another pencil.

SCORE [   ]

II. Reading

B. Read the article about fitness and then decide if the statements that follow are true (T) or false (F). (6 points)

Reporter Beth Jennings berichtet:

In den USA rollt die Fitnesswelle. Man muss nicht dünn *(thin)* aussehen, um sportlich zu sein, sondern Muskeln haben. Das ist auch bei Frauen „in".

Bei einem Health Club in Connecticut waren wir zum Workout eingeladen. Da gab es *(there were)* stationäre Fahrräder und einen Apparat zum stationären Skilaufen. Die Direktorin des Health Clubs sagte: „Das ist doch praktischer als mit dem Auto in die Berge *(mountains)* zu fahren und Ski zu laufen."

Quiz 4-2B

Wir haben eine junge Frau im Health Club gefragt, ob *(whether)* es Spaß macht, auf einem computergeregelten Laufband zu trainieren. Sie sagte: „Eigentlich nicht, aber ich muss mich fit halten. Ich bin Modedesignerin *(fashion designer)* und da ist es wichtig, dass ich gut aussehe.“

_____ 5. Frauen wollen jetzt auch Muskeln haben.

_____ 6. Das stationäre Skilaufen ist praktischer als das Skilaufen in den Bergen.

_____ 7. Es ist nicht wichtig, wie die Modedesignerin aussieht.

SCORE ☐

III. Writing

C. You are discussing something with a German friend. Complete the exchange by writing sentences as indicated. (12 points)

ER Du machst keinen Sport.

Say that you do! Explain how often and what kind(s).

8. DU _____

ER Aber du schaust ziemlich viel Fernsehen.

Agree, but explain what else you do.

9. DU _____

Now it's your turn. Ask your friend a question that will elicit the answer below.

10. DU _____

ER Wie ich mich fit halte? Ich mache natürlich Sport und ernähre mich richtig!

SCORE ☐

IV. Culture

D. You are an exchange student living with a host family in Germany. Answer the following questions by writing the German word in the blanks provided. (4 points)

11. Your host mother has special dietary needs and has asked you to buy her a few groceries.
To which store should you go? _____

12. A friend of yours from the **Gymnasium** is having a birthday party tonight. You want to bring something to snack on, but you know he or she eats only organic, all-natural foods.
To which store should you go? _____

SCORE ☐

TOTAL SCORE ☐

Name _____ Klasse _____ Datum _____

4 Gesund leben

■ Dritte Stufe

Maximum Score: 35

Grammar and Vocabulary

A. Give the German equivalents of the following English words. Don't forget to include the articles and plural forms! (Note: not every word below will have a plural form.) (13 points)

cherry	**1.**	_____
beef	**2.**	_____
mushroom	**3.**	_____
blueberry	**4.**	_____
cauliflower	**5.**	_____
chicken	**6.**	_____
carrot	**7.**	_____
apricot	**8.**	_____
rice	**9.**	_____
food (prepared meal)	**10.**	_____
broccoli	**11.**	_____
trout	**12.**	_____
strawberry	**13.**	_____

SCORE ☐

B. Fill in the blanks below with the appropriate forms of **kein** and **dürfen**. (10 points)

Heiko, **14.** _____ du denn **15.** _____ Eis essen?

Ich **16.** _____ **17.** _____ Pralinen essen.

Die Daniela **18.** _____ **19.** _____ Alkohol trinken.

Frau Weber, **20.** _____ Sie **21.** _____ Kartoffelsuppe essen?

Ihr **22.** _____ **23.** _____ Spinat essen.

SCORE ☐

KAPITEL 4

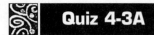

Quiz 4-3A

C. Complete the following sentences, using the English phrases in parentheses as prompts. (12 points)

Sie dürfen kein Fleisch essen, denn es ...

(is fattening)   24. _____.

(isn't good for their health)   25. _____.

(has too much fat)   26. _____.

Wir dürfen keinen Kuchen essen, weil er ...

(has too many calories)   27. _____.

(doesn't taste good to us)   28. _____.

(has too much sugar)   29. _____.

SCORE _____

TOTAL SCORE _____

4 Gesund leben

Dritte Stufe

Maximum Score: 30

I. Listening

A. Class 8b at the **Realschule** has been planning a trip. Their homeroom teacher receives a call from a parent. Listen to the conversation, and then decide whether the statements below are true (T) or false (F). Answer question 5 briefly in English. (10 points)

_____ 1. The students in 8b want to experience life on a farm.

_____ 2. The mother wants Bernd to go, but he's afraid of cows.

_____ 3. Bernd is not allowed to drink milk, but he can eat cheese.

_____ 4. In addition to being allergic to milk, Bernd has several other allergies.

5. What does the mother seem to be suggesting at the end of this conversation?

_____

SCORE [   ]

II. Reading

B. The following article provides information for those who suffer from nickel allergy. Read the article and then decide which of the items listed on page 90 may aggravate a nickel allergy. Write the letters of those items in the blanks. (12 points)

Was kann man bei einer Nickel-Allergie tun?

Nickel kommt in vielen Lebensmitteln und Metalllegierungen vor. Allergische Symptome werden durch Hautkontakt *(skin contact)*, das Einatmen *(breathing in)* von nickelhaltigem Rauch oder durch das Essen von nickelhaltigen Lebensmitteln verursacht.

– Vermeiden Sie deshalb Modeschmuck, Knöpfe (z.B. an Jeans), Ohrringe, Ringe und anderen Schmuck. Verwenden Sie nur Kochgeschirr aus Glas und Behälter *(containers)* aus Holz und Plastik. Verwenden Sie auch keine Kaffeemaschine.

– Rauchen Sie nicht und vermeiden Sie verrauchte Räume. Jedes Kilogramm Zigaretten enthält 2 bis 5,4 Milligramm Nickel, davon gehen 20 Prozent in den Rauch über.

– Vermeiden Sie Lebensmittel, die besonders nickelhaltig sind. Essen Sie keinen Käse und keine Schokolade. Vermeiden Sie Brokkoli, Pilze, Zwiebeln, Tomaten und Spinat. Essen Sie keine Kirschen und keine Birnen. Auch Brot, Kuchen, und Müsli enthalten Nickel.

Quiz 4-3B

Sie dürfen essen: Fleisch, Huhn, Fisch, Eier, Reis, Margarine, Milch, Joghurt, Butter, Kartoffeln, Gurken, Salat und frisches Obst (außer Kirschen und Birnen).

_____ 6.

_____ 7.

_____ 8.

a. beef
b. cigarettes
c. mushrooms
d. cooking pot made out of glass
e. coffee made in a coffee machine
f. rice

SCORE [   ]

III. Writing

C. You have been reading about and discussing health and fitness. Write a list of four rules to remind yourself of what you should do, have to do, or are not allowed to do. Write complete sentences using **sollen, dürfen,** and **müssen.** [8 points]

9. _____

_____

10. _____

_____

11. _____

_____

12. _____

_____

SCORE [   ]

TOTAL SCORE [   ]

Name _____ Klasse _____ Datum _____

4 Gesund leben

Chapter Test

I. Listening

Maximum Score: 30 points

A. A reporter for the school paper at the Hans-Böckler-Schule is interviewing students for his article **Schule und Stress**. Read the statements below, and then listen to the interview, marking each statement true (**a**) or false (**b**). (20 points)

The interviewee, Johannes,

_____ 1. realizes that breakfast is an important meal.

_____ 2. rushes through a big breakfast in the morning.

_____ 3. drinks coffee.

_____ 4. drives a moped to school instead of riding his bike.

_____ 5. takes a short walk during the morning school break.

_____ 6. eats a **Semmel** during break.

_____ 7. eats a healthy light lunch.

_____ 8. eats lunch at the café downtown.

_____ 9. would like to eat a nutritious midday meal.

_____ 10. says he does not have time during the usual school day to do healthy things for himself.

SCORE _____

B. Read the statements below and then listen as a teacher from the Therese-Erhardt-Schule reads the school rules on the first day of classes. For each statement, mark **a)** for "allowed" and **b)** for "not allowed." (10 points)

_____ 11. entering the school building before 8:20 a.m.

_____ 12. staying in the classroom during the morning break

_____ 13. standing around in the school yard before 8:20 am

_____ 14. waiting in the gym before school on rainy days

_____ 15. buying a morning snack at school

SCORE _____

Chapter Test

II. Reading

Maximum Score: 30 points

C. For each set of responses, choose the one that is NOT an appropriate reply. (20 points)

16. Ich halte mich mit Langlauf fit.
    a. Das freut mich sehr.
    b. Ich bin froh, dass du vernünftig isst.
    c. Ich finde es gut, dass du Sport machst.
    d. Schön, dass du etwas für deine Gesundheit tust.

17. Du trinkst keine Milch?
    a. Doch! Jeden Tag fast einen Liter.
    b. Doch! Aber nur Magermilch.
    c. Na und? Du trinkst ja auch keine!
    d. Stimmt nicht! Ich trinke doch nie Milch.

18. Ernährst du dich richtig?
    a. Ja, ich esse ziemlich viel Obst und Gemüse.
    b. Ja, ich esse ganz wenig Fett.
    c. Ja, ich esse alles, was mir schmeckt.
    d. Nein, ich esse eigentlich sehr oft in einer Imbissstube.

19. Geht's dir heute besser?
    a. Danke, ich fühle mich wieder sehr wohl.
    b. Ja, ich bin wieder ganz gesund.
    c. Nein, leider fühle ich mich überhaupt nicht wohl.
    d. Nein, ich finde es gar nicht gut.

20. Fühlt ihr euch hier in München wohl?
    a. Ja, danke, wir sind alle sehr gesund.
    b. Ja, die Stadt gefällt uns sehr.
    c. Klar! München ist doch toll.
    d. Nein, nicht so sehr. Wir kennen noch niemanden hier.

21. Raucht Herr Holzmann nicht?
    a. Eigentlich raucht er nur Zigarre.
    b. Nein, er ist doch Raucherfeind.
    c. Ja, er raucht. Er ist ja Gesundheitsfanatiker.
    d. Doch! Er ist ja ein Gesundheitsmuffel.

22. Hast du genügend geschlafen?
    a. Ich bin jeden Abend früh ins Bett gegangen.
    b. Ja, jede Nacht acht Stunden.
    c. Leider habe ich nur wenig Schlaf bekommen.
    d. Ja, ich bin ganz müde.

23. Ich bin allergisch gegen Milch.
   a. Dann sollst du auch Käse vermeiden.
   b. Dann musst du Vollmilch trinken.
   c. Also darfst du keine Butter essen?
   d. Dann gehen wir lieber nicht Eis essen.

24. Ich mache zweimal in der Woche Gymnastik.
   a. Ich treibe auch regelmäßig Sport.
   b. Schade, dass du selten Sport machst.
   c. Gymnastik macht mir auch Spaß.
   d. Gehst du auch zum Trimm-dich-Pfad?

25. Dürfen wir hier im Korridor laufen?
   a. Nein, das sollt ihr draußen auf dem Schulhof machen.
   b. Nein, hier darf man nicht laufen.
   c. Nein, ihr könnt hier laufen.
   d. Nein! Das wisst ihr doch schon!

SCORE [   ]

D. Read the passage below once. Then read it again and note the letter of the sentence(s) in which you can find the following information. (10 points)

_____ 26. A fifteenth-century method of cooking spinach

_____ 27. Some modern attitudes about eating fatty foods

_____ 28. The controversy over defining healthy foods

_____ 29. A fifteenth-century doctor's ideas on eating right

_____ 30. Modern ideas about eating fresh fruits and vegetables

a) Vernünftig essen — das will jeder. Aber auch die medizinischen Wissenschaftler *(scientists)* streiten sich *(argue)* darüber, was „vernünftig" ist. Was bedeutet „vernünftig essen"? Was muss man wirklich für die Gesundheit tun?

b) Im fünfzehnten Jahrhundert hat ein englischer Arzt *(physician)* geschrieben: Bitteres Essen beruhigt *(soothe)* den Magen *(stomach)*. Frisches Obst und Gemüse irritiert den Magen.

c) Heute meinen fast alle, dass frisches Obst und Gemüse für die Gesundheit sehr wichtig ist. Sogar Brokkoli und Blumenkohl sollen ungekocht gegessen werden.

d) Im fünfzehnten Jahrhundert hat man den Spinat zum Beispiel zuerst lange in Wasser gekocht und dann in Fett gebraten *(fried)*, damit er besser schmeckt.

e) Heute wissen wir, dass fettiges Essen nicht gesund ist, aber wir essen doch zu viel Fett.

SCORE [   ]

Chapter Test

KAPITEL 4

III. Culture

Maximum Score: 10 points

E. Based on your cultural knowledge of German-speaking countries, choose the best answers from among the alternatives given. (10 points)

31. Where would you go if you wanted to buy organic produce?
    a. **Supermarkt**
    b. **Obst- und Gemüseladen**
    c. **Bioladen**
    d. **Vollwertkost**

32. When grocery shopping in Germany it is common to
    a. pay only with credit cards.
    b. bring your own grocery bag or basket.
    c. tip the bagger.
    d. bring small bills because the cashiers don't have change.

33. **Vollwertkost** refers to
    a. the cost of whole grains.
    b. a type of store.
    c. unprocessed, all-natural foods.
    d. a type of bread.

34. **Reformhaus** refers to
    a. a meeting place for politically active people.
    b. a church committed to changing the world.
    c. a reformed community dating from the sixteenth century.
    d. a grocery store that sells food for people with special diets.

35. Imagine you are a German teenager. An American friend of yours is visiting from the United States. You go grocery shopping together, and your friend notices several people putting excess food packaging into bins at the front of the store. Your friend wants to know what's going on. What would you tell him or her?

    _____

    _____

    _____

    _____

    _____

SCORE [   ]

Chapter Test

IV. Writing

Maximum Score: 30 points

F. You are talking to your German friend Rolf on the telephone. Complete the conversation by following the directions below. (15 points)

Greet him and ask how things are going.

36. DU _____

   ER Eigentlich geht's mir ganz schlecht.

Ask if he is not feeling well.

37. DU _____

   ER Nun, ich habe Kopfschmerzen und Fieber. Ich glaube, ich habe mich erkältet.

Give him some advice. Tell him he should get enough sleep and drink a lot of water.

38. DU _____

39.   [und] _____

   ER Ja, das mache ich gleich.

Tell him he should also avoid the sun.

40. DU _____

   ER Ja, mache ich auch. Danke!

SCORE ☐

KAPITEL 4

Chapter Test

G. A friend of yours is taking some serious risks with his or her health. You are worried. Write a short note in which you mention how you feel about this in general. Then mention three things he or she does or does not do, and give him or her three pieces of advice about how to improve his or her health. Write five or more complete sentences. (15 points)

_____

_____

_____

_____

_____

_____

_____

_____

_____

SCORE [ ]

TOTAL SCORE [ ]

KAPITEL 4 Chapter Test Score Sheet

Circle the letter that matches the most appropriate response.

I. Listening
Maximum Score: 30 points

A. (20 points)

1. a b
2. a b
3. a b
4. a b
5. a b

6. a b
7. a b
8. a b
9. a b
10. a b

SCORE [   ]

B. (10 points)

11. a b
12. a b
13. a b
14. a b
15. a b

SCORE [   ]

II. Reading
Maximum Score: 30 points

C. (20 points)

16. a b c d
17. a b c d
18. a b c d
19. a b c d
20. a b c d

21. a b c d
22. a b c d
23. a b c d
24. a b c d
25. a b c d

SCORE [   ]

D. (10 points)

26. a b c d e
27. a b c d e
28. a b c d e
29. a b c d e
30. a b c d e

SCORE [   ]

III. Culture
Maximum Score: 10 points

E. (10 points)

31. a b c d
32. a b c d
33. a b c d
34. a b c d

35. _____
_____
_____
_____
_____
_____

SCORE [   ]

IV. Writing

Maximum Score: 30 points

F. (15 points)

36. _____

_____

37. _____

_____

38. _____

_____

39. _____

_____

40. _____

_____

SCORE _____

G. (15 points)

_____

_____

_____

_____

_____

_____

_____

_____

_____

_____

_____

_____

_____

_____

SCORE _____

TOTAL SCORE _____

Quiz 4-1B Kapitel 4 Erste Stufe

I. Listening

A.   VATER   Abend, Ulrike! Was liest du da?

      ULRIKE   Abend, Vati! Ich lese gerade ein Gesundheitsmagazin.

      VATER   Und? Hast du was gelernt?

      ULRIKE   Hier steht's, man soll keine Zigaretten rauchen und nur wenig Alkohol trinken.

      VATER   Nun, wir sind alle Nichtraucher, und Alkohol trinken Mutti und ich auch nicht.

      ULRIKE   Ja, und man soll wenig Fett essen, aber viel Obst und Gemüse — besonders Salat.

      VATER   Na, meine Mutter — deine Großmutter — hat immer gesagt, dass zum Beispiel Butter gesund macht. Und Gurkenscheiben esse ich eigentlich oft auf meinem Brot.

      ULRIKE   Ach Vati! Nun, sehr wichtig für das Herz ist es eben, dass man sich durch Sport fit hält, also richtig trainiert. Und das tust du aber nicht.

      VATER   Doch! Ich kegle jeden Freitag, und wenn das Wetter schön ist, gehe ich immer spazieren.

      ULRIKE   Nein, Vati, ich finde, dass du nicht genug für deine Gesundheit tust!

Quiz 4-2B Kapitel 4 Zweite Stufe

I. Listening

A. CORNELIA   Michael, ich habe eine Frage: Hast du meine Zeichenstifte genommen?

     MICHAEL   Deine Stifte? Eigentlich schon, aber ich habe gedacht, du brauchst die Stifte nicht.

     CORNELIA   Hör mal, mein Lieber, es steht geschrieben: Du sollst nicht stehlen! Besonders nicht von deiner Schwester.

     MICHAEL   Mensch, ich habe sie doch nicht gestohlen.

     CORNELIA   Und meinen Radiergummi? Hast du dir den auch geborgt?

     MICHAEL   Ja ja.

     CORNELIA   Sag mal, warum hast du eigentlich keine Stifte und keinen Radiergummi? Kauf sie dir doch mal! Findest du das nicht auch besser?

     MICHAEL   Ja klar, aber ich habe kein Geld.

     CORNELIA   Wie steht's denn mit deinem Taschengeld?

     MICHAEL   Das Taschengeld ist alle.

     CORNELIA   Also, du sollst nicht gleich alles am Anfang des Monats ausgeben. Du sollst einen Teil von deinem Geld bis zum Ende des Monats aufheben.

     MICHAEL   Das kann sein, aber es ist nicht leicht, du, weil alles sehr teuer ist. Aber du hast Recht, Cornelia. Nun, sag mal, kannst du mir drei Euro geben, damit ich Stifte kaufen kann?

     CORNELIA   Also! So ein Schlitzohr bist du! Nein. Kommt nicht in Frage! Ich habe sowieso bis zum Ersten nur noch einen Euro.

Quiz 4-3B Kapitel 4 Dritte Stufe

I. Listening

A.   LEHRER   Guten Tag, Frau Albrecht! Was darf ich für Sie tun?

     MUTTER   Ja, wissen Sie, mein Sohn Bernd ist bei Ihnen in der Klasse 8b. Er hat uns gesagt, die Klasse will einen Bauernhof besuchen und dort übernachten.

     LEHRER   Ja, die Schüler wollen auf dem Lande wohnen und die Tiere sehen und füttern und so was.

     MUTTER   Nun, wissen Sie, Bernd ist allergisch gegen Haustiere. Ich glaube, dass er wahrscheinlich auch gegen Kühe allergisch ist.

     LEHRER   Das ist aber schade!

     MUTTER   Bernd darf gar keine Milch trinken. Käse und Butter soll er auch vermeiden, verstehen Sie? Und gegen Heu und verschiedene Gräser hat er auch Allergien.

     LEHRER   Ja, Frau Albrecht, dann darf Ihr Sohn natürlich nicht mit auf die Klassenfahrt kommen. Am besten bleibt er im Unterricht in der Parallelklasse, in der 8a, bei Herrn Pfost für drei Tage.

     MUTTER   Aber das gefällt dem Bernd doch bestimmt nicht! Wir machen nie Urlaub auf dem Land, sondern fahren woandershin. Wir wollen nicht, dass Bernd zu Hause bleiben muss, verstehen Sie?

     LEHRER   Ja, Frau Albrecht, es gibt aber noch 29 andere Schüler in der 8b ...

ANSWERS Quiz 4-1A

A. (14 points; 2 points per item)
Answers will vary. Possible answers:
1. Gisela, tust du viel für die Gesundheit?
2. Herr Becker joggt jeden Morgen.
3. Anke und Jens, esst ihr vernünftig?
4. Ich lebe sehr gesund.
5. Schläft er genügend?
6. Sie trinken keinen Alkohol.
7. Renate macht jeden Abend Gymnastik.

B. (8 points; 2 points per item)
Answers will vary. Possible answers:
8. Ich finde es toll
9. Es ist schade
10. Ich freue mich
11. Ich finde es nicht gut

C. (13 points; 1 point per item)
Answers will vary. Possible answers:
12. uns
13. in der Clique
14. sich
15. in dieser Stadt
16. dich
17. überhaupt nicht wohl
18. mich
19. in der Klasse
20. sich
21. in der Fußballmannschaft
22. euch
23. großartig
24. sich

ANSWERS Quiz 4-1B

I. **Listening** (10 points: 2 points per item)
A.

Gesundheitstipps	
☐ Rad fahren	☑ Sport machen
☐ die Sonne vermeiden	☑ nicht rauchen
☑ viel Obst und Gemüse essen	☐ genügend schlafen
☑ fettes Essen vermeiden	☑ wenig Alkohol trinken

II. **Reading** (12 points: 4 points per item)
B. 1. c
2. a
3. d

III. **Writing** (12 points: 4 points per item)
C. 4. Wie fühlst du dich?/ Wie geht es dir?
5. Ernährst du dich richtig?
6. Du sollst Fisch vermeiden.

IV. **Culture** (6 points)
D. Answers will vary. Possible answer: Germans like to do many of the same things that Americans do to stay healthy. For example, skateboarding and jogging are both popular in Germany.

ANSWERS Quiz 4-2A

A. (10 points; 1 point per item)
1. jedes
2. Jeder
3. jedem
4. alle
5. jeder
6. Jeden
7. jeden
8. Jede
9. allen
10. jedem

B. (6 points; 1 point per item)
11. Sag
12. Frage
13. steht's
14. eigentlich
15. Darf
16. etwas

C. (6 points; 2 points per item)
Answers will vary. Possible answers:
17. Das stimmt, aber ich esse oft Gemüse.
18. Eigentlich schon, aber ich trinke auch viel Saft.
19. Ja, das kann sein, aber ich ernähre mich richtig.

D. (8 points; 2 points per item)
Answers will vary. Possible answers:
20. Sara und Uwe, esst ihr selten Obst und Gemüse?
21. Gewöhnlich trinkt Herr Bauer jeden Tag Milch.
22. Ich bin froh, dass sie sich normalerweise fit halten.
23. Meistens essen wir vernünftig, aber jedes Wochenende essen wir Fleisch oder Wurst.

ANSWERS Quiz 4-2B

I. Listening (8 points: 2 points per item)
A. 1. c
2. a
3. c
4. a

II. Reading (6 points: 2 points per item)
B. 5. T
6. T
7. F

III. Writing (12 points: 4 points per item)
C. 8. Doch! Ich spiele Fußball zweimal in der Woche.
9. Das kann sein, aber ich mache auch jeden Tag Gymnastik.
10. Wie hältst du dich fit?

IV. Culture (4 points: 2 points per item)
D. 11. Reformhaus
12. Bioladen

KAPITEL 4

ANSWERS Quiz 4-3A

A. (13 points; 1 point per item)
1. die Kirsche, –n
2. das Rindfleisch
3. der Pilz, –e
4. die Blaubeere, –n
5. der Blumenkohl
6. das Huhn, –̈er
7. die Möhre, –n
8. die Aprikose, –n
9. der Reis
10. die Speise, –n
11. der Brokkoli
12. die Forelle, –n
13. die Erdbeere, –n

B. (10 points; 1 point per item)
14. darfst
15. kein
16. darf
17. keine
18. darf
19. keinen
20. dürfen
21. keine
22. dürft
23. keinen

C. (12 points; 2 points per item)
24. macht dick
25. ist nicht gut für die Gesundheit
26. hat zu viel Fett
27. zu viele Kalorien hat
28. uns nicht schmeckt
29. zu viel Zucker hat

ANSWERS Quiz 4-3B

I. **Listening** (10 points: 2 points per item)
A. 1. T
   2. F
   3. F
   4. T
   5. The mother seems to be implying that the teacher should change his plans, so that her son does not have to miss out on the trip.

II. **Reading** (12 points: 4 points per item)
B. 6.-8. b, c, e

III. **Writing** (8 points: 2 points per item)
C. Answers will vary. Possible answers:
   9. Ich soll wenig Fleisch essen.
   10. Ich muss acht Stunden schlafen.
   11. Ich darf keine Schokolade essen.
   12. Ich soll die Sonne vermeiden.

I. Listening

A.

INTERVIEWER Tag, Johannes! Darf ich dich etwas fragen?

JOHANNES Ja, klar.

INTERVIEWER Was isst du am Morgen, also zum Frühstück?

JOHANNES Eigentlich nichts.

INTERVIEWER Wusstest du, dass Frühstück unsere wichtigste Mahlzeit ist?

JOHANNES Ist das wahr? Na, das kann sein, aber ich habe keine Zeit, am Morgen zu essen. Ich muss schon morgens um halb acht abfahren. Vorher trinke ich eine Tasse Kaffee.

INTERVIEWER Und du fährst mit dem Auto zur Schule?

JOHANNES Mit dem Moped natürlich. Das ist ganz schön frustrierend. Manchmal dauert es 20 Minuten.

INTERVIEWER Also könntest du fast so schnell mit dem Fahrrad zur Schule kommen?

JOHANNES Stimmt!

INTERVIEWER Und gehst du in der Pause spazieren oder laufen oder so was?

JOHANNES In der Pause? Wir haben nur fünfzehn Minuten. Ich habe nur Zeit, meine Semmel schnell aufzuessen.

INTERVIEWER Nur noch eine Frage: Was isst du gewöhnlich zu Mittag?

JOHANNES Mittagessen? Ich esse in einer Imbissstube, Pommes frites, ein Paar Bratwürstchen. Mehr nicht. Ich möchte lieber in ein Café gehen und etwas Gesundes essen, Salat oder Suppe, aber ...

INTERVIEWER Aber du hast keine Zeit dazu?

JOHANNES Richtig!

B.

[read slowly and clearly as if at a school assembly]

Die Hausordnung:

Erstens: Schüler dürfen nicht in der Schule oder auf dem Schulhof rauchen. Auch das Mitbringen von Tabakwaren ist strengstens verboten.

Zweitens: Während der Pause müssen die Schüler auf dem Schulhof bleiben. Sie dürfen in der Pause nicht im Klassenzimmer bleiben.

Drittens: Auf den Korridoren und im Treppenhaus dürfen die Schüler nicht laufen. Sie sollen ruhig gehen und Rücksicht aufeinander nehmen.

Viertens: Schüler dürfen nicht vor acht Uhr zwanzig ins Hauptgebäude kommen. Schüler, die vor acht Uhr zwanzig ankommen, sollen sich auf dem Schulhof oder bei schlechtem Wetter in der Sporthalle aufhalten.

Fünftens: Schüler dürfen ein Pausenbrot von zu Hause mitbringen oder in der Pause sich etwas zu essen kaufen. Speisereste, Butterbrotpapiere, leere Milch- und Saftbeutel, Joghurtbecher und dergleichen müssen in die Mülleimer auf dem Schulhof hineingegeben werden. Sie dürfen nicht in die Papierkörbe in den Klassenzimmern kommen.

Answers to Chapter Test Kapitel 4

I. Listening Maximum Score: 30 points

A. (20 points: 2 points per item)   **B.** (10 points: 2 points per item)
1. b
2. b
3. a
4. a
5. b
6. a
7. b
8. b
9. a
10. a

11. b
12. b
13. a
14. a
15. a

II. Reading Maximum Score: 30 points

C. (20 points: 2 points per item)   **D.** (10 points: 2 points per item)
16. b
17. d
18. c
19. d
20. a
21. c
22. d
23. b
24. b
25. c

26. d
27. e
28. a
29. b
30. c

III. Culture Maximum Score: 10 points

E. (10 points: 2 points per item)
31. c
32. b
33. c
34. d
35. For both economic and environmental reasons, people try to take with them only the minimum amount of packaging necessary. They are allowed to leave the rest at the store where it will be recycled.

IV. Writing Maximum Score: 30 points

F. (15 points: 3 points per item)
Answers will vary. Possible answers:
36. Tag, Rolf! Wie geht's? / Wie geht's dir?
37. Fühlst du dich nicht wohl? / Ist dir schlecht?
38-39. Du sollst genügend schlafen und auch viel Wasser trinken.
40. Du sollst auch die Sonne vermeiden.

G. (15 points: 3 points per sentence)
Answers will vary. Possible answer:
Ich finde es schlecht, dass du so wenig für deine Gesundheit tust. Du isst kein Obst und Gemüse, und du isst zu viel Fett. Du schläfst auch nicht genug und machst keinen Sport. Du sollst mehr Gemüse essen, und du darfst nicht rauchen. Vermeide auch die Sonne!

Holt German 2 Komm mit!, Chapter 4

5 Gesund essen

Quiz 5-1A

Erste Stufe

Maximum Score: 35

Grammar and Vocabulary

A. You are in a crowded checkout line at a supermarket and overhear fragments of a conversation between one of the customers in front of you and the cashier. Complete their conversation by filling in each blank with an appropriate word from the box. (10 points)

| dieser | preiswert | halt | diesen | habe |
| teuer | Laden | nur | kostet | 30 Cent |

CUSTOMER   Was? So viel?

CASHIER   Es tut mir Leid, **1.** _____ Joghurt kostet jetzt 80 Cent.

CUSTOMER   Das ist viel zu **2.** _____ !

CASHIER   Der Joghurt ohne Früchte kostet **3.** _____ 45 Cent.

CUSTUMER   Ich will aber **4.** _____ Joghurt mit Erdbeeren.

CASHIER   Ich bedaure, er **5.** _____ 80 Cent.

CUSTOMER   Ich **6.** _____ aber nur 50 Cent.

CASHIER   Dann müssen Sie **7.** _____ den Joghurt ohne Früchte nehmen.

CUSTOMER   Ich will aber...

SECOND
CUSTOMER   Hier haben Sie **8.** _____ . Zahlen Sie endlich!

CUSTOMER   Danke schön! Teurer Laden hier. Morgen geh ich in den

   9. _____ um die Ecke.

CUSTOMER   So kann man **10.** _____ einkaufen.
(mumbling to himself)

SCORE [   ]

B. Your friend Siegfried is giving a party. He quickly runs out of drinks! It is his first party and you try to be nice about his lack of planning. Answer his statements by giving the German equivalents of the expressions in parentheses. (15 points)

SIEGFRIED   Ich hab keine Cola mehr.

DU   (I'll drink milk instead.) **11.** _____

SIEGFRIED   Ich hab auch keine Milch.

DU   (In that case I'll take juice.) **12.** _____

Quiz 5-1A

SIEGFRIED	So ein Pech! Ich habe auch keinen Saft mehr.
DU	(That's not so bad.) **13.** _____
SIEGFRIED	Du trinkst doch Mineralwasser, oder?
DU	(Not necessarily!) **14.** _____
SIEGFRIED	Schade! Willst du vielleicht einen Kakao?
DU	(Of course! Thanks!) **15.** _____

SCORE ☐

C. You are in the restaurant *Der Blaue Bock* and your friend Maria doesn't like what's on her plate. Complete the following conversation between Maria and the waiter (**Bedienung**) by filling in each blank with the correct form of the demonstrative **dieser**. (10 points)

MARIA Was soll denn das sein, **16.** _____ Fleisch da?

BEDIENUNG Probieren Sie erst **17.** _____ Fleisch da. Es ist Rindfleisch.

MARIA Ich bedaure, **18.** _____ Fleisch schmeckt mir nicht. Und was

ist in **19.** _____ Gemüse?

BEDIENUNG In **20.** _____ Gemüse sind Erbsen.

MARIA **21.** _____ Erbsen mag ich auch nicht.

BEDIENUNG Ich bedaure, dass Ihnen das Essen nicht schmeckt.

MARIA (*pointing to your plate*) Ich möchte **22.** _____ Fisch. Was ist

das für ein Fisch?

BEDIENUNG **23.** _____ Fisch ist eine Forelle.

MARIA Gut, ich will eine Forelle. (*still pointing to your plate*) Und was ist

24. _____ Gemüse da?

BEDIENUNG Das sind Süßkartoffeln. Möchten Sie **25.** _____ Kartoffeln?

MARIA Ja, bitte bringen Sie mir eine Forelle mit Kartoffeln.

SCORE ☐

TOTAL SCORE ☐

5 Gesund essen

■ Erste Stufe

Maximum Score: 30

I. Listening

A. Edgar and Katrin had arranged to meet at a seafood restaurant for lunch. Listen to their conversation twice and then mark each statement below true (**T**) or false (**F**). (10 points)

_____ 1. Katrin has been waiting for Edgar for half an hour.

_____ 2. They had planned to eat mussels.

_____ 3. The restaurant is out of paella.

_____ 4. Katrin is very upset that there is no more paella.

_____ 5. Edgar is familiar with paella.

SCORE _____

II. Reading

B. Read the article and then decide if the statements that follow are true (T) or false (F). (8 points)

Gesund essen ohne Fleisch?

Immer mehr Menschen verzichten auf Fleisch und Wurst. Bekommen diese Menschen genug Nährstoffe *(nutrients)*? Fleisch und Fleischwaren sind eiweißreich *(protein-rich)* und haben viele Vitamine und Mineralstoffe. Wer auf Fleisch und Wurst verzichtet, muss deshalb andere eiweißreiche Lebensmittel optimal kombinieren. Fisch, Milch, Milchprodukte und Eier enthalten wichtige Nährstoffe wie Eiweiß, Vitamin B12, Calcium und Jod *(iodine)*. Sie können Kartoffeln mit Eiern oder mit Milch oder Milchprodukten (zum Beispiel Pellkartoffeln mit Quark) kombinieren, um genug Eiweiß zu bekommen. Sie können auch Getreide *(grains)* mit Milch kombinieren.

Ohne Fleisch ist es leider schwierig, genug Eisen *(iron)* zu bekommen. Eisen aus pflanzlichen Produkten ist schwieriger aufzunehmen *(to take in)* als Eisen aus tierischen Produkten. Vitamin C hilft bei der Aufnahme. Daher *(for that reason)* müssen Sie eisenreiche Lebensmittel, wie Brot oder Gemüse, zusammen mit Obst essen.

_____ 6. Meat and meat products do not have any nutrients the body really needs.

_____ 7. It is easier for us to take in iron from vegetables than from meat.

_____ 8. Potatoes combined with eggs supply as much protein as meat.

_____ 9. Vitamin C helps the body take in iron from plants.

SCORE _____

Quiz 5-1B

III. Writing

C. You want to buy a snack, but it's almost closing time at the snack bar. The **Verkäuferin** is out of almost everything you want. Downplay your disappointment, and then order something else. (8 points)

10.   DU _____

    VERKÄUFERIN Ich bedaure, die Milch ist alle.

11.   DU _____

SCORE [   ]

IV. Culture

D. Based on what you learned in the **Landeskunde** section of **Kapitel 5**, answer the following two questions. (4 points)

12. **Hausmannskost** refers to:
    a. the cost of a cleaning man
    b. the cost of home repairs
    c. home-style cooking
    d. a simple diet

Decide if the following statement is true **(T)** or false **(F)**.

_____ 13. In Germany, it is considered impolite to leave your lower arm on the table while eating.

SCORE [   ]

TOTAL SCORE [   ]

KAPITEL 5

KAPITEL 5

Gesund essen

■ Zweite Stufe

Grammar and Vocabulary

A. The cafeteria at your school is trying to make its selection more appealing to students. You were asked by the cafeteria's supervisor to interview your classmates about their food preferences. Fill in each blank with the correct form of a possessive. (15 points)

DU	Heiko, was magst du auf **1.** _____ Sandwich?
HEIKO	Ich mag Quark mit Schnittlauch.
DU	Und du, Udo?
UDO	**2.** _____ Vater macht **3.** _____ Pausenbrot!
DU	Und du, Anna, macht **4.** _____ Vater auch
	5. _____ Brot?
ANNA	Nein, meine Mutter. Ich kaufe aber oft **6.** _____ Joghurt in der Cafeteria.
DU	Und ihr, Peter und Hans, was mögt ihr auf **7.** _____ Brot?
PETER und HANS *(in unison)*	Wir mögen nur Wurst auf **8.** _____ Pausenbrot.
DU	Peter, was mag **9.** _____ Schwester auf
	10. _____ Brot?
PETER	Sie mag Tilsiter Käse. Und **11.** _____ Bruder Erwin mag
	Camembert Käse auf **12.** _____ Brot.
DU	Danke für die Information, Peter. Maria, was magst du auf
	13. _____ Sandwich?
MARIA	Auf **14.** _____ Sandwich mag ich am liebsten Tomaten und Sojasprossen.
DU	Gut! Und ich selbst mag am liebsten Himbeermarmelade auf
	15. _____ Brot.
DU	Ah, das wird aber eine lange Liste: Quark mit Schnittlauch, Wurst, Tilsiter Käse, Camembert Käse, Tomaten und Sojasprossen, Himbeermarmelade.

SCORE ☐

Quiz 5-2A

B. It is a warm, sunny day and you and your friend Ingo decide to have a picnic. To buy food for the picnic, you and Ingo go to the nearest supermarket. Complete the conversation by filling in the blanks with appropriate words or expressions from the box. (15 points)

| mal | lieber | dieses | los | Echt | lecker | Hör | Café Freizeit |
| kaufen | Sojasprossen | CD | Tilsiter Käse | zuerst | Prima | Was denn |

INGO   Schau 16. _____ !

DU   Ja? 17. _____ ?

INGO   Na, 18. _____ Gemüse!

DU   Aber das sind doch nur 19. _____ .

INGO   Die sehen überhaupt nicht 20. _____ aus.

DU   Was magst du eigentlich gern essen?

INGO   Ich mag Wurst und Käse.

DU   Magst du 21. _____ ?

INGO   Ja, aber Camembert mag ich 22. _____ .

DU   23. _____ mal!

INGO   Was ist denn 24. _____ ?

DU   Na, die Musik!

INGO   Ach, das ist die neue CD von den Fantastischen Vier.

DU   Stark! 25. _____ stark!

INGO   Schon gut! Wollen wir nicht Wurst und Brot 26. _____ ?

DU   Vergiss das Picknick! Gehen wir lieber in einen Musikladen. Ich will unbedingt diese

27. _____ kaufen.

INGO   Also gut! Aber ich will 28. _____ etwas essen und trinken.

DU   29. _____ ! Gehen wir ins

30. _____ und dann in den Musikladen um die Ecke.

SCORE ⬜

TOTAL SCORE ⬜

KAPITEL

5 Gesund essen

■ Zweite Stufe

I. Listening

A. Günther and Anke are eating in the school cafeteria. They see Luise come in for lunch. Read the questions below and then listen to the conversation twice. Choose the best answers from among the alternatives given. (6 points)

1. Anke has
   a. a sandwich from home.
   b. a "regular" hamburger.
   c. a vegetarian burger.
   d. nothing; she's sharing with Günther.

2. Luise thinks that
   a. Günther's food tastes better than Anke's.
   b. Anke's food tastes better than Günther's.
   c. neither Anke's nor Günther's food is edible.
   d. Anke's and Günther's food tastes exactly alike.

3. Luise's attitude is:
   a. she will never change her mind
   b. she'll take advantage of a good deal
   c. Anke and Günther are very pushy people
   d. one has to have meat for lunch every day

SCORE

KAPITEL 5

II. Reading

B. Read the following passage and then mark the statements on page 112 true (T) or false (F). (12 points)

Warum vegetarisch essen? Es gibt fast so viele verschiedene Antworten auf diese Frage, wie es Vegetarier gibt. Einige Leute wollen aus religiösen Gründen alle Lebewesen (*living beings*) respektieren. Diese Vegetarier essen gewöhnlich kein Fleisch, keinen Fisch und keine Eier, aber viele von ihnen trinken Milch.

Manche (*some*) Leute essen „halb" vegetarisch und vermeiden prinzipiell das Fett von Tieren. Andere Leute sind sehr tierlieb und wünschen, dass man keine Säugetiere (*mammals*) (zum Beispiel Delphine und Walfische) tötet (*kill*). Noch andere Vegetarier denken mehr an die Umwelt. Sie glauben, dass die Tierzucht (*animal breeding*) für die Umwelt schlecht ist.

Die meisten Vegetarier glauben, dass der Mensch gesünder lebt, wenn er vegetarisch isst. Eine mittelgroße Scheibe Vollkornbrot mit Erdnussbutter hat, zum Beispiel, mehr Nährwert (*nutritional value*) als eine Bratwurst mit einer Semmel.

Quiz 5-2B

_____ **4.** There are many different reasons why people are vegetarians.

_____ **5.** Strict vegetarians don't eat eggs.

_____ **6.** Most vegetarians who do not eat beef, fish, and eggs also do not drink milk.

_____ **7.** Some people are vegetarians for environmental reasons.

_____ **8.** Most vegetarians think that a diet that includes meat is actually healthier than a diet that does not include meat.

_____ **9.** A slice of whole-wheat bread with peanut butter has less nutritional value than a roll with sausage.

SCORE [   ]

III. Writing

C. Your German pen pal is curious about what you eat at school. Tell your pen pal if you eat at school or go home for lunch, and whether your school has a cafeteria, snack bar, or just vending machines (**Automaten**). Also say what you usually eat, whether you like it or not, and why. (16 points)

_____

_____

_____

_____

_____

SCORE [   ]

IV. Culture

D. You are living in Düsseldorf and some German friends are coming to visit you for the entire day tomorrow. You have planned the following meals. Now you need to decide when you should serve each one. Write the correct lettered choice in the blanks provided. (6 points)

_____ **10.** leftovers and **Butterbrote**

_____ **11.** **Brötchen** with cheese and assorted cold cuts

_____ **12.** veal cutlets with potatoes and red cabbage

a. breakfast
b. lunch
c. dinner

SCORE [   ]

TOTAL SCORE [   ]

KAPITEL 5

5 Gesund essen

■ Dritte Stufe

Maximum Score: 35

Grammar and Vocabulary

A. You want to cook dinner for your friends. Before deciding on the menu you ask your friends about their food preferences. Complete the following conversation by filling in each blank with the correct form of the personal pronoun or **welcher**. (10 points)

DU   Ich lade euch morgen zum Abendessen ein. Sagt 1. _____ bitte, was ihr gern esst. Erika, 2. _____ Fleisch magst du am liebsten?

ERIKA   Eigentlich mag ich nur Hackfleisch.

DU   Und du, Beate, 3. _____ Gemüse isst du gern?

BEATE   Hm, Tomaten schmecken 4. _____ am besten.

DU   Und Holger, was schmeckt 5. _____ besser, Nudeln oder Reis?

BEATE   Er mag Nudeln lieber.

DU   Franz, 6. _____ Käse magst du am liebsten?

FRANZ   Ich mag am liebsten italienischen Käse, Parmesan oder Mozzarella.

DU   Ausgezeichnet! 7. _____ Obst magst du gern?

FRANZ   Ich mag Beeren.

DU   8. _____ Beeren magst du? Erdbeeren oder Blaubeeren?

FRANZ   Erdbeeren mag 9. _____ am liebsten.

DU   Beate, 10. _____ Saft magst du am liebsten?

BEATE   Ach du, ich trinke am liebsten Spezi.

SCORE ☐

B. Give the German equivalents of the following phrases. (10 points)

Which cheese do you (informal, singular) prefer?

11. _____

Beef tastes better to me.

12. _____

Which bread is your (informal, singular) favorite?

13. _____

Which vegetable tastes the best to you (informal, singular)?

14. _____

Quiz 5-3A

For dessert I eat yogurt with strawberries.

15. _____

C. You are interviewing the swimmer Franzi about her food preferences. Fill in the blanks with appropriate words from the box. (15 points)

welches	Lieblingsspeise	manchmal welche	Kartoffelsuppe
worüber	einen	teuer	isst
lieber	Vanillemilch	Pommes frites Heilbutt	Schnittlauch Nachtisch

DU   Hallo, Franzi! Darf ich dir ein paar Fragen stellen?

FRANZI   Ja, 16. _____ denn?

DU   Was 17. _____ du gewöhnlich zu Mittag und warum?

FRANZI   Ich esse oft 18. _____ Salat oder eine Suppe.

DU   Und 19. _____ Suppe magst du am liebsten?

FRANZI   Am liebsten mag ich 20. _____ mit viel

           21. _____ .

DU   Und 22. _____ Gemüse magst du am liebsten?

FRANZI   Tomaten und Kartoffeln.

DU   Was isst du zum 23. _____ ?

FRANZI   Hm, 24. _____ Joghurt, aber meistens Obst und Käse.

DU   Trinkst du gern Milch?

FRANZI   Ich trinke Milch, aber 25. _____ trink ich Kakao

           und am liebsten trink ich 26. _____ .

DU   Isst du Kaviar?

FRANZI   Kaviar ist mir zu 27. _____ .

DU   Magst du Fisch?

FRANZI   Ja, ich mag 28. _____ mit Bratkartoffeln.

           Bratkartoffeln sind echt meine 29. _____ .

DU   Magst du auch 30. _____ ?

FRANZI   Ja, ich mag Kartoffeln in allen Variationen.

Name _____ Klasse _____ Datum _____

Gesund essen

Dritte Stufe

Maximum Score: 30

I. Listening

A. Martin and Monika are a young, newly married couple. They are doing their weekend shopping in the supermarket. Listen to the conversation twice and then mark each statement below true (**T**) or false (**F**). (10 points)

_____ 1. Jam is on sale.

_____ 2. They selected Monika's favorite jam.

_____ 3. They already selected cold cuts and quark.

_____ 4. Another lady tries to take their shopping cart.

_____ 5. The lady is very upset about the mix-up.

SCORE [   ]

II. Reading

B. Read the article and then answer the questions that follow. (8 points)

Deutsche Lieblingsspeisen

Viele deutsche Lieblingsspeisen kommen aus dem Ausland *(foreign country)*. Die Kartoffel kommt aus Südamerika und ist heute die Beilage *(side dish)* zu fast allen Gerichten. Die Tomate kommt aus Mexiko und Peru und ist heute eine Zutat in vielen deutschen Gerichten. Die Zwiebel stammt aus dem Orient. Schwarzer Pfeffer kommt aus Indonesien und Malaysia. Heute findet man ihn aber auch in Brasilien. Salz und Pfeffer sind wohl die wichtigsten deutschen Gewürze *(spices)*.

Die Deutschen essen auch gern Fastfood. Am liebsten mögen sie Currywurst und Pommes frites. Der Curry hat seine Heimat in Südostasien, Sri Lanka und Malaysia. Man weiß nicht genau, woher die Pommes frites kommen, vielleicht aus Frankreich oder Belgien. Vielen Deutschen schmeckt auch der Döner Kebab aus der Türkei. Und natürlich essen die Deutschen Pizza. Die Pizza kommt eigentlich aus Italien.

Das liebste Fleisch vieler Deutschen ist das Huhn, das es in fast jeder Imbissstube gibt. Das Huhn gibt es schon lange in Deutschland, aber es kommt ursprünglich *(originally)* aus Asien.

6. What are the most important German spices?
   a. curry
   b. black pepper
   c. salt and pepper
   d. onions

Quiz 5-3B

7. Where do French fries come from?
   a. from France
   b. maybe from France or Belgium
   c. maybe from Turkey
   d. from Belgium

8. From where comes a favorite German side dish?
   a. Mexico and Guatemala
   b. Far East
   c. Indonesia and Malaysia
   d. South America

9. What meat is served in almost every snack bar in Germany?
   a. Döner Kebab
   b. chicken
   c. turkey
   d. beef

SCORE _____

III. Writing

C. Look at the menu below from a formal banquet. You were at the banquet, and want to write your pen pal about where you were and what you liked and didn't like about the meal. (Remember this took place in the past.) [12 points]

Forelle *trout*
Rehrücken *venison*

Hotel Schwarzwälderhof
Samstag, den 28. Oktober
20 Uhr

Ochsenschwanzsuppe
Gurkensalat
Forelle blau
Rehrücken mit Preiselbeersoße, Salzkartoffeln
Zitroneneis
Käse und frisches Obst
Kaffee

SCORE _____

TOTAL SCORE _____

KAPITEL 5

KAPITEL

5 Gesund essen

Chapter Test

I. Listening

Maximum Score: 30 points

A. Thorsten has come from the hair stylist's to the café where his friends usually meet. Listen to their conversation twice and mark each statement true (**a**) or false (**b**). (15 points)

_____ 1. Thorsten's friends hardly recognize him at first.

_____ 2. His friends are laughing about his clothes.

_____ 3. Thorsten is very upset about his friends' reaction.

_____ 4. Thorsten must have had his hair cut very short.

_____ 5. Thorsten's hair is green.

_____ 6. Thorsten's family wants to give his grandmother a photo of him.

_____ 7. His sister does not have to have her picture taken.

_____ 8. Thorsten is worried that he'll look "different" for a good many months.

_____ 9. Thorsten's sister is having a serious problem with her hair.

_____ 10. Thorsten's sister is in a good mood, even though she has a problem.

SCORE [   ]

B. Alice is traveling by train from Frankfurt to Milan, Italy. The train is crowded, but, fortunately, she has a reserved seat. Listen to the conversation twice and as you listen mark each statement true (**a**) or false (**b**). (15 points)

_____ 11. Alice had reserved a window seat.

_____ 12. She is traveling alone.

_____ 13. The other passenger's ticket has the same seat number as Alice's.

_____ 14. Alice is in the right place.

_____ 15. The man has the wrong seat ticket.

_____ 16. This train car only goes as far as Zurich.

_____ 17. Alice speaks German very well.

_____ 18. The man offers Alice help.

_____ 19. The man has been very patient.

_____ 20. The young man finally becomes irritated and yells at Alice.

SCORE [   ]

Chapter Test

II. Reading

Maximum Score: 30 points

C. In each group, choose the one alternative that is **NOT** an appropriate response. (10 points)

21. Welche Suppe isst du am liebsten?
    a. Ich habe Tomatensuppe furchtbar gern.
    b. Lieber Tomatensuppe als Hühnersuppe.
    c. Am liebsten Hühnersuppe.
    d. Am liebsten möchte ich eine Suppe.

22. Mutti, guck mal her!
    a. Ja, was ist denn?
    b. Was gibt's?
    c. Ja, ich höre schon.
    d. Was hast du denn?

23. Du willst Auto fahren, oder?
    a. Ja, eigentlich möchte ich fahren.
    b. Möchtest du lieber fahren?
    c. Mit dem Bus oder mit der Bahn?
    d. Ja, gern.

24. Hör mal zu!
    a. Das ist doch Klaviermusik.
    b. Ach ja. Das ist das Telefon wieder.
    c. Bitte! Hier ist die Kassette.
    d. Ich höre noch immer nichts.

25. Die Orangen sind schon alle.
    a. Macht nichts. Dann esse ich halt eine Banane.
    b. Ich bedaure.
    c. Schon gut.
    d. Nicht so schlimm. Eigentlich habe ich keinen Hunger mehr.

SCORE ☐

D. Before you read the passage on page 119, look at the following words and their unmatched translations. As you read **"An das Brot"** the first time, match each word with the correct translation. (12 points)

_____ 26. Butterbrot   **a.** dinner

_____ 27. Abendbrot   **b.** snack

_____ 28. Pausenbrot   **c.** dark rye bread

_____ 29. Schwarzbrot   **d.** bread with butter

Holt German 2 Komm mit!, Chapter 5

_____ 30. Vollkornbrot

_____ 31. Franzbrot

_____ 32. Katenbrot

_____ 33. Brotlaib

a. cottage-style bread

b. loaf of bread

c. multi-whole-grain bread

d. French bread

> **abgefunden** *settled for*
> **weder ... noch ...** *neither ... nor ...*

An das Brot

(Ode to Bread)

Wenn ich um unser tägliches Brot bete, dann denke ich wortwörtlich an das B r o t. Denn Brot ist ja die Substanz des Lebens, von der wir den Körper ernähren — in traditionellen Familien, wie unserer, bis zu dreimal am Tag.

Morgens essen wir zum Frühstück Brot oder Brötchen. Vormittags hat man das Pausenbrot, ein Butterbrot, das man in die Schule mitnimmt. Abends gibt es das Abendbrot. Nur zum Mittagessen wird kein Brot gegessen.

Und was für Brot! Das deutsche Brot ist etwas Handfestes. Es hat Gewicht. Man kauft beim Bäcker fast immer ein Kilo, einen Brotlaib, der sich in der Einkaufstasche bemerkbar macht.

Zwar hat man sich in Wien und in Salzburg, oder meinetwegen in der Schweizer Stadt Zürich, mit dem Franzbrot abgefunden, aber hier in Westfalen verstehen wir unter „Brot" in erster Linie Vollkornbrot. Davon essen wir am meisten. Katenbrot mit Körnern oder Schwarzbrot aus Roggenmehl kosten etwas mehr, sind aber weder nahrhafter, noch herzhafter.

KAPITEL 5

SCORE _____

E. Reread the passage above, and then answer these questions. (8 points)

34. On an average weekday, the author typically eats bread at all of the following times EXCEPT
    a. breakfast.
    b. mid-morning snack.
    c. lunch.
    d. dinner.

35. The author normally thinks of buying bread
    a. by weight.
    b. in packages.
    c. pre-cut.
    d. in long, thin, lightweight loaves.

Chapter Test

36. The author says people in Westphalia prefer
    a. multi-whole-grain bread.
    b. French bread.
    c. cottage-style bread.
    d. dark rye bread.

37. The author's opinion seems to be:
    a. You'll never go hungry as long as you have bread.
    b. People in Austria and Switzerland live better than North Germans.
    c. People in France eat better bread.
    d. Children naturally like white bread.

SCORE [   ]

III. Culture

Maximum Score: 9 points

F. Based on your cultural knowledge of German-speaking countries, mark the following statements true (**a**) or false (**b**). (9 points)

If you are staying with a German family:

_____ 38. You will probably eat some kind of bread at least twice a day.

_____ 39. You can't count on being served your favorite sugar-frosted cereal for breakfast.

_____ 40. You'll usually eat "dinner," that is, the main hot meal, in the middle of the day.

_____ 41. You won't have any problem going to a restaurant and getting a cold sandwich for lunch.

_____ 42. You should remember to keep your left hand "in sight" on the table while eating.

_____ 43. You should say **Danke** to your host to indicate when you have enough food on your plate.

_____ 44. You will find that steak, baked potatoes, salad, and a vegetable is a common evening meal.

_____ 45. Lunch will usually be served at 1 o'clock.

If you have a German house guest:

_____ 46. You should serve fresh rolls, boiled eggs, and cold cuts for breakfast, if you want to make him or her feel at home.

SCORE [   ]

KAPITEL 5

Chapter Test

IV. Writing

Maximum Score: 31 points

G. You're staying with your friend's brother, a university student, for the weekend. It's morning and he's busy getting ready, and you're supposed to help yourself to breakfast. Write a connected conversation, following the directions below. (16 points)

ER   Ich glaube, es ist noch etwas Müsli da.

[The muesli is all gone. Tell him so, but that it's okay and you'll have rolls.]

47. DU _____

48. _____

49. _____

ER   Brötchen habe ich leider nicht gekauft.

[That's okay too. Tell him you'll have some bread and ask what there is to put on the bread.]

50. DU _____

51. _____

52. _____

ER   Schau doch mal in den Kühlschrank!

[You look in the refrigerator and ask him if you may eat something you see in there.]

53. DU _____

ER   Ja, klar. Nimm doch, bitte. So ein Pech, dass ich keine Zeit zum Einkaufen habe!

[Ask if you can help out by going shopping for him.]

54. DU _____

ER   Ach danke! Ja, eigentlich schon.

SCORE [   ]

KAPITEL 5

Chapter Test

H. You have just spent a weekend with a German family. You had a great time, and the food was excellent. Both the mother and father are great cooks. Write a thank you note mentioning how much you enjoyed the city and the food. Write four complete sentences and an appropriate salutation and closing. (15 points)

_____

_____

_____

_____

_____

_____

_____

_____

_____

_____

SCORE [   ]

TOTAL SCORE [   ]

KAPITEL 5

Name _____ Klasse _____ Datum _____

KAPITEL 5 Chapter Test Score Sheet

Circle the letter that matches the most appropriate response.

I. Listening
Maximum Score: 30 points

A. (15 points)

1. a b
2. a b
3. a b
4. a b
5. a b

6. a b
7. a b
8. a b
9. a b
10. a b

SCORE _____

B. (15 points)

11. a b
12. a h
13. a b
14. a b
15. a b

16. a b
17. a b
18. a b
19. a b
20. a b

SCORE _____

II. Reading
Maximum Score: 30 points

C. (10 points)

21. a b c d
22. a b c d
23. a b c d
24. a b c d
25. a b c d

SCORE _____

D. (12 points)

26. a b c d
27. a b c d
28. a b c d
29. a b c d
30. a b c d

31. a b c d
32. a b c d
33. a b c d

SCORE _____

E. (8 points)

34. a b c d
35. a b c d
36. a b c d
37. a b c d

SCORE _____

III. Culture
Maximum Score: 9 points

F. (9 points)

38. a b
39. a b
40. a b
41. a b
42. a b

43. a b
44. a b
45. a b
46. a b

SCORE _____

KAPITEL 5

IV. Writing

Maximum Score: 31 points

G. (16 points)

47. _____

_____

48. _____

_____

49. _____

_____

50. _____

_____

51. _____

_____

52. _____

_____

53. _____

_____

54. _____

_____

SCORE [   ]

H. (15 points)

_____

_____

_____

_____

_____

_____

_____

SCORE [   ]

TOTAL SCORE [   ]

KAPITEL 5

Listening Scripts for Quizzes 5-1B, 5-2B, 5-3B

Quiz 5-1B Kapitel 5 Erste Stufe

I. Listening

A.

EDGAR	Du, es tut mir furchtbar Leid! Wirklich! Wartest du schon lange?
KATRIN	Wo warst du denn? Es ist ja schon halb zwei. Ich bin um eins gekommen, wie wir gesagt haben.
EDGAR	Hast du schon bestellt?
KATRIN	Nein, noch nicht.
BEDIENUNG	Möchten Sie jetzt bestellen?
EDGAR	Ja, wir wollen doch Muscheln essen, nicht wahr?
KATRIN	Ja, ich freue mich schon darauf.
BEDIENUNG	Ich bedaure sehr, aber die Muscheln sind alle.
KATRIN	Schon gut. Dann esse ich eben Paella.
EDGAR	Was soll denn das sein, diese Paella?
BEDIENUNG	Es tut mir sehr Leid, aber Paella gibt es auch nicht mehr.
KATRIN	Nicht so schlimm. Dann nehme ich halt ein Fischfilet. Gegrillt.
BEDIENUNG	Wir haben nur noch den Heilbutt frisch. Den können Sie aber gerne gegrillt bekommen.
EDGAR	Also, zweimal Heilbutt. Und einen grünen Salat.

Quiz 5-2B Kapitel 5 Zweite Stufe

I. Listening

A.

GÜNTHER	Guck mal, Anke, da kommt Luise. Hallo, Luise! Komm! Setz dich einen Moment zu uns.
LUISE	Was ist denn?
GÜNTHER	Luise, du hast gestern gesagt, du magst keinen Tofu, nicht wahr? Und nichts aus Soja, oder?
LUISE	Ja, das stimmt. Wieso fragst du?
GÜNTHER	Sagen wir dir gleich. Zuerst sollst du Ankes Hamburger probieren und dann meinen. Dann sag mal, welcher dir besser schmeckt.
LUISE	Ja, gut.
ANKE	Bitte.
LUISE	Danke ... Hmmm. Ankes Hamburger schmeckt ganz gut.
GÜNTHER	Nun einen Biss von meinem.
LUISE	Danke. Der schmeckt genau so gut wie Ankes Hamburger.
GÜNTHER	Anke, sag, was hast du in deinem Hamburger?
ANKE	Na, Hackfleisch, ganz klar, das ist doch ein Hamburger.
LUISE	Aber Günthers Hamburger ist auch Hackfleisch, nicht wahr? Er schmeckt genau wie Ankes.
GÜNTHER	Eben nicht! Mein Burger ist ein Sojaburger. Kostet 40 Cent weniger.
LUISE	Stimmt das? Dann hole ich mir halt so einen Sojaburger. Und für die 40 Cent kann ich noch eine Cola kaufen.

Quiz 5-3B Kapitel 5 Dritte Stufe

I. Listening

A.

MONIKA	Schau mal, Martin!
MARTIN	Was ist?
MONIKA	Marmelade: Heute im Sonderangebot.
MARTIN	Schön. Nehmen wir doch ein Glas.
MONIKA	Was für Marmelade schmeckt dir am besten?
MARTIN	Erst mal schauen, welche Sorten es gibt ... Hmmm ... Himbeer, Erdbeer, Pfirsich, Pflaumen. ... Ja, mir ist's ziemlich gleich. Welche magst du lieber?
MONIKA	Am liebsten Himbeer. Die schmeckt mir am besten. Tust du bitte gleich zwei Gläser in den Einkaufswagen?
MARTIN	Ja, ... warte mal! Das ist doch nicht unser Wagen!
MONIKA	Wieso nicht?
MARTIN	Ja, in unserem Wagen müsste doch Aufschnitt und Quark sein, oder?
MONIKA	Ja, klar.
MARTIN	Nun, in diesem Wagen ist aber kein Quark, nur Tofu und Brot.
MONIKA	Wo ist denn bloß unser Wagen geblieben?
FRAU X	Entschuldigen Sie, aber ich glaube, Sie haben meinen Einkaufswagen da. Mit Tofu, nicht wahr? Und Vollkornbrot?
MARTIN	Stimmt schon! Verzeihung!
FRAU X	Ist das Ihr Wagen da drüben?
MONIKA	Ja, vielen Dank!
FRAU X	Bitte. Das ist nicht so schlimm.

ANSWERS Quiz 5-1A

A. (10 points; 1 point per item)
1. dieser
2. teuer
3. nur
4. diesen
5. kostet
6. habe
7. halt
8. 30 Cent
9. Laden
10. preiswert

B. (15 points; 3 points per item)
Answers will vary. Possible answers:
11. Dann trink ich halt Milch.
12. Dann nehm ich eben Saft.
13. Nicht so schlimm!
14. Nicht unbedingt!
15. Aber sicher! Danke.

C. (10 points; 1 point per item)
16. dieses
17. dieses
18. dieses
19. diesem
20. diesem
21. Diese
22. diesen
23. Dieser
24. dieses
25. diese

ANSWERS Quiz 5-1B

I. Listening

A. (10 points: 2 points per item)
1. T
2. T
3. T
4. F
5. F

II. Reading

B. (8 points: 2 points per item)
6. F
7. F
8. T
9. T

III. Writing

C. (8 points: 4 points per item)
Answers will vary. Possible answers:
10. Haben Sie noch Milch?
11. Das macht nichts. Dann nehme ich eben einen Saft.

IV. Culture

D. (4 points: 2 points per item)
12. c
13. F

KAPITEL 5

Answers to Quizzes 5-2A, 5-2B

ANSWERS Quiz 5-2A

A. (15 points; 1 point per item)
1. deinem
2. Mein
3. mein
4. dein
5. dein
6. meinen
7. euerem
8. unserem
9. deine
10. ihrem
11. mein
12. seinem
13. deinem
14. meinem
15. meinem

B. (15 points; 1 point per item)
16. mal
17. Was denn
18. dieses
19. Sojasprossen
20. lecker
21. Tilsiter Käse
22. lieber
23. Hör
24. los
25. Echt
26. kaufen
27. CD
28. zuerst
29. Prima
30. *Café Freizeit*

ANSWERS Quiz 5-2B

I. Listening

A. (6 points: 2 points per item)
1. b
2. d
3. b

II. Reading

B. (12 points: 2 points per item)
4. T
5. T
6. F
7. T
8. F
9. F

III. Writing

C. (16 points: 4 points per item)
Answers will vary. Possible answers:
In meiner Schule essen wir alle in einer Cafeteria, aber es gibt auch Automaten. Es gibt gewöhnlich Hamburger und Pizza und auch Obst und Salat. Ich esse diese nicht so gern, weil sie sehr fettig sind.

IV. Culture

D. (6 points: 2 points per item)
10. c
11. a
12. b

KAPITEL 5

Answers to Quizzes 5-3A, 5-3B

ANSWERS Quiz 5-3A

A. (10 points; 1 point per item)
1. mir
2. welches
3. welches
4. mir
5. ihm
6. welchen
7. Welches
8. Welche
9. ich
10. welchen

B. (10 points; 2 points per item)
Answers will vary. Possible answers:
11. Welchen Käse magst du lieber?
12. Rind schmeckt mir besser.
13. Welches Brot magst du am liebsten?
14. Welches Gemüse schmeckt dir am besten?
15. Zum Nachtisch esse ich Joghurt mit Erdbeeren.

C. (15 points; 1 point per item)
16. worüber
17. isst
18. einen
19. welche
20. Kartoffelsuppe
21. Schnittlauch
22. welches
23. Nachtisch
24. manchmal
25. lieber
26. Vanillemilch
27. teuer
28. Heilbutt
29. Lieblingsspeise
30. Pommes frites

ANSWERS Quiz 5-3B

I. Listening

A. (10 points: 2 points per item)
1. T
2. T
3. T
4. F
5. F

II. Reading

B. (8 points: 2 points per item)
6. c
7. b
8. d
9. b

III. Writing

C. (12 points: 4 points per item)
Ich habe letzte Woche im Hotel Schwarzwälderhof gegessen. Das Essen war prima! Die Ochsenschwanzsuppe hat mir am besten geschmeckt.

KAPITEL 5

Scripts for Chapter Test Kapitel 5

I. Listening

A.

ELKE	Schau mal!
SUSA	Ja, was denn?
ELKE	Das ist doch der Thorsten, oder?
SUSA	Wo denn? Ich sehe ihn nicht. Ach doch! Aber er sieht so komisch aus — das Haar.
ELKE	Thorsten, wie siehst du denn aus? Hast du einen neuen Haarschnitt?
SUSA	*[laughs sarcastically as she says this]* Wie bist du aber schön!
THORSTEN	Schon gut.
ELKE	Nur eine Frage: Was hast du bloß mit deinem Haar gemacht?
THORSTEN	Ich muss mich fotografieren lassen. Meine Familie will meiner Oma zu Weihnachten ein Foto schenken. Ein Foto von meiner Schwester und mir.
ELKE	Dann ist mir alles klar! Weg mit den langen, struppigen Haaren, nicht wahr? Ich finde, du siehst eigentlich gar nicht so schlecht aus. Ist dir aber nicht ein bisschen kalt so um die Ohren?
THORSTEN	Ach, Elke! Es ist nicht so schlimm, wie es aussieht! Meine Haare wachsen doch furchtbar schnell. Meine Schwester ist aber ganz schön schlecht gelaunt.
SUSA	Warum denn?
THORSTEN	Ja, sie hat sich die Haare gefärbt — und nun sind sie grün. Und jetzt muss sie sich fotografieren lassen.
SUSA	Ach du meine Güte! Was für ein Pech!
ELKE	Grüne Haare. Na, grün passt doch prima zu Weihnachten, oder? *[laughter]*

B.

HERR	Guten Tag! Entschuldigen Sie, bitte. Ich glaube, das ist mein Platz.
ALICE	Dieser hier? Der Fensterplatz? Nein. Das tut mir Leid. Ich habe diesen Fensterplatz reserviert.
HERR	Schon gut. Dann nehme ich eben diesen Platz hier.
ALICE	Leider geht das auch nicht. Der Platz ist auch reserviert. Er gehört meiner Freundin. Sie kommt gleich wieder.
HERR	Ja? Schauen Sie doch mal. Hier ist meine Platzkarte: 3C, also, drittes Abteil, Platz C.
ALICE	Sehen Sie sich meine Platzkarte an: 3C! Bitte schön!
HERR	Ich bedaure, aber auf Ihrer Karte steht Wagen 173, nach Milano, nicht wahr?
ALICE	Ja, das stimmt, wir fahren nach Milano, in Italien.
HERR	Ja, sehen Sie, dieser Wagen ist Nummer 170 und fährt nur nach Zürich, in die Schweiz. Also, kann dieser nicht Ihr Platz sein. Sie müssen doch zuerst den richtigen Wagen suchen, dann finden Sie und Ihre Freundin schon Ihre Plätze.
ALICE	Ach, Verzeihung!
HERR	Nicht so schlimm. Darf ich Ihnen helfen? Sie sind ja nicht von hier, oder?
ALICE	Nein, eigentlich sind wir aus Amerika — aus den Staaten, meine ich.
HERR	Sie sprechen aber sehr gut Deutsch.
ALICE	Danke!
HERR	Darf ich mich vorstellen? Ich heiße Saeh Al-Harbin.

Answers to Chapter Test Kapitel 5

I. Listening Maximum Score: 30 points

A. (15 points: 1 ½ points per item) **B.** (15 points: 1 ½ points per item)

1. T		11. T	
2. F		12. F	
3. F		13. T	
4. T		14. F	
5. F		15. F	
6. T		16. T	
7. F		17. T	
8. F		18. T	
9. T		19. T	
10. F		20. F	

II. Reading Maximum Score: 30 points

C. (10 points: 2 points per item) **D.** (12 points: 1 ½ points per item) **E.** (8 points; 2 points per item)

21. d	26. d	34. c
22. c	27. a	35. a
23. c	28. b	36. a
24. c	29. c	37. a
25. b	30. c	
	31. d	
	32. a	
	33. b	

III. Culture Maximum Score: 9 points

F. (9 points: 1 point per item)

38. T
39. T
40. T
41. F
42. T
43. T
44. F
45. F
46. T

IV. Writing Maximum Score: 31 points

G. (16 points: 2 points per item)

47. Das Müsli ist alle.
48. Aber das macht nichts.
49. Ich esse halt Brötchen.
50. Das ist auch nicht schlimm.
51. Ich esse eben Brot.
52. Was kann ich auf mein Brot tun?
53. Darf ich den Käse essen?
54. Kann ich für dich einkaufen gehen?

H. (15 points: 3 points per item)
Liebe Herr und Frau ... !
Köln hat mir sehr gut gefallen, und ich habe viel Spaß gehabt. Das Essen war sehr gut. Ihre Suppe hat mir am besten geschmeckt. Danke für alles!
        Herzliche Grüße
        [*student's name*]

Holt German 2 Komm mit!, Chapter 5

6 Gute Besserung!

Name _____ Klasse _____ Datum _____

Quiz 6-1A

Maximum Score: 35

■ Erste Stufe

Grammar and Vocabulary

A. Give the German equivalents of the following questions and answers. (15 points)

How do you feel?

1. _____

I am not doing well.

2. _____

What's wrong with you?

3. _____

I have a cough and stuffy nose.

4. _____

You must stay at home in bed.

5. _____

SCORE _____

B. Fill in the blanks in the statements and questions below with the correct form of the modal verb **sollen**. (5 points)

Du 6. _____ heute einkaufen gehen.

7. _____ wir zu Hause bleiben?

Ich 8. _____ am Wochenende zu meiner Oma fahren.

9. _____ ihr nicht in die Drogerie gehen?

10. _____ sie (sing) nicht in die Schule gehen?

SCORE _____

Holt German 2 Komm mit!, Chapter 6

Testing Program **131**

Quiz 6-1A

C. You work in a pharmacy and people call in describing their ailments and asking your advice. Fill in the blanks in the conversations with the appropriate words from the box. (15 points)

> Erkältung   Apotheke   helfen   soll   Fieber   Saft   schlecht
> Bauchschmerzen   tun   mir   Auf Wiederhören   Kirche   sofort
> Warum   krank

DU   Hier **11.** _____ *Rachengold.* Was kann ich für Sie tun?

KRANKE   Ach, Frau Apothekerin, ich habe eine **12.** _____

und Fieber. Was **13.** _____ ich nur tun?

DU   Nehmen Sie eine Aspirin und trinken Sie viel

14. _____ .

KRANKE   Danke. **15.** _____ !

Das Telefon klingelt wieder.

DU   Hallo?

KRANKER   Grüß Gott! Bitte **16.** _____ Sie mir, ich habe

furchtbare **17.** _____ . Mir ist auch sehr

18. _____ und ich habe hohes

19. _____ .

DU   Ja, da müssen Sie **20.** _____ ins Krankenhaus.

Wo wohnen Sie? Ich rufe einen Krankenwagen (*ambulance*).

KRANKER   In der Marienstaße, gleich neben der **21.** _____

DU   Der Krankenwagen ist gleich bei Ihnen.

Das Telefon klingelt schon wieder.

DU   Guten Morgen. Was kann ich für Sie **22.** _____ ?

Sind Sie **23.** _____ ?

ANRUFER   Nein, es geht **24.** _____ ausgezeichnet.

DU   **25.** _____ rufen Sie mich dann an?

ANRUFER   *(etwas verwirrt)* Ach, ich... ich wollte die Elke zu meiner Fete am Samstag einladen.

DU   Sie haben leider die falsche Nummer. Hier ist die Apotheke *Rachengold.*

ANRUFER   Entschuldigen Sie!

SCORE _____

TOTAL SCORE _____

KAPITEL 6

Name _____ Klasse _____ Datum _____

Gute Besserung!

■ Erste Stufe

Maximum Score: 40

I. Listening

A. Hanno is running errands today. Listen to his conversations twice and mark the statements below true (**T**) or false (**F**). (10 points)

_____ 1. Hanno went to a drugstore (**Drogerie**) first.

_____ 2. Hanno's mother needs something for her headache.

_____ 3. Hanno had to pick up prescription medicine.

_____ 4. Hanno bought suntan lotion at the pharmacy.

_____ 5. Hanno still has another errand to run.

SCORE [＿＿＿]

II. Reading

B. Read the following article and answer the questions that follow. (8 points)

Was tun bei einer Erkältung?

In der nasskalten Jahreszeit kommt es oft zu Erkältungen. Die Symptome einer Erkältung sind Halsschmerzen, Husten, Schnupfen, Bronchitis, Fieber und Abgeschlagenheit.

Normale Erkältungen können durch Selbstmedikation behandelt werden (*be treated*).
   *Machen Sie eine Schwitzkur: Decken Sie sich warm zu und trinken sie heißen Kamillentee!
   *Lutschen Sie Hustenbonbons mit kühlendem Effekt! Eukalyptus- und Mentholbonbons lindern (*soothe*) den Hustenreiz.
   *Sie brauchen auch ein feuchtes (*humid*) Raumklima. Trockene Luft (*dry air*) schadet erkälteten Menschen.

Was können Sie tun, um eine Erkältung zu vermeiden? Härten Sie sich schon in der warmen Sommerzeit ab: Gehen Sie viel schwimmen und besuchen Sie oft die Sauna! In Erkältungszeiten meiden Sie Orte mit vielen Menschen.

6. In what season are colds most frequent?
   a. in winter when the weather is cold and wet
   b. in summer when the weather is hot and humid
   c. in fall when the weather is wet and warm
   d. in spring when the weather is dry and cool

Quiz 6-1B

7. Which of the following is NOT listed as a cold symptom?
   a. sore throat   **b.** cough   **c.** fever   **d.** earache

8. What is recommended as treatment for the cold?
   a. sweating it out   **c.** resting in dry air
   b. drinking plenty of ice-cold water   **d.** eating a box of candy

9. What should people do to avoid catching a cold during cold season?
   a. They should take a steam bath once a week.
   b. They should go swimming.
   c. They should avoid crowds.
   d. They should eat lots of fruits and vegetables.

SCORE [   ]

III. Writing

C. You have had a cold and missed a few days of school. Write your pen pal about it. Tell him or her about what you have, how you feel in general, and some of your symptoms. [12 points]

_____

_____

_____

_____

SCORE [   ]

IV. Culture

D. List two facts that you have learned about the national health care system in Germany. [4 points]

10. _____

   _____

Briefly explain the difference between an **Apotheke** and a **Drogerie**. Also mention one item you can buy at an **Apotheke** but not at a **Drogerie**. [6 points]

11. _____

   _____

SCORE [   ]

TOTAL SCORE [   ]

KAPITEL 6

6 Gute Besserung!

■ Zweite Stufe

Maximum Score: 30

Grammar and Vocabulary

A. Fill in the correct case in the questions below, using the prompts in parentheses. (5 points)

(your mother)   Was tut **1.** _____ weh, Petra?

(he)   Schmeckt **2.** _____ die Erbsensuppe?

(your sister)   Hilfst du manchmal **3.** _____ ?

(his grandfather)   Was fehlt **4.** _____ ?

(they)   Hat es **5.** _____ in Dresden gefallen?

SCORE [   ]

B. Fill in the blanks in the statements below by providing the correct dative reflexive pronoun. (5 points)

Ich habe **6.** _____ den Arm gebrochen.

Du hast **7.** _____ den Knöchel verstaucht.

Ulrike hat **8.** _____ den Fuß gebrochen.

Peter hat **9.** _____ das Knie verletzt.

Ihr habt **10.** _____ den Arm gebrochen.

SCORE [   ]

C. Give the German equivalents of the statements below. (15 points)

She washes her hands.

11. _____

He combs his hair.

12. _____

Monika brushes her teeth.

13. _____

Name _____ Klasse _____ Datum _____

Quiz 6-2A

My grandmother cleans the windows.

14. _____

My mother washes my shirt.

15. _____

SCORE [   ]

D. Fill in the blanks below with the correct form of the verb **brechen**. (5 points)

Wer hat sich beim Fußballspielen etwas **16.** _____ ?

Hans **17.** _____ sich nie was.

Ihr **18.** _____ euch noch den Hals.

Wie oft hast du dir schon den Fuß **19.** _____ ?

Was **20.** _____ du dir oft?

SCORE [   ]

TOTAL SCORE [   ]

Holt German 2 Komm mit!, Chapter 6

6 Gute Besserung!

■ Zweite Stufe

Maximum Score: 30

I. Listening

A. Erik is at the doctor's office. Listen to the conversation twice and then choose the best answers from the alternatives given. (6 points)

1. Erik has injured the following body parts:
   a. his arm and foot
   b. his arm and leg
   c. his leg and foot
   d. his arm only

2. Erik has the following kinds of injuries:
   a. a sprain and a surface injury
   b. a broken bone and a sprain
   c. a broken bone and a cut
   d. only cuts and bruises

3. Erik has a real problem with his injuries because he had planned
   a. to go swimming in two days.
   b. to go to the beach for vacation.
   c. to take a hiking trip this weekend.
   d. to run in a marathon in three weeks.

SCORE _____

II. Reading

B. Read the diary entry of an emergency clinic doctor and then answer the questions that follow. (8 points)

Montag, den 18. Juli

Heute hatte ich in der Unfallklinik viel Arbeit. Ein alter Mann ist gekommen, der starke Bauchschmerzen hatte. Die Untersuchung zeigte, dass er eine schwere Lebensmittelvergiftung hat. Er hat Kartoffelsalat gegessen, den er schon letzte Woche zubereitet hatte. Leider hat er den Kartoffelsalat nicht im Kühlschrank aufbewahrt. Kurz vor dem Mittagessen ist ein kleines Mädchen gekommen, das Halsschmerzen und hohes Fieber hatte. Ich habe der Mutter ein Rezept für ein Antibiotikum ausgestellt und ihr gesagt, dass sie ihre Tochter sofort ins Bett stecken muss. Am frühen Nachmittag ist ein junger Mann in die Klinik gekommen. Er beklagte sich über starke Kopfschmerzen und einen Sonnenbrand auf den Schultern und dem Rücken. Er war wohl viel zu lange in der heißen Sonne. Ich gab ihm ein Schmerzmittel und eine Heilcreme für den Sonnenbrand. Eine Minute vor dem Ende meiner Schicht *(shift)* wurde eine Frau gebracht, die kaum atmen konnte. Eine Biene *(bee)* hatte sie gestochen und sie hatte eine Insektengiftallergie. Ich habe ihr sofort eine Adrenalininjektion gegeben und in einer halben Stunde ist es ihr gleich wieder besser gegangen.

Quiz 6-2B

4. What is **Lebensmittelvergiftung?**
   a. a stomach injury
   b. indigestion
   c. food poisoning
   d. a food allergy

5. What did the doctor prescribe for the little girl's illness?
   a. pain medication
   b. cortisone
   c. an antibiotic
   d. cough syrup

6. What is a **Sonnenbrand?**
   a. sunset
   b. sunbathing
   c. a skin rash
   d. a sunburn

7. What was wrong with the woman who was brought in at the end of the shift?
   a. She was allergic to adrenalin.
   b. She had an allergic reaction to a bee sting.
   c. She had a bad cough.
   d. She could no longer swallow.

SCORE [   ]

III. Writing

C. You are babysitting your neighbor's seven-year-old daughter. She doesn't look very chipper, so you try to find out what's wrong. (16 points)

Ask her what's wrong with her:

8. DU _____

   SIE Es geht mir nicht gut.

Ask her if something hurts:

9. DU _____

   SIE Ja, mein Knie!

Ask her if she's injured her knee:

10. DU _____

   SIE Ja, ich bin vom Fahrrad gefallen. Heute Nachmittag.

Ask her if she has washed her knee.

11. DU _____

   SIE Nein, noch nicht.

SCORE [   ]

TOTAL SCORE [   ]

6 Gute Besserung!

Name _____ Klasse _____ Datum _____

Dritte Stufe

Maximum Score: 35

Grammar and Vocabulary

A. Complete the sentences below by using the prompts in parentheses. [15 points]

Ich vermeide die Sonne, weil ich **1.** _____

_____ . (to have a sunstroke)

Ulrike schläft lange, weil sie **2.** _____ . (to be tired)

Heinz isst etwas, weil er **3.** _____ . (to be hungry)

Sie geht zum Arzt, weil sie **4.** _____ . (to be sick)

Ich mag die Seife nicht, weil sie **5.** _____ . (to be perfumed)

SCORE _____

B. Your friend Heiko complains about various ailments and you give him advice. Use the cues in parentheses, changing them to the **du**-form of the imperative. [15 points]

HEIKO   Meine Stirn ist so heiß.

DU   **6.** _____
(to take one's temperature)

HEIKO   Ich bin auch so müde.

DU   **7.** _____
(to take a break)

HEIKO   Der Hals tut mir auch weh.

DU   **8.** _____
(to stay at home)

HEIKO   Aber ich brauche Medizin!

DU   **9.** _____
(to go to the pharmacy)

HEIKO   Aber ich bin zu krank, um aus dem Haus zu gehen.

DU   **10.** _____
(to call the doctor)

SCORE _____

Quiz 6-3A

C. Your friend Petra is going on a vacation to Mallorca. You spent your vacation there last year and now you give her some last-minute advice. Fill in the blanks in the conversation using words from the box. (5 points)

Lichtschutzfaktor	mitnehmen	Shampoo	hoffe	hoffentlich

DU   Ich 11. _____ , du nimmst eine Sonnencreme mit

hohem 12. _____ mit.

PETRA   Ach, 13. _____ ist Faktor 8 hoch genug?

DU   Ich glaube schon. Vergiss auch nicht dein 14. _____ .

PETRA   Was soll ich sonst noch 15. _____ ?

DU   Tja, vor allem lässige Klamotten.

SCORE [   ]

TOTAL SCORE [   ]

KAPITEL 6

Gute Besserung!

◾ Dritte Stufe

Maximum Score: 30

I. Listening

A. Katje has been invited to a costume ball for **Karneval**. As you listen to her conversation with her friend, mark the statements below true (**T**) or false (**F**). (10 points)

_____ 1. Katje wants advice about how to get out of going to the ball.

_____ 2. Her friend suggests she go as a clown.

_____ 3. She doesn't want to have to spend a lot on a costume.

_____ 4. A fox (**Fuchs**) costume would be too expensive.

_____ 5. All three of Werner's suggestions are "inspired" by Katje's red hair.

SCORE _____

II. Reading

B. Read the article and then decide if the statements that follow are true (T) or false (F). (8 points)

Der richtige Lichtschutzfaktor (LSF)

Die Größe des Lichtschutzfaktors hängt *(depends on)* vom Hauttyp ab:

—Menschen mit heller Haut, Sommersprossen, blonden oder hellroten Haaren, blauen oder grünen Augen brauchen mindestens LSF 15.

—Menschen mit heller Haut, blonden Haaren, blauen oder grünen Augen brauchen in den ersten Sonnentagen mindestens LSF 14, später *(later)* LSF 9-14.

—Menschen mit dunklen Haaren und braunen Augen brauchen in den ersten Sonnentagen mindestens LSF 8, später LSF 5-8.

—Menschen, die von Natur aus dunkle Haut, dunkle oder schwarze Haare und braune Augen haben, brauchen in den ersten Sonnentagen mindestens LSF 4, später LSF 2-4.

Der sonnenunempfindliche Hauttyp ist natürlich nicht immun gegen Sonnenbrand *(sunburn)*. Faktoren wie geographische Lage und Jahres- und Tageszeit spielen auch eine wichtige Rolle bei der Bestimmung *(determination)* des richtigen Lichtschutzfaktors. Sie brauchen zum Beispiel in Italien einen höheren LSF als in Hamburg. Die UV-Strahlung ist mittags höher als in den Morgenstunden. Man braucht deshalb mittags einen höheren LSF.

_____ 6. Menschen mit schwarzen Haaren und braunen Augen bekommen keinen Sonnenbrand.

_____ 7. Menschen mit heller Haut brauchen einen hohen LSF.

Quiz 6-3B

_____ **8.** Zur Bestimmung des richtigen Lichtschutzfaktors muss man den Hauttyp wissen.

_____ **9.** Menschen mit dunklen Haaren und braunen Augen brauchen in den ersten Sonnentagen mindestens LSF 5.

SCORE [   ]

III. Writing

C. Your pen pal has had a serious accident in which he broke his foot. He is just out of the hospital. Write a short letter in which you ask how he's feeling and if anything still hurts. Also express your hopes for his speedy recovery. (12 points)

_____

_____

_____

_____

_____

_____

SCORE [   ]

TOTAL SCORE [   ]

KAPITEL 6

Gute Besserung!

Chapter Test

I. Listening

Maximum Score: 29 points

A. Karl and Luise Stegmüller were out late last night and overslept this morning. Their small son, Emil, woke up at 7:30 as usual. Listen as he tells his mother about his morning routine and put the activities below in the order in which Emil did them. (15 points)

    a. sich die Ohren und den Hals gewaschen
    b. sich die Haare gekämmt
    c. sich die Haare gewaschen
    d. Frühstück gegessen
    e. sich die Zähne geputzt

_____ 1.

_____ 2.

_____ 3.

_____ 4.

_____ 5.

SCORE [ ]

B. Michael meets Beate, who is walking with her dog, Polo. Read the following statements before you listen to the conversation. After you listen to the conversation twice, mark the statements true (**a**) or false (**b**). (14 points)

_____ **6.** Polo hat sich das Bein gebrochen.

_____ **7.** Er hinkt (*limps*) nur auf einem Bein.

_____ **8.** Er kann laufen und Ball spielen.

_____ **9.** Ein Auto hat Polo überfahren.

_____ **10.** Das rechte Vorderbein tut dem Hund noch weh.

_____ **11.** Der Hund hat gelernt: wenn man sich verletzt, lenkt man Aufmerksamkeit (*attention*) auf sich.

_____ **12.** Michael meint, Beates Hund ist ganz clever.

SCORE [ ]

Chapter Test

II. Reading

Maximum Score: 30 points

C. Read the questions below and then read the following passage twice. Choose the best answers from among the alternatives given. (15 points)

ERSTE HILFE

Wenn ein Unfall *(accident)* passiert, ist es natürlich am besten, wenn man einen Arzt oder einen Krankenwagen anruft. Doch gibt es Situationen, in denen Freunde oder Passanten einen Verletzten ins Krankenhaus transportieren müssen. In solchen Fällen soll man prinzipiell das verletzte Glied *(limb)* (Arm oder Bein) vor dem Transport einschienen *(provide a splint)*.

Beim Schienen soll man das verletzte Glied so wenig wie möglich *(as little as possible)* bewegen *(move)*. Zweitens soll man das Glied nicht so fest *(tight)* binden, dass der Blutkreislauf *(circulation)* gestört wird. Die Schiene kann ein Stück Holz sein, aufgerolltes Zeitungspapier oder auch das gesunde Bein.

Wenn es keine offene Wunde gibt, soll man Eis auf das verletzte Glied legen. Ansonsten *(otherwise)* soll man den Verletzten während des Transports mit einer Decke oder einem Mantel warm halten. Auf keinen Fall soll man ihm Alkohol oder Schmerzmittel geben, nicht einmal Aspirin.

WICHTIG: Wenn der Verletzte eine Kopfwunde hat, oder sich den Rücken verletzt hat, soll man den Verletzten überhaupt nicht bewegen.

13. The first-aid advice in this article pertains to
    a. how to stop bleeding.
    b. head injuries.
    c. caring for injured persons before transporting them.
    d. preventing injuries.

14. An emergency splint could be made from all of the following EXCEPT
    a. rolled-up magazines.
    b. a broomstick.
    c. the uninjured leg.
    d. an ice pack.

15. The principles of splinting a limb include all of the following EXCEPT
    a. choosing a stable splint.
    b. moving the injured limb as little as possible.
    c. pulling the bone back into correct alignment.
    d. checking to make sure circulation isn't cut off by the splint.

16. Additional things you should do for the victim include
    a. giving the victim a painkiller if you have one.
    b. keeping the victim warm.
    c. putting an ice pack on open wounds.
    d. giving the victim alcohol before transporting him or her.

KAPITEL 6

17. In case of head wounds or back injuries, one should
    a. check to see if there is also a leg injury.
    b. make sure the injured person is not moved.
    c. place the injured person in a more comfortable position.
    d. carry the patient immediately to a warm spot.

SCORE [   ]

D. Read the questions below and then read the following passage twice. Choose the best answers from among the alternatives given. (15 points)

> entdecken *to discover*
> sich entwickeln *to develop*

ANTIBIOTIKA: WUNDER ODER KEIN WUNDER?

1929 hat Sir Richard Fleming zum ersten Mal den medizinischen Nutzen von Penizillin zeigen können. Eine neue Epoche begann bei der Behandlung von Infektionen und anderen Krankheiten.

In den Jahren nach dem Zweiten Weltkrieg wurden immer neue Antibiotika entdeckt, was wichtig war, weil ziemlich viele Patienten allergisch gegen Penizillin waren. Penizillin hat auch viele Nebenwirkungen. Auch war es wichtig, weil neue Arten von Bakterien sich schnell entwickelten, die gegen die alten Antibiotika immun waren.

Heutzutage bekommen unsere Milchkühe, Rinder, Schweine und Hühner kleine aber regelmäßige Dosen von Antibiotika in ihr Futter, damit wir sie leicht und bequem gesund halten können. Wenn wir also Tierprodukte essen, zum Beispiel Fleisch oder Eier, dann nehmen wir auch kleine Mengen Antibiotika mit dieser Nahrung auf.

18. The first paragraph focuses on
    a. the discovery of the medical uses of penicillin.
    b. infectious diseases.
    c. the life of Sir Richard Fleming.
    d. important events of 1929.

19. The second paragraph focuses on
    a. how bacteria become immune.
    b. medical milestones during World War II.
    c. allergies and the growth of pollutants following World War II.
    d. the importance of the discovery of new antibiotics.

20. The third paragraph focuses on
    a. the use of antibiotics in animal feed.
    b. the use of antibiotics in milk.
    c. the effects of penicillin on animals.
    d. how to keep animals from getting lung infections.

Read the second paragraph again more closely and answer the following two questions.

KAPITEL 6

Chapter Test

21. One of the problems with penicillin was
    a. it was not very effective.
    b. it had many side effects.
    c. it was developed for animals only.
    d. it was limited to the treatment of pneumonia.

22. One reason new antibiotics were needed fairly soon was that
    a. the early antibiotics were not very powerful.
    b. a lot of patients resisted injections.
    c. penicillin can't be administered to animals.
    d. new strains of bacteria soon developed that were immune to penicillin.

SCORE [   ]

III. Culture

Maximum Score: 9 points

E. Based on your knowledge of German culture, mark the following statements true (a) or false (b). (9 points)

_____ 23. Employers pay a large amount of the costs in Germany's national health care system.

_____ 24. College students and housewives are not covered in the national health care system in Germany.

_____ 25. An **Apotheke** sells nothing but prescription medicine.

_____ 26. A **Drogerie** sells items such as shampoo and soap.

_____ 27. A **Bad** usually features mineral or hot springs of some sort.

_____ 28. Some of the most famous German places called **Bad** were once Roman baths.

_____ 29. Traditionally, a trip to a **Bad** was taken for health reasons.

_____ 30. **Kur** is the same thing as **Urlaub** or **Ferien**.

_____ 31. You will be allowed to stay in Germany as an exchange student without having health insurance.

SCORE [   ]

Chapter Test

IV. Writing

Maximum Score: 32 points

F. You must call your boss to say that you're sick and can't go to work today. Complete the conversation using the cues given. (16 points)

      ER   Hier Goetze.

[You greet your boss and explain that you are calling in sick.]

32. DU _____

33.   _____

      ER   Das tut mir aber Leid! Was fehlt Ihnen denn?

[You explain what's the matter with you. Remember, you are too sick to work!]

34. DU _____

35.   [und] _____

36.   [und] _____

      ER   Sind Sie schon beim Arzt gewesen?

[Explain whether or not you have been or are going to the doctor.]

37. DU _____

      ER   Schon gut. Also, wann kommen Sie denn wieder?

[Give an estimate. Explain any conditions you know of that will influence how long you'll have to miss work.]

38. DU _____

      ER   Also dann, gute Besserung!

39. DU _____

SCORE [ ]

Chapter Test

G. A German student who is staying in your home was hurt playing soccer and now has his arm in a sling. You were there when it happened and went to the hospital with him. Write a short note to his parents explaining

a) what happened

b) how it happened

c) what the doctor said he should do

d) and how he's feeling now.

Write five complete sentences. Be sure to use an appropriate salutation and closing. (16 points)

_____

_____

_____

_____

_____

_____

_____

_____

_____

_____

_____

_____

_____

_____

SCORE [ ]

TOTAL SCORE [ ]

Holt German 2 Komm mit!, Chapter 6

KAPITEL 6

KAPITEL 6 Chapter Test Score Sheet

Circle the letter that matches the most appropriate response.

I. Listening
Maximum Score: 29 points

A. (15 points)

1. a b c d e
2. a b c d e
3. a b c d e
4. a b c d e
5. a b c d e

SCORE [ ]

B. (14 points)

6. a b
7. a b
8. a b
9. a b
10. a b

11. a b
12. a b

SCORE [ ]

II. Reading
Maximum Score: 30 points

C. (15 points)

13. a b c d
14. a b c d
15. a b c d
16. a b c d
17. a b c d

SCORE [ ]

D. (15 points)

18. a b c d
19. a b c d
20. a b c d
21. a b c d
22. a b c d

SCORE [ ]

III. Culture
Maximum Score: 9 points

E. (9 points)

23. a b
24. a b
25. a b
26. a b
27. a b

28. a b
29. a b
30. a b
31. a b

SCORE [ ]

K A P I T E L 6

IV. Writing

F. (16 points)

32. _____

_____

33. _____

_____

34. _____

_____

35. _____

_____

36. _____

_____

37. _____

_____

38. _____

_____

39. _____

_____

SCORE [   ]

G. (16 points)

_____

_____

_____

_____

_____

_____

_____

_____

_____

SCORE [   ]

TOTAL SCORE [   ]

KAPITEL 6

Quiz 6-1B Kapitel 6 Erste Stufe

I. Listening

A.

APOTHEKERIN	Was darf's sein, bitte?
HANNO	Ich habe hier einen Abholschein für ein Medikament. Bitte!
APOTHEKERIN	Von Doktor Wertmüller. Hmmm. Das Rezept ist aber nicht für Sie, oder?
HANNO	Nein. Ich hole es für meine Mutter. Der Arzt hat ihr Tabletten gegen Kopfschmerzen verschrieben.
APOTHEKERIN	Moment, bitte. So, bitte schön. Sagen Sie aber Ihrer Mutter, wenn sie diese Tabletten einnimmt, darf sie nicht Auto fahren.
HANNO	Danke, sag ich ihr. Wiedersehen!
	[street noises as Hanno heads for home]
HANNO	Hallo, Mutti! Hier sind die Tabletten.
MUTTER	Danke! Hast du die Sonnencreme für dich auch gekauft?
HANNO	Ach, so was Blödes! Nein, die Sonnencreme hab ich vergessen.
MUTTER	Na ja, Junge. Was man nicht im Kopf hat ...
HANNO	... muss man in den Beinen haben. Also, ich gehe jetzt in die Drogerie in der Schillerstraße. Das ist doch nicht so schlimm.

Quiz 6-2B Kapitel 6 Zweite Stufe

I. Listening

A.	ÄRZTIN	Nun, was fehlt Ihnen heute?
	ERIK	Mir tut der Arm weh.
	ÄRZTIN	Nun, lassen Sie mich mal schauen.
	ERIK	Aua!
	ÄRZTIN	Tut das weh?
	ERIK	Und wie!
	ÄRZTIN	Ja, wir wollen natürlich eine Röntgenaufnahme machen. Ich befürchte, dass Sie sich den Arm gebrochen haben. Tut sonst was weh?
	ERIK	Ja, mein Fuß.
	ÄRZTIN	Ach ja. Ich seh's. Sie haben sich auch den Fuß verstaucht. Dafür brauchen Sie einen Verband. Und zwei Tage nicht laufen. Und um den Arm bekommen Sie einen Gipsverband. Nehmen Sie Aspirin gegen Schmerzen. Vermeiden Sie die Sonne und trinken Sie auch keinen Kaffee. Schlecht für den Magen! Ach ja, und mindestens drei Wochen dürfen Sie nicht baden gehen. Der Gips darf nicht nass werden.
	ERIK	Drei Wochen! Aber ich gehe nächste Woche in Urlaub, nach Frankreich. Wir wollten einen Strandurlaub machen an der atlantischen Küste!
	ÄRZTIN	Ja, das tut mir furchtbar Leid!

Quiz 6-3B Kapitel 6 Dritte Stufe

I. Listening

A.	KATJE	Du, Werner, meine Tante hat mich nach Köln eingeladen, zum Karneval. Wir gehen sogar auf einen Maskenball.
	WERNER	Prima, Mensch!
	KATJE	Aber sag mir doch, was ich bloß für ein Kostüm anziehen soll.
	WERNER	Du solltest dich vielleicht als Clown verkleiden. Deine wilden roten Haare passen ausgezeichnet dazu.
	KATJE	Ach, nee!
	WERNER	Clown passt dir nicht? Dann gehst du am besten als die englische Königin Elisabeth. Die war auch rothaarig.
	KATJE	Dann muss ich mir aber unbedingt ein tolles Ballkleid mieten. Das ist mir doch zu teuer.
	WERNER	Ja, so ein Kostüm ist dir wahrscheinlich auch zu steif und unbequem. Ich weiß was! Du solltest als Fuchs gehen! Wir können dir eine Fuchsmaske basteln. Das kostet auch nicht viel. Und du hast doch diesen rotbraunen Trainingsanzug vom Schwimmclub. Wir basteln einen buschigen Schwanz hintendran. Dann siehst du echt lustig aus.
	KATJE	Gar nicht so schlecht. Meine Haare sind ja so fuchsrot-braun.

ANSWERS Quiz 6-1A

A. (15 points; 3 points per item)
Answers will vary. Possible answers:
1. Wie fühlst du dich?
2. Mir ist nicht gut.
3. Was fehlt dir?
4. Ich habe Husten und Schnupfen.
5. Du musst zu Hause bleiben, im Bett.

B. (5 points; 1 point per item)
6. sollst
7. Sollen
8. soll
9. Sollt
10. Soll

C. (15 points; 1 point per item)
11. Apotheke
12. Erkältung
13. soll
14. Saft
15. Auf Wiederhören
16. helfen
17. Bauchschmerzen
18. schlecht
19. Fieber
20. sofort
21. Kirche
22. tun
23. krank
24. mir
25. Warum

ANSWERS Quiz 6-1B

I. Listening

A. (10 points: 2 points per item)
1. F
2. T
3. T
4. F
5. T

II. Reading

B. (8 points: 2 points per item)
6. a
7. d
8. a
9. c

III. Writing

C. (12 points: 4 points per item)
Ich fühle mich ganz schlecht. Ich habe mich erkältet. Jetzt habe ich Kopfschmerzen und Halsschmerzen.

IV. Culture

D. (10 points)
Answers will vary. Possible answers:
10. Health insurance is relatively inexpensive. / Everyone is insured, even if they are not working.
11. A **Drogerie** is like an American drugstore, but you cannot buy prescription drugs there or medicine. / You must go to an **Apotheke** for that. / Any prescription drug.

KAPITEL 6

ANSWERS Quiz 6-2A

A. (5 points; 1 point per item)
  1. deiner Mutter
  2. ihm
  3. deiner Schwester
  4. seinem Großvater
  5. ihnen

B. (5 points; 1 point per item)
  6. mir
  7. dir
  8. sich
  9. sich
  10. euch

C. (15 points; 3 points per item)
  Answers will vary. Possible answers:
  11. Sie wäscht sich die Hände.
  12. Er kämmt sich die Haare.
  13. Monika putzt sich die Zähne.
  14. Meine Großmutter putzt die Fenster.
  15. Meine Mutter wäscht mein Hemd.

D. (5 points; 1 point per item)
  16. gebrochen
  17. bricht
  18. brecht
  19. gebrochen
  20. brichst

ANSWERS Quiz 6-2B

I. Listening

A. (6 points: 2 points per item)
  1. a
  2. b
  3. b

II. Reading

B. (8 points: 2 points per item)
  4. c
  5. c
  6. d
  7. b

III. Writing

C. (16 points: 4 points per item)
  8. Geht es dir nicht gut?
  9. Tut dir etwas weh?
  10. Hast du dir das Knie verletzt?
  11. Hast du dir das Knie schon gewaschen?

Answers to Quizzes 6-3A, 6-3B

ANSWERS Quiz 6-3A

A. (15 points; 3 points per item)
1. einen Sonnenstich habe
2. müde ist
3. Hunger hat
4. krank ist
5. parfümiert ist

B. (15 points; 3 points per item)
6. Miss dein Fieber!
7. Mach eine Pause!
8. Bleib zu Hause!
9. Geh zur Apotheke!
10. Ruf den Arzt an!

C. (5 points; 1 point per item)
11. hoffe
12. Lichtschutzfaktor
13. hoffentlich
14. Shampoo
15. mitnehmen

ANSWERS Quiz 6-3B

I. Listening

A. (10 points: 2 points per item)
1. F
2. T
3. T
4. F
5. T

II. Reading

B. (8 points: 2 points per item)
6. F
7. T
8. T
9. F

III. Writing

C. (12 points: 4 points per item)
Wie geht's dir denn? Tut dir der Fuß
noch weh? Ich hoffe, dass es dir bald
besser geht.

KAPITEL 6

I. Listening

A.

EMIL	Mutti! Mutti!!
MUTTER	Emil! Was ist denn Kind? Oh je! Schon neun Uhr!
EMIL	Ja, Mutti. Komm doch mal in die Küche!
MUTTER	Hast du Hunger?
EMIL	Nein. Ich habe schon gegessen.
MUTTER	Wer hat dir denn das Frühstück gemacht?
EMIL	Das Frühstück habe ich mir selbst gemacht.
MUTTER	Du hast dir ein Ei gekocht?
EMIL	Eigentlich nicht.
MUTTER	Und was ist bloß mit deinen Haaren? Die sehen ganz steif aus, Emil.
EMIL	Nach dem Frühstück habe ich mir die Haare gewaschen. Mit dem neuen Shampoo.
MUTTER	Ach so. Die sind ja voller Seife. Nicht so schlimm. Und hast du dich denn auch gebadet?
EMIL	Ja klar. Ich habe mir den Hals gut gewaschen, Mutti. Und die Ohren auch.
MUTTER	Prima! Aber was ist denn hier auf deinem Hemd? Das sieht ja wie Zahnpasta aus, oder?
EMIL	Stimmt. Ich habe mir die Zähne geputzt, und dann habe ich mir die Haare gekämmt. Habe ich alles ganz allein gemacht. Aber jetzt komm doch endlich in die Küche!
MUTTER	Gut, ich komme schon. Was ist denn dort?
EMIL	Ja ... weißt du ... ich wollte schon Eier kochen, aber die Eier sind mir aus den Händen gerutscht, und die Katze hat sie gefressen. Ihr geht es jetzt bestimmt ganz schlecht.

B.

MICHAEL	Was fehlt denn eurem Hund?
BEATE	Eigentlich nichts.
MICHAEL	Doch, doch. Er ist verletzt. Er hinkt ganz offensichtlich. Er hat sich bestimmt das Bein verletzt.
BEATE	Also, welches Bein hat er sich denn verletzt?
MICHAEL	Das rechte Vorderbein. Siehst du das nicht?
BEATE	Polo, komm her, Polo! Nun, schau mal, Michael! Auf welchem Bein hinkt er jetzt?
MICHAEL	Auf dem linken.
BEATE	Na, siehst du. Du hast vorher gesagt, er hat sich das rechte Bein verletzt.
MICHAEL	Das ist aber ganz komisch. Vielleicht tun ihm beide Beine weh.
BEATE	Glaube ich nicht. Laufen kann er ganz prima. Und Ball spielen.
MICHAEL	Wie kommt denn das?
BEATE	Unser Polo ist ein super Hund, aber er spielt ein bisschen Theater. Er hat sich letzte Woche wehgetan. Er ist gegen das Fahrrad von meinem Bruder gelaufen. Polo hat ein paar Mal gebellt. Dann hat mein Bruder ihn in die Arme genommen und ihn getröstet und liebkost und so weiter. Und das hat Polo sehr gut gefallen. Jetzt versucht er immer wieder, unsre Aufmerksamkeit auf sich zu lenken.
MICHAEL	Der ist ein ganz intelligenter Hund, finde ich. Manche Menschen machen das auch mit den Wehwehchen.

KAPITEL 6

Answers to Chapter Test Kapitel 6

I. Listening Maximum Score: 29 points

A. (15 points: 3 points per item) **B.** (14 points: 2 points per item)

1.	d	6.	b
2.	c	7.	b
3.	a	8.	a
4.	e	9.	b
5.	b	10.	b
		11.	a
		12.	a

II. Reading Maximum Score: 30 points

C. (15 points: 3 points per item) **D.** (15 points: 3 points per item)

13.	c	18.	a
14.	d	19.	d
15.	c	20.	a
16.	b	21.	b
17.	b	22.	d

III. Culture Maximum Score: 9 points

E. (9 points: 1 point per item)

23. a
24. b
25. b
26. a
27. a
28. a
29. a
30. b
31. b

IV. Writing Maximum Score: 32 points

F. (16 points: 2 points per item)
Answers will vary. Possible answers:
32. Hier *[student's name]*! Guten Tag, Herr Goetze!
33. Entschuldigen Sie, aber leider kann ich heute nicht arbeiten./Ich fühle mich gar nicht wohl.
34. Mir geht's ganz schlecht.
35. Ich habe Fieber und Kopfschmerzen.
36. Und der Hals tut mir weh.
37. Ich gehe heute zum Arzt.
38. Ich hoffe, dass ich wieder am Montag arbeiten kann.
39. Vielen Dank. Auf Wiederhören!

G. (16 points: 3 points per item plus 1 point for salutation and closing)
Answers will vary. Possible answer:
Lieber Herr und liebe Frau Hinz!
Heinz und ich haben Fußball gespielt, und dann hat Heinz sich den Arm gebrochen. Es tut mir sehr Leid. Wir sind ins Krankenhaus gegangen. Der Arzt hat gesagt, er soll drei Wochen keinen Sport machen. Jetzt geht es ihm gut, aber der Arm tut noch ein bisschen weh.
          Herzliche Grüße
          [student's name]

Holt German 2 Komm mit!, Chapter 6

Name _____ Klasse _____ Datum _____

I. Listening

Maximum Score: 30 points

A. Anna is expecting a visit from some relatives, and she wants her husband, Bernd, to go to pick them up. Listen to their conversation and choose the picture below that best matches the descriptions. Then mark each of the statements that follow **a) true** or **b) false**. (10 points)

_____ 1. Which of the following is most likely a picture of Anna's aunt and her son?

    a.   b.   c.   d.

_____ 2. Anna's aunt is tall.

_____ 3. The aunt has dark brown hair.

_____ 4. The aunt is in her mid 40s.

_____ 5. Her son has blue eyes.

B. Andreas, Beate, and Christoph are siblings. Christmas is coming and they have a problem. Listen to their conversation, and then complete the following statements by choosing the best answer from among the alternatives given. (10 points)

_____ 6. Andreas, Beate, and Christoph are having trouble choosing a gift for their grandmother because
    a. she doesn't have any interests or hobbies.
    b. she has a house full of things already.
    c. she doesn't like receiving presents.
    d. she's an unusual person.

_____ 7. They discuss all of the following ideas EXCEPT:
    a. photo album   **c.** clothing
    b. handmade crafts   **d.** music

_____ 8. Of her interests, the only one they can think of anything to buy for is
    a. hiking.   **c.** her little dog, Mops.
    b. gardening.   **d.** photography.

_____ 9. They finally decide to
    a. buy her a cassette.
    b. copy a piece from their own Telemann cassette.
    c. take her to a concert.
    d. record a cassette of themselves playing the flute.

_____ 10. They agree that
    a. the musical present is the best suggestion so far.
    b. making a cassette is too much trouble.
    c. she probably doesn't like to listen to their music.
    d. it would be better to get her a box of candy.

C. A reporter from a popular teen magazine is interviewing students about what they do for their health. Listen to the following interview with Marianne. After you listen to the interview, choose the best answers from among the alternatives below.

_____ 11. Marianne
    a. tut sehr wenig für ihre Gesundheit.
    b. ist eine Gesundheitsfanatikerin.
    c. lebt ziemlich gesund.
    d. soll sich vernünftiger ernähren.

_____ 12. Mariannes Mutter
    a. isst nur vegetarisch.
    b. kocht mit viel Fett.
    c. sorgt dafür, dass die Kinder richtig essen.
    d. kauft nicht genug frisches Obst und Gemüse.

_____ 13. Marianne treibt Sport
    a. nur, weil sie es muss.
    b. ziemlich oft.
    c. nur an Wochenenden.
    d. nur in der Sportstunde in der Schule.

_____ 14. Marianne fährt
    a. mit dem Rad zur Schule.
    b. lieber mit dem Bus als mit dem Rad.
    c. am liebsten mit dem Auto.
    d. in ihrer Freizeit Rad.

_____ 15. Der Reporter findet,
    a. Marianne lebt ganz gesund.
    b. Marianne tut zu viel für ihre Gesundheit.
    c. Marianne soll mehr für ihre Gesundheit machen.
    d. Mariannes Mutter soll besser auf Mariannes Gesundheit aufpassen.

II. Reading

Maximum Score: 30 points

A. Carefully read each of the questions below and choose the one response that would NOT be a logical reply. (10 points)

_____ 16. Wie findest du die Suppe?
    a. Ausgezeichnet! Schmeckt sie dir auch?
    b. Nicht besonders. Magst du sie?
    c. Lecker! Nudeln habe ich sehr gern.
    d. Eigentlich schon. Was machst du gern?

_____ 17. Möchten Sie jetzt bestellen?
    a. Nein, danke, ich möchte im Moment gar nichts.
    b. Ja, ich bekomme eine Limo.
    c. Ja, ich habe schon bezahlt.
    d. Für mich ein Stück Schwarzwälder Kirschtorte.

_____ 18. Sonst noch etwas? Noch etwas Brot?
    a. Nein, danke, ich habe schon zu viel gegessen.
    b. Nein, danke, ich habe keinen Durst mehr.
    c. Nein, danke, ich bin satt.
    d. Ja, bitte, aber nur eine kleine Scheibe.

_____ 19. Kann ich etwas für dich tun?
    a. Nein, danke. Ich muss das leider selbst machen.
    b. Kannst du bitte einkaufen gehen? Zum Metzger?
    c. Ja. Bringst du mir bitte ein Glas Wasser?
    d. Ja. Ich bekomme noch ein Pfund Tomaten.

_____ 20. London hat mir gar nicht gefallen.
    a. Das tut mir Leid. Warum denn nicht?
    b. Das freut mich aber sehr!
    c. Das ist doch schade! War alles zu teuer?
    d. Uns auch nicht.

_____ 21. Die Äpfel sind schon alle, was?
    a. Ja, ich bedaure.
    b. Es tut mir Leid. Die sind schon ausverkauft.
    c. Wir haben nur noch Orangen.
    d. Stimmt. Wir haben diese Äpfel hier.

_____ 22. Mutti, schau doch mal her!
    a. Nicht unbedingt.
    b. Ja, was gibt's denn?
    c. Was ist denn, Junge?
    d. Moment, bitte, ich gucke gleich.

_____ 23. Wie fühlt sich die Patientin?
    a. Überhaupt nicht wohl, sagt sie.
    b. Na, im Moment schläft sie ganz ruhig.
    c. Sie freut sich doch sehr.
    d. Eigentlich geht's ihr etwas besser.

_____ 24. Was fehlt dir denn?
    a. Das Knie tut mir furchtbar weh.
    b. Mir ist ganz schlecht.
    c. Ich habe Bauchschmerzen.
    d. Ich fühle mich wunderbar.

_____ 25. Haben Sie sich verletzt?
    a. Ja, ich habe Husten, und der Hals tut mir weh.
    b. Ja, ich habe mir den Fuß verstaucht.
    c. Nein, ist schon in Ordnung.
    d. Ich weiß nicht, aber die Schulter tut mir echt weh!

B. Before you read, look at the five questions on page 160. After reading the passage twice, choose the best answers from among the alternatives given. (10 points)

Wilhelm Tells Schwester

HELGA Was wisst ihr über Wilhelm Tell?

JOACHIM Ja, nur das, was jeder weiß: dass Schiller ein Stück über ihn geschrieben hat, und Rossini hat eine Oper komponiert, und dass Tell der Schweizer Nationalheld ist.

KARL Weil er für die Freiheit und Unabhängigkeit der Schweizer gekämpft hat.

JOACHIM Ja, und die Geschichte mit dem Apfel ...

KARL ... die aber keine wahre Geschichte ist, sondern eine Legende.

HELGA Und das ist alles? Dann habt ihr bestimmt nicht gewusst, dass der Wilhelm eine Schwester hatte. Für sie war Schweizer Patriotismus und Schweizer Einheit genau so wichtig wie für ihren Bruder, aber sie konnte keine Freiheitskämpferin werden, weil sie eine Frau war.

JOACHIM Was meinst du überhaupt damit?

HELGA Ich meine, die Schwester von Tell war vielleicht ein sehr intelligentes Mädchen. Aber weil sie ein Mädchen war, hat es vieles gegeben, was sie nicht machen durfte. Zu Hause hat sie gekocht und Küchendienst gemacht, die Wäsche gewaschen und gebügelt. Sie ist natürlich zum Markt gegangen dort im Dorf, und sonntags in die Kirche, aber sie hat nie eine größere Stadt gesehen, ist nie in die Welt hinausgegangen. Wahrscheinlich hat sie im Sommer im Garten und auf dem Feld gearbeitet wie die anderen Bauersfrauen auch und hat Käse und Butter für die Familie und für den Markt produziert, aber sie hat bestimmt kein Geld dafür bekommen.

KARL Hör mal, Helga, wo hast du denn das alles gelesen?

HELGA Habe ich in einem Buch gelesen. Bei Heinemanns. Da bin ich heute Nachmittag babysitten gewesen, und die Franzi wollte, dass ich ihr und ihrem Bruder eine Geschichte vorlese.

KARL Und das mit der Schwester von Tell war da drin? Wie heißt sie denn? Wilhelmina? Das ist doch der reinste Unsinn, Mensch! Wir wissen nicht mal, ob der Tell wirklich einen Sohn hatte.

_____ 26. According to the story that Helga read,
  a. Tell's sister was not patriotic.
  b. Tell's sister may have been quite intelligent.
  c. Tell's sister never wanted to be a freedom fighter.
  d. Tell's sister liked babysitting.

_____ 27. Helga says that Tell's sister
  a. probably went to a bigger town to do her shopping.
  b. was only allowed to work indoors.
  c. learned to read from her grandmother.
  d. produced goods and services for her family without pay.

_____ 28. Helga read the story about Tell's sister
  a. because it was assigned at school.
  b. while she was babysitting.
  c. for fun.
  d. while the children were busy playing games.

_____ 29. According to Karl, nobody knows
  a. if William Tell really had a son.
  b. that Schiller wrote a play about William Tell.
  c. that Rossini is the composer of the opera *William Tell*.
  d. that William Tell is the national hero of Switzerland.

_____ 30. Based on Helga's conversation with her brothers, we can assume that she
  a. does not believe that William Tell had a sister.
  b. believes that girls and women should only do volunteer work.
  c. believes that Tell's sister could have also become a hero, given the opportunity.
  d. thinks that Tell's sister probably was not very intelligent.

C. Read the article and then determine whether each statement is **a) true** or **b) false**. Mark **c)** if the article does not provide information on the statement made. (10 points)

Richtig vor dem Computer sitzen

Vor dem Computer sitzen ist bestimmt keine sportliche Aktivität. Man ist nicht an der frischen Luft *(air)* und benutzt die Muskeln und den Kreislauf *(circulation)* nur wenig. Aber dafür ist das Sitzen vor dem Computer nicht gefährlich *(dangerous)*. Schließlich kann man sich nicht, wie etwa beim Skilaufen, Fußball oder Joggen, verletzen. Oder doch?

Was sagen die Experten? Zu lange und zu oft am Computer sitzen kann viele schädliche *(harmful)* Konsequenzen haben. Man kann Haltungsschäden *(back injuries)* von einer falschen Sitzpositur bekommen. Man kann auch Augen-, Nerven- und Muskelschmerzen bekommen. Hier sind ein paar Tipps, wie man Computerschäden vermeiden kann.

- Aufrecht *(upright)* sitzen, und die Schultern nicht nach vorne beugen *(bend)*.
- Den Bildschirm *(screen)* in Augenhöhe einstellen, damit man den Kopf nicht vor- oder zurückbeugen muss.
- Ellbogen und Unterarme etwas höher als die Tastatur *(keyboard)* halten, damit die Finger ganz natürlich auf die Tasten *(keys)* „fallen".
- Handgelenke *(wrists)* locker *(relaxed)* halten.
- Alle 50 bis 55 Minuten aufstehen, die Augen ein paar Minuten schließen *(close)* und Schultern, Arme und Hände bewegen *(move)*. Man soll sich fünf Minuten lang entspannen *(relax)*.

Wenn man diese Tipps beachtet *(keep in mind)*, kann das Sitzen vor dem Computer zum Vergnügen werden. Man wird nicht so leicht müde und man kann für lange Zeit am Computer arbeiten, ohne Langzeitschäden *(long-term injuries)* davonzutragen.

_____ 31. Vor dem Computer sitzen ist gefährlicher für Frauen als für Männer.

_____ 32. Der Computerbildschirm soll höher sein als der Kopf.

_____ 33. Die Ellbogen sollen höher liegen als die Tasten.

_____ 34. Wenn man einen Computer benutzt, soll man alle 50 bis 55 Minuten aufstehen und sich fünf Minuten entspannen.

_____ 35. Alle Leute, die vor dem Computer sitzen, bekommen Computerschäden.

III. Culture

Maximum Score: 10 points

A. Complete the following statements by choosing the best answer from among the alternatives given. (5 points)

_____ 36. If you order a **Limo** in Germany, you will get
    a. fresh homemade lemonade.   **c.** a kind of taxi.
    b. tea with lemon.   **d.** a kind of soft drink.

_____ 37. You need to know your German size (34, 36, 38, etc.) in order to buy a
    a. T-shirt.   **c.** suit or formal dress.
    b. sweat shirt.   **d.** pair of jogging pants.

_____ 38. If you plan to attend a German school, you should probably
    a. save some money to buy school uniforms.
    b. gather some conservative clothes to wear to school.
    c. pack the clothes you wear to school in the United States.
    d. buy all of your clothes in Germany.

_____ 39. In German families today
    a. boys are not expected to help in the kitchen.
    b. girls are not expected to help in the yard.
    c. teens aren't expected to do housework, because they have so much homework.
    d. both boys and girls are expected to help around the house.

_____ 40. **Fachwerk** is a style of
    a. older German architecture.
    b. traditional German cooking.
    c. modern German architecture.
    d. traditional German clothing.

_____ 41. A **Pension** is most similar to
    a. an American motel.
    b. an American hotel.
    c. a bed and breakfast.
    d. a retirement home.

_____ 42. A **Gasthof** is a place where
    a. you can get a room and/or meals.
    b. you can get cheap dormitory accommodations.
    c. you can eat main meals only.
    d. you can get drinks but no meals.

_____ 43. A **Bioladen** is a
    a. shop that specializes in herbal medicines.
    b. store that sells organic produce and health foods.
    c. recycling center.
    d. store that specializes in synthetic vitamins and food supplements.

_____ 44. An **Apotheke** is similar to
    a. a hospital.   **c.** a drugstore.
    b. a pharmacy.   **d.** a department store.

_____ 45. If you are an exchange student in Germany, you'll need to adjust to
    a. eating a hot breakfast every morning.
    b. eating your main meal at noon.
    c. eating three meals a day and nothing in between.
    d. doing without any junk foods.

IV. Writing

A. A visiting older relative (**der Besuch**) is criticizing your habits. Stand up for yourself politely but firmly. For each item below, agree and say what you should do differently, agree but with reservations and explain why you do what you do, or disagree and set the record straight. (10 points)

1. BESUCH Was tust du denn für deine Gesundheit? Du isst nicht besonders vernünftig.

   DU _____

   _____

2. BESUCH Du sitzt aber den ganzen Abend vor dem Fernseher. Treibst du eigentlich keinen Sport?

   DU _____

   _____

3. BESUCH Und deine Zähne! Wenn du immerzu Pralinen isst und Kaugummi kaust, werden deine Zähne ganz schlecht.

   DU _____

   _____

4. BESUCH Na, schon gut. Aber wie steht es mit deinen Haaren und mit der Haut? Du willst doch eine schöne Haut haben, oder?

   DU _____

   _____

5. BESUCH Das kann sein, aber ich finde es nicht schön, dass ihr in der Freizeit immer mit dem Auto fahrt oder mit dem Bus oder der Bahn. Ihr sollt mal wandern gehen oder eine Radtour machen!

   DU _____

   _____

B. Look at the following itinerary for a group tour of the city of Hannover in Niedersachsen. Pretend that you took this tour and write a short note to a friend, relating what you did and how you liked it. (Be sure to use the past tenses!) (10 points)

FREITAG:	
Vormittag:	• Stadtrundfahrt, inkl. **Opernhaus** (1845-1852 gebaut, 1943 ausgebrannt, 1950 wieder aufgebaut) **Marktkirche** (Mitte des 14. Jhs. gebaut, 1943 ausgebrannt, 1952-1961 wieder aufgebaut) **Rathaus** (16. Jh. gebaut, 1943 ausgebrannt, 1954/55 wieder aufgebaut **Berufsschul-Zentrum am Waterlooplatz** (1952, ff. gebaut) **Niedersachsen-Stadion am Maschsee** (1951-54 gebaut) **Mittagessen in der Maschsee — Gaststätte am Nordufer des Sees**
Nachmittag:	• Schloss Herrenhausen - Königsgärten, Galeriegebäude (17. Jh. gebaut, 1952 erneuert) • Deutsche Industrie-Messe/ Messe-Haus der Elektro-Industrie
SAMSTAG:	
Vormittag:	• Besuch in der Leibnizschule (Oberschule) und in der Gerrit-Engelke Volksschule
Nachmittag:	• Frei zum Shopping, u.s.w.

Name _____ Klasse _____ Datum _____

_____

_____

_____

_____

_____

_____

_____

_____

C. Look at the doctor's memo. Write a short paragraph with five or more complete sentences in which you describe what happened to the patient, his present condition, and what he should do now to get better. (10 points)

Name: *Ulrich Hinkebein*

Alter: *16*

Beruf: *Realschüler*

Beschwerden: *Knöchel geschwollen/ Schmerzen bei Bewegung*

Diagnose: *verstauchter Knöchel*

Empfehlung: *ACE Binde/ Eis/ 3 Wochen lang kein Fußball!*

Unterschrift _____

_____

_____

_____

_____

_____

_____

_____

_____

_____

Name _____ Klasse _____ Datum _____

Midterm Exam Score Sheet

Circle the letter that matches the most appropriate response.

I. Listening
Maximum Score: 30 points

A. (10 points)

1. a b c d
2. a b
3. a b
4. a b
5. a b

SCORE ☐

B. (10 points)

6. a b c d
7. a b c d
8. a b c d
9. a b c d
10. a b c d

SCORE ☐

C. (10 points)

11. a b c d
12. a b c d
13. a b c d
14. a b c d
15. a b c d

SCORE ☐

II. Reading
Maximum Score: 30 points

A. (10 points)

16. a b c d
17. a b c d
18. a b c d
19. a b c d
20. a b c d
21. a b c d
22. a b c d
23. a b c d
24. a b c d
25. a b c d

SCORE ☐

B. (10 points)

26. a b c d
27. a b c d
28. a b c d
29. a b c d
30. a b c d

SCORE ☐

C. (10 points)

31. a b c
32. a b c
33. a b c
34. a b c
35. a b c

SCORE ☐

Holt German 2 Komm mit!, Midterm Exam

Name _____ Klasse _____ Datum _____

III. Culture

Maximum Score: 10 points

A. (10 points)

36. a b c d

37. a b c d

38. a b c d

39. a b c d

40. a b c d

41. a b c d

42. a b c d

43. a b c d

44. a b c d

45. a b c d

SCORE [   ]

IV. Writing

Maximum Score: 30 points

A. (10 points)

1. _____
   _____

2. _____
   _____

3. _____
   _____

4. _____
   _____

5. _____
   _____

SCORE [   ]

B. (10 points)

_____
_____
_____
_____
_____
_____
_____
_____
_____
_____

SCORE [   ]

C. (10 points)

_____
_____
_____
_____
_____
_____
_____
_____
_____
_____

SCORE [   ]

TOTAL SCORE [   ]

Listening Scripts for Midterm Exam

I. Listening

A.

ANNA Du, ich habe morgen Vormittag keine Zeit. Kannst du bitte Tante Lisa und ihren Sohn vom Bahnhof abholen? Sie kommen um 9 Uhr 35 an, Bahnhof Friedrichstraße.

BERND Kann ich machen. Aber wie soll ich sie erkennen? Im Bahnhof Friedrichstraße sind ja immer sehr viele Menschen. Wie sehen sie aus?

ANNA Ich habe sie auch schon seit 8 Jahren nicht mehr gesehen. Aber Tante Lisa ist ziemlich groß, 1,70 bis 1,75, glaube ich, und schlank mit dunkelbraunen Haaren und braunen Augen.

BERND Also, ungefähr deine Größe.

ANNA Ja, eine ziemlich große Frau.

BERND Und wie sieht dein Cousin aus?

ANNA Von ihm hat uns die Tante ein Bild geschickt. Schau her.

BERND Ganz schön dick ist der Junge!

ANNA Ja, auf diesem Bild schon. Aber das ist auch alt. Sie hat geschrieben, dass er ziemlich schlank geworden ist. Auf jeden Fall hat er blonde Haare und braune Augen. Und er ist jetzt — warte mal — 20 Jahre alt.

BERND Und deine Tante, so mitte 40?

ANNA Ich glaube ja, so um die 45 herum, denke ich.

B.

ANDREAS Was schenken wir der Oma bloß zu Weihnachten?

BEATE Gute Frage! Was schenkt man einer Frau, die alles hat? Omas Haus ist doch überfüllt mit Sachen, die ihr verschiedene Leute geschenkt haben.

CHRISTOPH Am besten etwas, was nur wir ihr schenken können.

ANDREAS Na, Bilder von uns „Kindern" hat sie ja schon genügend.

BEATE Und ganz viele selbst gebastelte Sachen auch. Außerdem sind wir ja nicht mehr in dem Alter, in dem man schlecht gemachte Handarbeiten verschenkt.

CHRISTOPH Stimmt. Ja, was hat sie eigentlich gern? ... Ihren Garten, den Mopshund, im Sommer das Wandern ...

ANDREAS Und Fotografieren ... Vielleicht ein Album für ihre Fotos?

BEATE Lieber nicht. Fotoalben kauft sie sich selbst, wenn sie welche braucht.

CHRISTOPH Musik hat sie gern. Sie hört sogar unsere Hausmusik auf der Blockflöte ganz gern.

BEATE Na, so schlecht spielen wir ja auch nicht!

ANDREAS Moment! Ich habe eine Idee. Wir üben ein Stück ein — sagen wir mal eins von Telemann, den hört sie doch sehr gern. Und dann nehmen wir das auf eine Kassette auf und schenken sie ihr. Was meint ihr dazu?

BEATE Prima Idee, du!

CHRISTOPH Da müssen wir aber viel üben. Aber für unsre Oma, na, es geht schon. Gefällt ihr doch bestimmt besser als Pralinen.

ANDREAS Finde ich auch.

C.

REPORTER Darf ich dich fragen, was du für deine Gesundheit tust?

MARIANNE Ja, gerne. Nur tue ich eigentlich nicht besonders viel. Ich rauche nicht und trinke keinen Alkohol, aber ich bin keine Gesundheitsfanatikerin.

REPORTER Ja, aber, was isst du zum Beispiel? Ernährst du dich vernünftig?

MARIANNE Oh ja, meine Mutter sorgt schon dafür. Wir essen viel Salat zu Hause und frisches Obst auch. Und Fleisch gibt es selten, und wenn, dann nur mageres. Außerdem trinken wir Magermilch und essen überhaupt keine Butter. Wir kaufen nur Margarine aus Sonnenblumenöl, und wir essen den kalorienreduzierten Streichkäse. Aber vegetarisch essen, das wollen wir eigentlich nicht so gern.

REPORTER   Das finde ich aber schon sehr gut, was ihr macht. Und treibst du Sport?

MARIANNE   Ja, aber nur, weil es mir Spaß macht und auch hier in der Schule, in der Sportstunde natürlich. Und dann spiele ich auch sehr gern Tennis und Handball. Und ich schwimme viel, zwei- oder dreimal in der Woche — meistens im Hallenbad.

REPORTER   Nun, das freut mich aber wirklich sehr. Und wie kommst du zur Schule? Fährst du mit dem Rad?

MARIANNE   Nein, ich fahre mit dem Bus. Aber nach der Schule und am Wochenende fahre ich viel mit dem Rad. Wenn es etwas zu besorgen gibt, dann fahre ich mit dem Rad. Und auch nur deshalb, weil es mir Spaß macht.

REPORTER   Also, du tust doch eine ganze Menge für deine Gesundheit! Vielen Dank für das Interview.

Answers to Midterm Exam

I. Listening   Maximum Score: 30 points

A. (10 points: 2 points per item)
1. c
2. a
3. a
4. a
5. b

B. (10 points: 2 points per item)
6. b
7. c
8. d
9. d
10. a

C. (10 points: 2 points per item)
11. c
12. c
13. b
14. d
15. a

II. Reading   Maximum Score: 30 points

A. (10 points: 1 point per item)
16. d
17. c
18. b
19. d
20. b
21. d
22. a
23. c
24. d
25. a

B. (10 points: 2 points per item)
26. b
27. d
28. b
29. a
30. c

C. (10 points: 2 points per item)
31. c
32. b
33. a
34. a
35. b

III. Culture   Maximum Score: 10 points

A. (10 points: 1 point per item)
36. d
37. c
38. c
39. d
40. a
41. c
42. a
43. b
44. b
45. b

IV. Writing   Maximum Score: 30 points

A. (10 points: 2 points per item) Answers will vary.
B. (10 points) Answers will vary.
C. (10 points) Answers will vary.

K A P I T E L

7 Stadt oder Land?

■ Erste Stufe

Maximum Score: 35

Grammar and Vocabulary

A. You overhear a conversation between your little brother and his friend Manfred as they compare their rooms. Complete their conversation by filling in each blank with the comparative form of the adjective given in parentheses. [10 points]

BRUDER   Mein Zimmer ist **1.** _____ (big) als dein Zimmer.

MANFRED   Ja, aber mein Zimmer ist viel **2.** _____ (clean) als dein Zimmer.

BRUDER   Hm, das stimmt. Mein Zimmer ist **3.** _____ (dirty) als dein Zimmer.

MANFRED   Meine Möbel sind auch **4.** _____ (expensive) als deine Möbel.

BRUDER   Tja, meine Möbel sind **5.** _____ (cheap) als deine Möbel, aber deine Stereoanlage ist **6.** _____ (small) als meine.

MANFRED   Ja, auch der Lärm von deiner Stereoanlage ist **7.** _____ (great).

BRUDER   Meine Lautsprecher sind halt **8.** _____ (good).

MANFRED   Dafür ist dein Fernseher **9.** _____ (old) als mein Fernseher.

BRUDER   Ja, aber mein Schrank ist viel **10.** _____ (beautiful) als dein Schrank.

MANFRED   Ja, aber.... (*notices that you are listening in and signals your brother to be quiet*)

SCORE [   ]

B. Listen to your friends describe the places where they would like to live. Match their statements with the places listed in the right column. [3 points]

_____ 11. Dort gibt es viele Berge und man kann viel wandern. Es gibt auch nicht viel Verkehr.

_____ 12. Da kann man schwimmen und Boot fahren.

_____ 13. Das ist eine Großstadt.

a. New York

b. Schwarzwald

c. Bodensee

SCORE [   ]

KAPITEL 7

Quiz 7-1A

C. Your summer vacation is coming up and you and your friends share information about places you have visited in the past. Complete each of the following statements, filling in the blanks with appropriate words from the box. Be sure to use the comparative form of the adjectives. (10 points)

sauber	viel	am liebsten		zu Hause		Alpen	Verkehr
		wenig	ruhig		gut	Auto	

HEIDI   Ich fahre **14.** _____ an den Plattensee, weil dort die Luft

viel **15.** _____ (cleaner) ist als in Hamburg.

MELANIE   Ich fahre auch gern an den Plattensee, weil dort **16.** _____

(less) Verkehr ist. Auch ist das Leben dort **17.** _____ .

ULRIKE   Also ich fahr gern nach New York, weil dort **18.** _____ los

ist als in Bietigheim. Auch gibt es dort **19.** _____ (better)

Geschäfte und Restaurants.

PETRA   Also, ich fahr lieber in die Berge, vor allem in die

20. _____ . Dort gibt es keine U-Bahn und keinen

21. _____ .

MEIKE   Ich bleibe am liebsten **22.** _____ . Da ist es billiger und

ich kann mir dann ein **23.** _____ kaufen.

SCORE ☐

D. Write complete sentences with the words and phrases below. (12 points)

vorziehen / eine Stadt / ich / wie Hamburg

24. _____

gern haben / Ingrid / die Berge / so...wie / die Großstadt

25. _____

lieber wohnen / in einer Großstadt / Peter / als / in einer Kleinstadt

26. _____

größer sein / die Häuser / oft / in einer Stadt / in einem Dorf / als

27. _____

SCORE ☐

TOTAL SCORE ☐

KAPITEL

7 Stadt oder Land?

■ Erste Stufe

Maximum Score: 40

I. Listening

A. Frau Gingereich is unhappy with her hotel room in Zurich. She has decided to speak to the management about it. Listen to the conversation twice and then check the three advantages that the second room would have. (8 points)

quieter		better air	
view of the mountains		a larger bed	
cheaper		view of the lake	

What reason does Frau Gingereich give for possibly not moving to a new room?

_____

SCORE _____

II. Reading

B. Read the description of Mittenwald and answer the questions that follow. (8 points)

Urlaub in Mittenwald!

Mittenwald ist der höchstgelegene Luftkurort in den Bayerischen Alpen. Dieses Ferienparadies liegt ungefähr 100 km südlich von München und hat 8.197 Einwohner. Hier ist der Himmel blau, die Seen klar, die Luft staubfrei, das Klima gesund und der Nebel selten. Die Stadt ist umgeben von der Bergkulisse des Karwendels. Die Berge beschützen Mittenwald vor rauhen Winden und deshalb dauert der Sommer hier etwas länger. Genießen Sie den Blick auf bunte Gärten und kunstvolle Lüftlmalereien. Besuchen Sie eine der schönsten Dorfkirchen von Josef Schmutzer. Die Kirche hat einen reich bemalten Turm und eine barocke Ausstattung. Für die Einwohner von Mittenwald ist aber die Landwirtschaft genauso wichtig wie die Berge. Die Gemeinde und die Bauern arbeiten zusammen, um die Kulturlandschaft zu erhalten (*conserve*). Deshalb wurde Mittenwald aus 299 Bewerbern ausgewählt und mit dem Henry Ford European Conservation Award 1999 prämiert.

1. What is the English equivalent of **Nebel**?
   a. rain
   b. dust
   c. air
   d. fog

2. Why did Mittenwald receive the Henry Ford European Conservation Award 1999?
   a. because is the most beautiful city in the Bavarian Alps
   b. because the city and the farmers keep traditions and customs alive
   c. because Mittenwald is a quiet city with clean air and clear lakes
   d. because Mittenwald has one of the most beautiful churches

KAPITEL 7

Quiz 7-1B

3. Why do summers last longer in Mittenwald?
   a. because Mittenwald is perched on a mountaintop
   b. because Mittenwald is protected against raw winds
   c. because Mittenwald is 100 km south of Munich
   d. because the air is free of dust and other pollutants

4. In Mittenwald, one thing you won't see is
   a. churches.   c. skyscrapers.
   b. gardens.   d. hotels and spas.

SCORE [ ]

III. Writing

C. If you were going to live in Germany for a year, where would you like to live? Describe your preference in as much detail as possible. Why would you like to live there? (Name two advantages.) Also mention one disadvantage of living there. (16 points)

_____

_____

_____

_____

_____

SCORE [ ]

IV. Culture

D. Based on the cultural information in **Kapitel 7**, answer the following questions. (8 points)

5. Which country has a higher population density: the United States or Germany?

   _____

6. What percentage of the population in Germany is bothered by noise pollution?
   a. less than 50%   c. about 30%
   b. more than 50%

7. Teens in Germany want to live
   a. in Großstädten.   c. auf dem Land.
   b. in Kleinstädten.   d. in all three places mentioned.

8. The four students interviewed for **Kapitel 7** all felt that a big disadvantage of living in a

   city was _____

SCORE [ ]

TOTAL SCORE [ ]

Stadt oder Land?

■ Zweite Stufe

Maximum Score: 35

Grammar and Vocabulary

A. Your parents are talking about building a house in a little town outside of Berlin. At dinner, you discuss with your family what the "ideal" house for your family would include. Give the German equivalents of the following statements made by different family members. (15 points)

VATER   Peter, what would you wish for?

1. _____

PETER   I wish for my own room and my own bathroom.

2. _____

MUTTER   I wish for a large porch and a pool.

3. _____

SABINE   I wish for a cozy living room.

4. _____

PETER
UND   We wish for a large garden with bushes and trees.
SABINE

5. _____

VATER   And I wish for a large income to build this house!

SCORE [   ]

Quiz 7-2A

B. While doing a writing assignment about the future of the world, you and your friend
Max exchange ideas about what an ideal world should be like. Fill in the blanks in the
conversation by giving the German equivalents of the prompts in parentheses.
(20 points)

DU   Es gibt 6. _____ (no more war).

MAX   Ja, und auch 7. _____ (no more poverty).

DU   Es gibt auch 8. _____ (no more hunger).

MAX   Und alle Leute haben 9. _____ (a secure income) und

10. _____ (to be healthy).

DU   Alle haben 11. _____ (a peaceful life).

MAX   12. _____ · (The environment is clean.)

DU   Ja, es gibt 13. _____ (no more cars) und alle Leute

fahren mit magnetischen Bahnen.

MAX   Auch hat jeder 14. _____ (a good education) und

15. _____ (a great job).

DU   Wir haben dann einen Computer für alles, fürs Kochen und Saubermachen, und dieser

Computer könnte sogar unsere Hausaufgaben machen.

MAX   Mensch, das wäre wirklich toll!

SCORE [ ]

TOTAL SCORE [ ]

K A P I T E L

7 Stadt oder Land?

■ Zweite Stufe

I. Listening

A. Three students from Berlin, ages 13-17, have been sent to a village in the Black Forest (population 397) to spend a few weeks for their health. As you listen to their conversation, decide which of the following things they like (write YES) and which they don't like (write NO). Then listen again and answer the last two questions. (10 points)

_____ 1. food

_____ 2. the lake

_____ 3. activities offered

4. The students would probably rather be ... right now.
   a. on a farm
   b. at the lake
   c. sitting outside on the terrace
   d. in a big city

5. The students would probably enjoy doing all of the following right now EXCEPT:
   a. playing cards
   b. going to a café
   c. paddle boating
   d. going to a disco with other friends

SCORE _____

II. Reading

B. Monika is an exchange student in Japan. She describes the home to which she has been invited. After reading the passage twice, choose the best answers from among the alternatives given. (8 points)

Schon im Flur ist alles pieksauber. Man muss sich hier die Schuhe ausziehen, denn die meisten Zimmer haben schöne Matten aus Reisstroh auf dem Fußboden, anstatt Parkett mit Teppichen. Das Haus hat eine Küche, ein Bad und ein WC. Die anderen sechs Zimmer sind alle Wohn-Schlafzimmer. Das heißt, man kann tagsüber dort plaudern, fernsehen, Karten spielen, essen oder sonst was. Abends stellt man dann den Tisch in die Ecke und legt das Bettzeug auf die Matten, und man hat ein Schlafzimmer.

Allerdings haben viele japanische Familien jetzt ihr „westliches" Wohnzimmer mit Parkettboden und Sofas, genauso wie wir in Deutschland. Aber meine Gastgeber sind vielleicht traditioneller als die Leute in den Großstädten.

Das schönste Zimmer — mit dem besten Blick auf den Garten — gehört den Großeltern. Dort haben wir Tee getrunken, was eine echte Ehre für mich war. Da hing ein wunderschönes chinesisches Bild an der Wand. Und wenn man auf den Garten hinausblickte, fühlte man sich ruhig und wohl.

K A P I T E L 7

Quiz 7-2B

6. The house has a total of
   a. six rooms.
   b. three bedrooms.
   c. six rooms, plus kitchen, bath, and toilet.
   d. one big room, plus kitchen, bath, and toilet.

7. The **Wohn-Schlafzimmer** can be used for all of the following EXCEPT:
   a. watching TV
   b. sleeping
   c. eating
   d. cooking

8. Monika's hosts do not have a western-style living room, because
   a. they are more traditional.
   b. it's too expensive.
   c. only people in the cities can buy western-style furniture.
   d. they use all their extra rooms as bedrooms.

9. What advantage does the grandparents' room have that the other rooms don't have?
   a. a view of the garden
   b. beautiful mats on the floor
   c. it can be used for both entertainment and sleeping
   d. it is very clean

SCORE [   ]

III. Writing

C. You have just won the lottery! A dream home is high on your priority list. What kind of house would you wish for? Write three sentences describing your dream house in as much detail as possible. (12 points)

_____

_____

_____

_____

_____

SCORE [   ]

TOTAL SCORE [   ]

Stadt oder Land?

■ Dritte Stufe

Maximum Score: 30

Grammar and Vocabulary

A. In the statements below, fill in the first blank with the German equivalent of the adjective given in parentheses. Fill in the second blank with the comparative form of this adjective. (12 points)

(big)   Das ist ein **1.** _____ Haus, aber dort ist ein viel

2. _____ Haus.

(small)   Ich habe ein **3.** _____ Zimmer, aber dein Zimmer ist noch

4. _____ .

(much)   Ein LKW produziert **5.** _____ Lärm, aber ein Flugzeug produziert

noch **6.** _____ Lärm.

(fast)   Mein Bruder hat schon ein **7.** _____ Auto. Er will aber ein noch

8. _____ Auto.

(calm)   Meine Eltern haben ein **9.** _____ Leben in einer Kleinstadt. Aber

mein Bruder hat ein **10.** _____ Leben auf dem Land.

(cozy)   Unser Wohnzimmer ist sehr **11.** _____ . Ich glaube nicht, dass es

ein **12.** _____ Wohnzimmer gibt.

SCORE ☐

Quiz 7-3A

B. Give the German equivalents of the following sentences. (18 points)

Turn your engine off!

13. _____

She is taking the curve too fast!

14. _____

Mr. Rauch is slamming the trunk again!

15. _____

You (informal, sing.) are playing the car radio too loud!

16. _____

He should switch off the motor.

17. _____

I like a big city like Berlin because there are just more shops and museums there.

18. _____

_____

SCORE [   ]

TOTAL SCORE [   ]

Stadt oder Land?

■ Dritte Stufe

Maximum Score: 30

I. Listening

A. Which of the following are not permitted at the campground where Anna and Mark's family is staying for the night? Listen to this conversation between Anna and Mark. Then mark each statement true (**T**) or false (**F**). (6 points)

It is forbidden to:

_____ 1. drive private vehicles through the campground after 10 pm.

_____ 2. shower between 8 and 9 pm.

_____ 3. play your radio quietly at night.

SCORE [   ]

II. Reading

B. Read Karin's e-mail message to her friend Walter. Then reread the text and match each of the words below with the best definition. (8 points)

Lieber Walter:

Wir sind umgezogen. Wir wohnen jetzt in der Willy-Brandt Str. in Stuttgart. Unsere Wohnung hier ist viel größer als unsere alte Wohnung in Karlsruhe. Aber der Lärm hier ist <u>unausstehlich</u>. Unser Gebäude ist gleich gegenüber einer riesigen Baustelle *(construction site)*. Sogar wenn unsere Fenster geschlossen sind, hören wir den ganzen Tag den <u>ohren-zerreißenden</u> Lärm der Presslufthämmer. In der Nacht ist es zwar auf der Baustelle ruhig, aber dann hören wir den Lärm der Autos und Laster von der Straße: <u>heulende</u> Motoren, auf-dringliches Hupen und laute Autoradios. Hoffentlich werden wir nicht alle <u>schwerhörig</u>. Wir vermissen unsere kleine Wohnung in Karlsruhe. Dort war es viel ruhiger, denn wir haben gegenüber einem Park gewohnt. Ab und zu hörten wir das Läuten der Kirchenglocken, aber das haben wir ja gern in Kauf genommen.

Deine Karin

_____ 4. schwerhörig   **a.** unbearable

_____ 5. unausstehlich   **b.** earsplitting

_____ 6. heulend   **c.** roaring

_____ 7. ohrenzerreißend   **d.** hard of hearing

SCORE [   ]

Quiz 7-3B

III. Writing

C. You are sharing a dorm room with a German student who is a great lover of <u>loud</u> Beethoven symphonies. Complete the conversation below by following the cues provided. (12 points)

ER   Ja, was ist denn? Magst du Beethoven nicht?

[Say you do, but he should turn it down.]

8. DU _____

ER   So, ist das besser? Aber das Licht brauchen wir doch.

[Say that you suppose so, but it's late and you want to sleep.]

9. DU _____

ER   Im Studentenwohnheim kann man den Lärm eben nicht vermeiden, oder?

[Agree, but with reservations. For example, people shouldn't slam their room doors.]

10. DU _____

IV. Culture

D. Based on what you read about noise pollution in the **Dritte Stufe**, answer the following questions in English. (4 points)

11. The largest producer of noise pollution in Germany is:

_____

12. Which is responsible for more noise pollution: **PKWs,** or **LKWs** and buses?

_____

SCORE _____

TOTAL SCORE _____

KAPITEL 7

Stadt oder Land?

I. Listening

Maximum Score: 30 points

A. Simone is a student at the **Rosa-Luxemburg-Hauptschule** in Potsdam. Listen as she talks to her friend Holger about their plans for the future. Then choose the best answers from among the alternatives given. (10 points)

1. Holger's goals include all of the following EXCEPT
   a. getting practical job training.
   b. having a secure income.
   c. serving his country.
   d. buying his own home.

2. His dream house should include:
   a. a very modern kitchen
   b. a swimming pool
   c. a large garden
   d. old-fashioned furniture

3. Simone's goals seem to be
   a. practical
   b. focused on one thing
   c. materialistic
   d. idealistic

4. Her ideas for her future include all of the following EXCEPT
   a. working to end war.
   b. working for the environment.
   c. working to end world hunger.
   d. working on behalf of world peace.

5. Holger thinks that
   a. Alice should work for the United Nations.
   b. there's not much that one person can do to improve the world.
   c. a person should serve a noble cause.
   d. wars and poverty are definitely avoidable.

SCORE [   ]

B. Bärbel and Jens, two students at the **Immanuel-Kant-Gymnasium** in Zürich, are discussing their "dream homes." Listen to their conversation twice and then mark statements 6-13 true (**a**) or false (**b**). For questions 14 and 15, choose the best answers from among the alternatives given. (20 points)

_____ 6. Bärbel dreams of living in a mountain village.

_____ 7. The house she describes has a cow stall beneath the living quarters.

_____ 8. Jens has never had the chance to visit or live in the mountains.

_____ 9. Jens would rather have a view of a city than cow pastures.

_____ 10. His dream is a luxury condo in the city.

_____ 11. Bärbel doesn't like Zürich because there's too much going on there.

_____ 12. Jens thinks Geneva (**Genf**) might be a more interesting city.

_____ 13. People in Geneva speak Swiss German.

Chapter Test

14. Jens' wish list includes all of the following EXCEPT
   a. a sauna.
   b. a hobby room.
   c. a music room.
   d. a guest bedroom.

15. He also wants all of the following EXCEPT
   a. a big living room.
   b. a balcony with a view.
   c. a gallery for his art-collection-to-be.
   d. a state-of-the-art kitchen.

SCORE _____

II. Reading

Maximum Score: 30 points

C. Sabine has made the following two entries in her diary. Look at the questions on page 185 first and then read the entries twice. Think about the questions as you read and choose the best answers from among the alternatives given. (16 points)

27. Dezember 1998

In den Winterferien fahren wir in die Berge, ins Harzgebirge. Mutter zieht eigentlich die Alpen vor, aber Vater gefällt das Harzgebirge besser, weil es, wie er meint, nicht so viele Touristen dort gibt. Der Trude gefällt das eine so wenig wie das andere, weil sie für Silvester eine tolle Party mit ihren Freunden geplant hat und lieber zu Hause bleibt. Mich haben Mutter und Vater noch nicht gefragt, was ich lieber machen will.

4. Januar 1999

Also sind wir doch in den Harz gefahren, in ein Dorf in 1 000 Meter Höhe, nicht weit von Goslar. Skier, Schneeschuhe, Schneebrillen und einen Haufen von Anoraks, Schals, Handschuhen, Mützen usw. haben wir in den Wagen gepackt. Der Verkehr auf der Autobahn war scheußlich, aber wir — zumindest Mutter, Vater und ich — waren froh. Nur Trude war, wie immer, schlecht gelaunt.

Abends, als wir im Dorf ankamen, hat es geregnet. Am nächsten Morgen war der Regen zwar gefroren, aber es lag überall eine dünne, unglaublich schöne, aber gefährliche Eisschicht. Skilaufen auf dem Eis machte wenig Spaß. Doch hatte die Trude sich mit einem anderen Mädchen im Gasthof befreundet, und die beiden haben ein paar Jungen kennen gelernt. Sie haben eine Rodelpartie organisiert. Das hat uns allen riesig Spaß gemacht.

„Ende gut, alles gut", sagte Mutter heute. Mal sehen.

Chapter Test

For the following five questions, mark either
a) the mother,
b) the father,
c) the sister (Trude), or
d) Sabine

_____ 16. Wer hat den Harz besonders gern?

_____ 17. Wem gefällt es in den Alpen besser als im Harzgebirge?

_____ 18. Wer hat seine/ihre Meinung gar nicht gesagt?

_____ 19. Wer wollte gar nicht wegfahren?

_____ 20. Wer war auf der Hinreise in die Berge gar nicht froh?

21. What were the weather conditions the morning after they arrived?
    a. A foot of snow had fallen.
    b. There was a sheet of ice on all the mountains.
    c. It was wet and foggy.
    d. The weather was perfect for skiing.

22. Who or what saved Trude from total boredom?
    a. Her friends from Hamburg called.
    b. The peace and quiet of the mountains.
    c. She went skiing with three new friends.
    d. She and her new friends organized a sledding party.

23. Who enjoyed the new activity?
    a. Sabine's whole family
    b. only Trude
    c. only Sabine
    d. only Trude and her new friends

SCORE [   ]

D. Read the questions first and then read the following passage twice. Think about the questions as you read. Choose the best answers from among the alternatives given. (14 points)

Wir haben schon immer in Berlin gewohnt, meine Familie und ich. Meine Großeltern waren Arbeiter und haben in der Stadtmitte in einer Wohnung in einem Hinterhof gewohnt. (Dort bin ich geboren und habe bis zu meinem sechzehnten Lebensjahr gewohnt.) Vorne, an der Straße, war ein großes Haus und eine Mauer mit einem breiten Tor. Dahinter hat es einen Hof gegeben und dann noch zwei Häuser, rechts und links. Oma und Opa haben hinten rechts im dritten Stock gewohnt. Sie teilten die Treppe und das WC mit einer anderen Familie. (Die Toiletten waren damals im Treppenhaus, erzählte mir meine Mutter.)

In der Wohnung hatte Oma eine Küche, natürlich mit einem Esstisch, drei Schlafzimmer und ein schönes Zimmer mit einem Heizofen — einem Kachelofen, der

KAPITEL 7

Chapter Test

viel Platz einnahm. Da war's schön gemütlich. Die Wände waren sehr hoch, und sie hatten so schöne, breite Fenster. Es war hell und freundlich.

Wir Kinder spielten auf dem Hof. Und die Mütter konnten uns im Auge behalten und uns rufen, wenn etwas war. Die Wäscheleinen gingen von Haus zu Haus über den Hof. Die Nachbarn haben sich alle damals gekannt.

Später, nach dem Krieg, haben meine Großeltern eine Zentralheizung installiert, den Ofen weggeschafft und endlich auch ein eigenes Bad eingebaut. Mein Onkel und meine Tante wohnen jetzt dort.

Wir — meine Eltern und mein Bruder und ich — wohnen jetzt aber draußen in einem Vorort — in einer Wohnung. Da ist man ganz anonym eigentlich, und alle Wohnungen sehen gleich aus — verhältnismäßig modern und bequem, aber irgendwie anonym ...

24. Which of the following would be the best title for this essay?
    a. *Berlin Heute*
    b. *Das Leben in einem Berliner Hinterhof*
    c. *Die Geschichte der Stadt Berlin*
    d. *Berlin für Touristen*

25. The writer's family has lived in Berlin
    a. for at least three generations.
    b. since the end of World War II.
    c. since the writer started school.
    d. for about 10 years.

26. The family has never
    a. lived without a bathroom.
    b. owned a home of their own.
    c. been a working-class family.
    d. lived in downtown Berlin.

27. In the "old days" their living room was
    a. dark and dusty.
    b. light and cheerful.
    c. cold and formal.
    d. also used as a dining room.

28. The courtyard between the houses (**Hinterhof**) was
    a. the site of the outdoor toilets.
    b. planted with grass and flowers.
    c. a dangerous area.
    d. the children's playground.

29. The remodeling of the grandparents' apartment did NOT include
    a. putting in a private bath.
    b. getting rid of the big old tile stove.
    c. modernizing the heating system.
    d. dividing up one of the bedrooms.

KAPITEL 7

30. When describing her parents' apartment in a suburb, the writer seems to feel that
    a. it's much more pleasant than her grandparents' apartment.
    b. the neighborhood she lives in is friendly.
    c. it's relatively comfortable but somehow anonymous.
    d. it's her "dream house."

SCORE [   ]

III. Culture

Maximum Score: 10 points

E. Based on your knowledge of German culture, mark the following statements true
(**a**) or false (**b**). (5 points)

_____ 31. The single most common complaint that Germans have about city life is that the air
is bad.

_____ 32. Noise pollution is not a problem in German cities.

_____ 33. Children in Germany usually have a nice large playroom in their home.

_____ 34. The average child's bedroom is relatively small.

_____ 35. If you lived in the small town of Bietigheim, you'd probably have to go to another
town to do some of your shopping.

SCORE [   ]

F. In the **Landeskunde** section of **Kapitel 7** you learned that Germany's population
density is about eight times as high as that of the United States. Describe (in English) three ways in which Germany's dense population affects Germans' daily lives,
habits, or customs. (5 points)

_____

_____

_____

_____

_____

SCORE [   ]

KAPITEL 7

Chapter Test

IV. Writing

Maximum Score: 30 points

G. Your pen pal would like to know what you hope to be doing and where you hope to be living 10 years from now. Write a paragraph of least 5 sentences describing your goals and dreams. (15 points)

_____

_____

_____

_____

_____

_____

_____

SCORE ☐

H. Of the places where you have lived, which one appeals to you most? Write a paragraph (of at least five sentences) describing that place in terms of the advantages it has. Include a brief mention of any disadvantages and explain why you don't mind them so much. (The place you describe can be a house, an apartment, a town, a city, or even an entire state, as long as your description includes specific details.) (15 points)

_____

_____

_____

_____

_____

_____

_____

SCORE ☐

TOTAL SCORE ☐

KAPITEL 7

Name _____ Klasse _____ Datum _____

Circle the letter that matches the most appropriate response.

I. Listening   Maximum Score: 30 points

A. (10 points)   **B.** (20 points)

  1. a b c d   6. a b   11. a b

  2. a b c d   7. a b   12. a b

  3. a b c d   8. a b   13. a b

  4. a b c d   9. a b   14. a b c d

  5. a b c d   10. a b   15. a b c d

SCORE [＿＿＿]   SCORE [＿＿＿]

II. Reading   Maximum Score: 30 points

C. (16 points)   **D.** (14 points)

16. a b c d   24. a b c d

17. a b c d   25. a b c d

18. a b c d   26. a b c d

19. a b c d   27. a b c d

20. a b c d   28. a b c d

21. a b c d   29. a b c d

22. a b c d   30. a b c d

23. a b c d

SCORE [＿＿＿]   SCORE [＿＿＿]

III. Culture   Maximum Score: 10 points

E. (5 points)   **F.** (5 points)

31. a b   _____

32. a b   _____

33. a b   _____

34. a b   _____

35. a b   _____

SCORE [＿＿＿]   SCORE [＿＿＿]

IV. Writing

Maximum Score: 30 points

G. (15 points)

_____

_____

_____

_____

_____

_____

_____

_____

_____

SCORE [   ]

H. (15 points)

_____

_____

_____

_____

_____

_____

_____

_____

_____

_____

_____

_____

SCORE [   ]

TOTAL SCORE [   ]

KAPITEL 7

Listening Scripts for Quizzes 7-1B, 7-2B, 7-3B

Quiz 7-1B Kapitel 7 Erste Stufe

I. Listening

FRAU G.   Ich möchte bitte das Zimmer wechseln. Nummer 301 habe ich jetzt.

MANAGER   Ja, sicher. Also, was gefällt Ihnen an dem Zimmer nicht?

FRAU G.   Erstens kommt viel Lärm von der Straße herauf. Es gab fast die ganze Nacht Verkehr. Ich habe sehr schlecht geschlafen.

MANAGER   Dann ziehen Sie bestimmt ein Zimmer auf der Hinterseite des Hotels vor. Das kostet natürlich etwas mehr, aber dafür haben Sie einen schönen Blick auf den See hinaus. Es ist auch viel ruhiger. Kein Verkehrslärm.

FRAU G.   Ist die Luft auch besser? Die Luft war sehr stickig.

MANAGER   Sehen Sie, Zürich ist doch eine Großstadt. Aber wenn Sie die Luft vom See her bekommen, ist sie bestimmt frischer.

FRAU G.   Und was kostet ein Zimmer auf der Seeseite?

MANAGER   Nur zwanzig Prozent mehr als ein Zimmer auf der Straßenseite. Wirklich ganz preiswert. Und Sie können dort bei offenem Fenster schlafen.

FRAU G.   Zwanzig Prozent mehr? Das ist mir eigentlich zu teuer, aber ...

MANAGER   Es gefällt Ihnen bestimmt!

Quiz 7-2B Kapitel 7 Zweite Stufe

I. Listening

CHRISTA   Also, ausgezeichnet war das Frühstück, wie immer hier. So viele Eier und Brötchen, wie man will. Und der Saft schmeckt ganz gut.

JOSEF   Das Essen schmeckt mir.

PAVEL   Mir auch. Ich habe schon wieder zu viel gegessen. Nun, sag mal, was wollen wir heute tun?

JOSEF   Was gibt's denn bloß zu machen? Hier ist nichts los! Auf der Terrasse oder im Garten herumsitzen macht mir keinen Spaß. Karten haben wir schon tausendmal gespielt. Langweilig ist das hier.

PAVEL   Wir können bis zum See wandern.

CHRISTA   Da waren wir doch schon. Da ist auch nichts los. Oder hast du denn was gesehen, was man dort machen kann? Ist da vielleicht ein Badestrand oder eine Wurstbude oder Paddelboote? Oder irgendwas Vernünftiges?

PAVEL   Eigentlich hat das Leben in einer Großstadt seine Vorteile. Ich möchte gern mal wieder ins Kino gehen oder in ein Café.

CHRISTA   Und ich wünsche mir wenigstens einen Brief von zu Hause! Schon vierzehn Tage hier und noch immer keine Post. Man könnte direkt Heimweh bekommen.

JOSEF   Das finde ich auch.

Quiz 7-3B Kapitel 7 Dritte Stufe

I. Listening

ANNA   Nachtruhe ab 22 Uhr steht hier geschrieben. Die Gäste sollen sich nach 22 Uhr so ruhig wie möglich verhalten.

MARK   Hoffentlich heißt das, dass keine Motorräder die Straße auf und ab rasen dürfen. Mich stört das auch tagsüber.

ANNA   Ja. Hier steht sogar: Nach 22 Uhr dürfen nicht mal PKWs durchfahren.

MARK   Freut mich. Verkehrslärm gehört ja nicht auf den Campingplatz.

ANNA   Ich kann dir nur zustimmen. Weiter steht hier: Die Duschen in den Baderäumen werden zwischen 21 Uhr und 6 Uhr abgestellt. Also muss ich mich etwas früher unter die Dusche stellen als zu Hause.

MARK   Ach, das ist doch nicht so schlimm. Also, kein Verkehrslärm, keine Motorräder, nachts keine Autotüren oder Kofferraumdeckel zuschlagen. Sonst noch etwas?

ANNA   Und Autoradios und Kofferradios um 22 Uhr ausmachen.

MARK   Ausmachen? Ganz?

ANNA   Ja, klar! Auch wenn du es ganz leise stellst, können es alle noch hören.

MARK   Na ja. Vielleicht hast du Recht.

ANSWERS Quiz 7-1A

A. (10 points; 1 point per item)
1. größer
2. sauberer
3. schmutziger
4. teurer
5. billiger
6. kleiner
7. größer
8. besser
9. älter
10. schöner

B. (3 points; 1 point per item)
11. b
12. c
13. a

C. (10 points; 1 point per item)
14. am liebsten
15. sauberer
16. weniger
17. ruhiger
18. mehr
19. bessere
20. Alpen
21. Verkehr
22. zu Hause
23. Auto

D. (12 points; 3 points per item)
Answers will vary. Possible answers:
24. Ich ziehe eine Stadt wie Hamburg vor.
25. Ingrid hat die Berge so gern wie die Großstadt.
26. Peter wohnt lieber in einer Großstadt als in einer Kleinstadt.
27. In einer Stadt sind oft die Häuser größer als in einem Dorf.

ANSWERS Quiz 7-1B

I. Listening
A. (8 points: 2 points per item)

quieter	✔	better air	✔
view of the mountains		a larger bed	
cheaper		view of the lake	✔

Reason: Es ist ihr zu teuer.

II. Reading
B. (8 points: 2 points per item)
1. d
2. b
3. b
4. c

III. Writing
C. (16 points: 4 points per item)
Answers will vary. Possible answer:
Ich möchte am liebsten in einer Großstadt im Stadtzentrum wohnen. Ich ziehe eine Großstadt vor, weil da mehr los ist und dort auch mehr Geschäfte sind. Aber die Luft ist auch schmutziger in einer Großstadt.

IV. Culture
D. (8 points: 2 points per item)
5. Germany
6. b
7. d
8. air pollution (**stickige Luft**)

ANSWERS Quiz 7-2A

A. (15 points; 3 points per item)
Answers will vary. Possible answers:
1. Peter, was wünschst du dir (mal)?
2. Ich wünsche mir ein eigenes Zimmer und ein eigenes Badezimmer.
3. Ich wünsche mir eine große Terrasse und einen Pool.
4. Ich wünsche mir ein gemütliches Wohnzimmer.
5. Wir wünschen uns einen großen Garten mit Sträuchern und Bäumen.

B. (20 points; 2 points per item)
Answers will vary. Possible answers:
6. keinen Krieg mehr
7. keine Armut mehr
8. keinen Hunger mehr
9. ein sicheres Einkommen
10. sind gesund
11. ein friedliches Leben
12. Die Umwelt ist sauber
13. keine Autos mehr
14. eine gute Ausbildung
15. einen tollen Job

ANSWERS Quiz 7-2B

I. Listening

A. (10 points: 2 points per item)
1. yes
2. no
3. no
4. d
5. a

II. Reading

B. (8 points: 2 points per item)
6. c
7. d
8. a
9. a

III. Writing

C. (12 points: 4 points per sentence)
Answers will vary.

Answers to Quizzes 7-3A, 7-3B

ANSWERS Quiz 7-3A

A. (12 points; 1 point per item)
1. großes
2. größeres
3. kleines
4. kleiner
5. viel
6. mehr
7. schnelles
8. schnelleres
9. ruhiges
10. ruhigeres
11. gemütlich
12. gemütlicheres

B. (18 points; 3 points per item)
Answers will vary. Possible answers:
13. Stellen Sie den Motor ab!
14. Sie fährt zu schnell in die Kurve!
15. Herr Rauch schlägt wieder den Kofferraumdeckel zu!
16. Du spielst das Autoradio zu laut!
17. Er soll den Motor abstellen!
18. Eine große Stadt wie Berlin gefällt mir gut, weil es da halt mehr Geschäfte und Museen gibt.

ANSWERS Quiz 7-3B

I. Listening

A. (6 points: 2 points per item)
1. T
2. F
3. T

II. Reading

B. (8 points: 2 points per item)
4. d
5. a
6. c
7. b

III. Writing

C. (12 points: 4 points per item)
8. Eigentlich schon, aber mach es bitte leiser!
9. Ja, aber es ist spät, und ich möchte schlafen.
10. Ich stimme dir zwar zu, aber man soll die Tür nicht immer zuschlagen.

IV. Culture

D. (4 points: 2 points per item)
11. traffic
12. **LKWs** and buses

Holt German 2 Komm mit!, Chapter 7

Scripts for Chapter Test Kapitel 7

I. Listening

A.

SIMONE Was wünschst du dir eigentlich im Leben, Holger?

HOLGER Ja, eine praktische Ausbildung, vielleicht als Elektrotechniker, aber das darf nicht allzu lange dauern. Und dann noch einen Job mit einem guten Einkommen.

SIMONE Und wo willst du wohnen?

HOLGER Ich möchte mein eigenes Haus haben, mit einer Terrasse oder einem Balkon und einem kleinen aber hübschen Garten. Ach ja, und eine sehr moderne Küche in ganz leuchtenden Farben. Alles soll sehr modern sein. Und du? Was hast du vor? Was wünschst du dir?

SIMONE Ich weiß nicht recht, was ich machen will. Ich möchte doch irgendwas unternehmen, denke ich, gegen Armut vielleicht, oder vielleicht etwas für die Umwelt tun. Ich bin nicht ganz sicher. Vielleicht setze ich mich dafür ein, dass Völker Krieg vermeiden und friedlich miteinander leben. Die Umwelt und Frieden unter den Menschen sind sehr wichtig für mich.

HOLGER Du denkst zu idealistisch. Was kannst du bloß als Einzelmensch tun, um die Welt besser zu machen? Kriege und Armut hat es schon immer gegeben, seit es Menschen gibt.

SIMONE Ja, ich stimme dir schon zu, aber man soll doch nicht immer so materialistisch denken. Ich meine, ein Haus zu haben und Sicherheit, das ist nicht alles im Leben, oder?

B.

JENS Wo möchtest du eigentlich am liebsten wohnen?

BÄRBEL Am allerliebsten in einem ganz kleinen Dorf in den Bergen. Ich wünsche mir ein Bauernhaus, wo die Leute oben im ersten Stock wohnen und Kühe unten im Stall sind. Und das Haus hat ein ganz schräges Dach mit Dachfenstern und einen Balkon mit bunten Blumentöpfen.

JENS Und das gefällt dir? Du willst lieber in den Bergen in einem Dorf leben als in der Stadt?

BÄRBEL Eigentlich ziehe ich Ruhe und gesunde Luft vor. Du nicht?

JENS Mir gefällt so was Langweiliges nicht. Meine Eltern haben ein Ferienhaus in Appenzell — in den Bergen. Wir fahren oft in den Ferien dahin, aber da ist nie was los. Ich wünsche mir eine Eigentumswohnung in Zürich mit einer Sauna im Haus, natürlich. Meine Wohnung soll auch einen Balkon haben, aber mit Blick auf die Stadt, nicht auf die Kuhweide.

BÄRBEL Ja, aber ich finde Zürich nicht so gut. Hier ist mir einfach zu viel los.

JENS Also gut. Dann lieber in Genf. Mit Blick auf den Genfer See. Die Stadt ist wenigstens international.

BÄRBEL Dann musst du aber Französisch lernen.

JENS Stimmt. Dann ziehe ich eben Hamburg vor — mit Blick auf den Hafen. Dort ist echt was los!

BÄRBEL Und wie viele Zimmer soll deine Wohnung haben?

JENS Hmm ... lass mal schauen. Aha: ein großes Wohnzimmer, mit Stereo-CD-Anlage und Video und so weiter. Und ein Schlafzimmer für mich und noch eins für die Gäste. Und dann muss ich noch einen Hobbyraum haben. Ja, und einen Raum für meine Kunstsammlung.

BÄRBEL Deine Kunstsammlung?

JENS Klar! Ich möchte dir doch was zeigen, wenn du zu Besuch kommst!

Answers to Chapter Test Kapitel 7

I. Listening Maximum Score: 30 points

A. (10 points: 2 points per item)   **B.** (20 points: 2 points per item)

1.	c	6.	a
2.	a	7.	a
3.	d	8.	b
4.	c	9.	a
5.	b	10.	a
		11.	a
		12.	a
		13.	b
		14.	c
		15.	d

II. Reading Maximum Score: 30 points

C. (16 points: 2 points per item)   **D.** (14 points: 2 points per item)

16.	b	24.	b
17.	a	25.	a
18.	d	26.	b
19.	c	27.	b
20.	c	28.	d
21.	b	29.	d
22.	d	30.	c
23.	a		

III. Culture Maximum Score: 10 points

E. (5 points: 1 point per item)

31. a
32. b
43. b
35. a
36. a

F. (5 points)
Answers will vary. Possible answers:
There are fewer large, one-family houses; most people live in apartments. Because of heavy traffic, many people ride bicycles instead of driving a car. Schools in different states have staggered vacation dates. Stores, restaurants, buses, and other public places are often crowded.

IV. Writing Maximum Score: 30 points

G. (15 points: 3 points per sentence)
Answers will vary.

H. (15 points: 3 points per sentence)
Answers will vary.

Mode? Ja oder nein?

■ Erste Stufe

Maximum Score: 35

Grammar and Vocabulary

A. Petra and Manfred are sitting outside *Café Freizeit* and commenting on the clothes of passers-by. Give the German equivalents of their comments. (15 points)

PETRA   Look! This woman wears a really cool blazer. It is conservative but witty.

1. _____

MANFRED   That's right. But her flowery pants look awful.

2. _____

PETRA   And look! She wears green shoes and a blue cap!

3. _____

MANFRED   The cap looks very fashionable and the shoes look sporty.

4. _____

PETRA   Hey, look, this young man wears a yellow parka and underneath a red shirt. And

his hair is blue!

5. _____

_____

MANFRED   Furchtbar! Wir sollten ihm einen Strafzettel *(ticket)* für diese Klamotten geben!

SCORE [   ]

B. Complete each of the following statements, filling in each blank with the correct form of **dieser** and the correct form of the adjective given in parentheses. (12 points)

(yellow)   6. _____ Wollhemd sieht phantastisch aus. Du

siehst auch gut aus in **7.** _____ Hemd.

(flowery)   8. _____ Krawatte steht dir aber wirklich nicht.

Sie passt nicht zu **9.** _____ Hemd.

(red)   Gib mir mal **10.** _____ Käppi. Es passt gut zu

11. _____ Anorak.

SCORE [   ]

Quiz 8-1A

C. Write complete sentences with the words below. Be sure to use the correct forms of verbs and correct endings of indefinite articles, adjectives, and **dies-**. (8 points)

anprobieren / Petra / Winterjacke / dies- / wollen / gelb-

12. _____

_____

Hans / tragen / ein- / grüne Hose / zu / dies- / blaue- Jacke

13. _____

_____

Ulrike / brauchen / ein- / weiß- / Hemd / zur / schwarz- / Jeans

14. _____

_____

Melanie / aussehen / fesch / in / dies- / blau- / Jeansweste

15. _____

_____

SCORE [ ]

TOTAL SCORE [ ]

KAPITEL 8

Mode? Ja oder nein?

■ Erste Stufe

Maximum Score: 40

I. Listening

A. Bärbel and her mother have just parked the car outside the school grounds. They're going to the school fair. Read the statements below and then listen to the conversation twice. As you listen, mark each statement true (**T**) or false (**F**). (10 points)

_____ 1. Bärbels Mutter meint, Bärbel muss sich wärmer anziehen.

_____ 2. Bärbel hat ihre gefütterte Jacke nicht an, weil es ihr schon zu warm ist.

_____ 3. Die Jacke von der Großmutter hat die gleiche (*same*) Farbe wie Bärbels Hose.

_____ 4. Bärbel findet, Großmutters Jacke sieht altmodisch aus.

_____ 5. Max findet die Kombination von grün und blau ganz fesch.

SCORE _____

II. Reading

B. The following is an "outline" of the reading passage. As you read, fill in the outline in English. (12 points)

6. Paragraph 1:

   It would be silly to say that the only function of clothing is to:

   _____

7. Paragraph 2:

   Most of us have fairly firm ideas about which kinds of clothes are "appropriate" for our:

   a. _____

   b. _____

   c. _____

8. Paragraph 3:

   When you wear clothes that don't match, you do so because you want to seem:

   a. _____

   b. _____

Quiz 8-1B

Welche Funktion erfüllen bei dir die Klamotten? Wenn du sagst: „Sie halten mich warm, schützen mich vor Wind und Regen, und sonst eigentlich nichts", so erlaubst du uns ein Grinsen, oder?

Denn du hast doch bestimmt ziemlich feste Vorstellungen (*ideas*) von der Kleidung, die zu deiner Altersgruppe, zu deinem Geschlecht (männlich oder weiblich) und auch zu deiner Clique passt. Sogar die Unisex Mode erlaubt mehr oder weniger feine Unterschiede zwischen „Damen-" und „Herrenstilen".

Außerdem hast du gewisse Vorstellungen von Kleidungsartikeln, Farben und Stoffmustern, die zueinander passen. Wenn du zu deiner rot-blau karierten Jacke einen knallgelb geblümten Schal anziehst, so tust du das, weil du eben ein bisschen „anders" aussehen willst als andere Leute — eben interessanter oder witziger.

SCORE [   ]

III. Writing

C. Your school is adopting a school uniform. What will it look like? Write at least three sentences describing what you think the uniform will look like and what you think about it. (12 points)

_____

_____

_____

_____

_____

SCORE [   ]

IV. Culture

D. What are two differences between the clothes you wear and the clothes teenagers in Germany wear for special occasions and to take part in sports activities? (6 points)

9. _____

_____

10. Which of the following would you most likely see on a holiday in Mittenwald?
    a. **ein weißes Outfit**
    b. **Tracht**
    c. **Reithosen und Stiefel**

SCORE [   ]

TOTAL SCORE [   ]

KAPITEL 8

KAPITEL 8

Mode? Ja oder nein?

▪ Zweite Stufe

Grammar and Vocabulary

A. Give the German equivalents of the following statements. (15 points)

I am not interested in fashion.

1. _____

What are you interested in?

2. _____

The white blouse goes really well with the black jeans.

3. _____

That looks great on you!

4. _____

It's too tight on him.

5. _____

SCORE _____

B. You were asked to write an article for your school newspaper about the interests of teens. You decide to do research on this topic by asking your friends about their interests. Fill in the blanks in the conversation with the correct form of the reflexive pronoun. (8 points)

DU   Udo, wofür interessierst du **6.** _____?

UDO   Ich interessiere **7.** _____ für Fußball.

DU   Petra und Maria, wofür interessiert ihr **8.** _____ ?

PETRA
UND   Wir interessieren **9.** _____ für die Umwelt.
MARIA

DU   Und wofür interessieren **10.** _____ eure Brüder, der Manfred und der Hans?

PETRA Sie interessieren **11.** _____ für Fußball.

DU   Der Hans, interessiert er **12.** _____ auch für die Umwelt?

PETRA Nein, er interessiert **13.** _____ nur für Sport.

DU   Vielen Dank für das Interview.

SCORE _____

KAPITEL 8

Quiz 8-2A

C. The mailman has left the latest issue of a fashion magazine at your doorstep. Unfortunately, rain has soaked the magazine to such a degree that some words have virtually disappeared. Fill in the blanks with appropriate words from the box. (7 points)

| ist trägt passt darunter |
| Lederjacke preiswert interessieren |

Diese 14. _____ aus weichem Nappa ist der Hit der Saison. Sie

15. _____ modisch und lässig. Man 16. _____ sie zur

Jeans, aber auch zum Kleid und Rock. Sie 17. _____ zu jedem Typen, jung

und alt. Sie ist gefüttert und man kann 18. _____ ein buntes Hemd oder

T-Shirt tragen. Auch Leute, die sich sonst nicht für Mode 19. _____ ,

finden diese Jacke scharf. Diese Jacke ist außerdem sehr 20. _____ . Sie

kostet nur 150 Euro. Kaufen sie diese Jacke noch heute!

SCORE _____

TOTAL SCORE _____

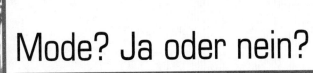

Mode? Ja oder nein?

■ Zweite Stufe

Maximum Score: 30

I. Listening

A. A woman on a TV show is giving advice about fashion. After you hear her talk, choose the best answers from among the alternatives given. (6 points)

1. She is specifically giving advice for:
   a. young men
   b. middle-aged and older men

2. The styles she talks about are:
   a. "radical chic"
   b. somewhat modern, but pretty moderate

3. She recommends:
   a. color and pattern contrasts
   b. white shirts and solid-color ties

SCORE [   ]

II. Reading

B. The following three students took a teen-magazine quiz. One of them always circled **a.** as his or her answer, another one always circled **b.** as his or her answer, and the other student always circled **c.** Read their descriptions in the boxes below and then the quiz on p. 204. Try to figure out which student circled which letter. (12 points)

4. Anita always circled _____

5. Susanne always circled _____

6. Helmut always circled _____

Anita hat lange Haare, ein Tatoo einer Rose auf der Schulter und eine Perle im Nasenloch. Sie trägt auch im Winter eine Sonnenbrille.	**Susanne** hat sehr kurze Haare, wird im Sommer sehr braun, weil sie viel schwimmt und viel Tennis spielt. Sie liest nie Modezeitschriften.	**Helmut** hat mittellange Haare, geht alle 14 Tage zum Friseur (*hair stylist*), trägt eine tolle Armbanduhr mit Alarm, Kalender, Stoppuhr und vielem mehr. Er geht nicht gern Klamotten kaufen.

Quiz 8-2B

Test: Welcher Mode-Typ Bist Du?

1. Was trägst du an den Füßen?
  a. Lederschuhe
  b. Armee-Stiefel
  c. Turnschuhe

2. Was ziehst du über deinem Hemd zu Jeans an?
  a. einen Blazer oder eine Jacke
  b. eine schwarze Lederjacke
  c. eine Windjacke oder einen Anorak

3. Wo kaufst du am liebsten Klamotten?
  a. aus dem Katalog
  b. in Secondhand-Läden
  c. in Sportwarengeschäften

SCORE _____

III. Writing

C. Your pen pal wonders if you're interested in fashion, and, if so, what kind. Write at least three sentences explaining what you and your friends wear most of the time. Be sure to use as many adjectives as possible to describe your style.
(12 points)

_____

_____

_____

_____

_____

_____

_____

_____

_____

SCORE _____

TOTAL SCORE _____

KAPITEL 8

KAPITEL 8

Mode? Ja oder nein?

■ Dritte Stufe

Maximum Score: 35

Grammar and Vocabulary

A. Your friend Albert asked you to come with him to *Billigmode* to help him buy clothes for the party on Saturday. Fill in the blanks with appropriate pronouns. (10 points)

DU   Warum kaufst du **1.** _____ nicht dieses Seidenhemd?

ALBERT   Das ist **2.** _____ viel zu teuer! Ich möchte **3.** _____ lieber ein billiges geblümtes Hemd kaufen.

DU   Aber das ist doch nicht modisch! Interessierst du **4.** _____ nicht für Mode?

ALBERT   Stimmt! Ich interessiere **5.** _____ überhaupt nicht für Mode.

DU   Mode ist **6.** _____ egal?

ALBERT   Ja, ganz egal!

DU   Probier doch mal das Seidenhemd an!

Albert probiert das Hemd an.

DU   Das steht **7.** _____ ausgezeichnet! Es passt **8.** _____ sehr gut!

ALBERT   Ist es **9.** _____ nicht zu eng?

DU   Nein, es passt prima!

ALBERT   Na gut, dann kaufe ich es **10.** _____ halt.

SCORE [   ]

B. Give the German equivalents of the following statements. (15 points)

Why don't you just buy a suit!

11. _____

Just don't wear anything made of silk!

12. _____

Just don't buy a business jacket out of wool!

13. _____

Go ahead and wear a pleated skirt out of linen!

14. _____

Why don't you wear a sporty jacket?

15. _____

SCORE [   ]

C. Write complete sentences with the words and phrases below. Be sure to use the correct form of the verbs and correct endings for nouns, pronouns, indefinite articles, and adjectives. (10 points)

Manuela / sich kaufen / ein- / blau- / Jacke / mit / Reißverschluss

16. _____

_____

Dies- / gelb- / Blouson / passen / prima / zur / braun- / Hose

17. _____

_____

Warum / sich kaufen / du / nicht / dies- / Wollhemd / mit / Druckknöpfe-

18. _____

_____

Ich / gern kaufen / fesch- / Klamotten / wenn / ich / haben / Geld

19. _____

_____

Dies- / kariert- / Hose / sein / dir / viel zu weit

20. _____

_____

SCORE [   ]

TOTAL SCORE [   ]

Mode? Ja oder nein?

■ Dritte Stufe

I. Listening

A. Anna and her sister, Katrin, are trying on clothes in a boutique. After you listen to the conversation twice, choose the best answers from among the alternatives given. (6 points)

1. Anna is trying on
   - **a.** a pants suit.
   - **b.** a dress.
   - **c.** just a blouse.
   - **d.** just a pair of slacks.

2. She already knows (and doesn't ask her sister)
   - **a.** what kind of shoes to wear with it.
   - **b.** whether it will have to be dry cleaned.
   - **c.** if the slacks fit.
   - **d.** how much it costs.

3. Actually, everything about the purchase would be wrong EXCEPT
   - **a.** the price.
   - **b.** the fabric/material.
   - **c.** the boots she would need.
   - **d.** the fit.

SCORE [   ]

II. Reading

B. Read the advertisement for business jackets and then answer the questions that follow. (8 points)

Modehaus Huber

Sakkos gewinnen dieses Jahr wieder an Bedeutung. Wir haben Sakkos für jeden Anlass und für jede Jahreszeit. Wir haben Sakkos in vielen Farben, auch in der Trendfarbe Anthrazit, und in allen Größen, auch in Spezialgrößen. Unsere Sakkos sind bequem und sitzen korrekt. Erlauben Sie uns, Ihnen unsere zwei Spitzenrenner vorzustellen:

Unser **Dinnersakko** ist ein eleganter Sakko mit zwei Innentaschen und ohne Rückschlitz. Das Material ist 55% Polyester, 25% Wolle und 20% Leinen. Das Futter ist 100% Viskose. Dieser Sakko kommt in Marine und Anthrazit. EUR 120

Unser 3-Knopf **Sakko Romeo** hat mehrere Innentaschen und zwei Seitenschlitze. Das Material ist 100% Schurwolle. Das Futter ist 100% Viskose. Dieser Sakko kommt in Anthrazit und hellem Grau. Diesen Sakko können sie sehr vorteilhaft zu einer schwarzen Hose tragen. EUR 140

Warten Sie nicht bis zum Schlussverkauf, um sich einen Sakko zu kaufen. Kommen Sie noch heute ins Modehaus Huber! Wir freuen uns auf Ihren Besuch.

4. What does **Futter** mean in this ad?
   - **a.** lining
   - **b.** feed
   - **c.** padded
   - **d.** button

Quiz 8-3B

5. What does **Schlitz** mean in this ad?
   a. slit   b. pocket   c. loop   d. snap

6. In addition to being comfortable, what other feature do Huber's jackets have?
   a. a very reasonable price   c. a correct fit
   b. luxurious material   d. versatility

7. What is **Anthrazit**?
   a. a fabric   b. a style   c. a color   d. an accessory

SCORE [   ]

III. Writing

C. You're shopping with your German host mother. She's hesitant about buying a blouse. You can tell she really wants it. Complete the conversation using the lines and directions given. (12 points)

[Tell her to go ahead and buy this blouse.]

8. DU _____

   SIE Ja, ich weiß nicht. Ich trage eigentlich nicht so oft Gelb.

[Tell her that yellow looks great on her.]

9. DU _____

   SIE [*She tries it on.*] Der Stil ist doch ein bisschen jung für mich, oder?

[Tell her it's not too youthful on her. Compliment her on how fashionable she looks.]

10. DU _____

    _____

    SIE Echt? Dann nehme ich sie doch.

SCORE [   ]

IV. Culture

D. Mark the following statements true (**T**) or false (**F**). (4 points)

According to what you have read in this chapter,

_____ 11. many German teens consider generosity and concern for others to be important characteristics.

_____ 12. when German teens think about what is most desirable in life, jewelry, houses, cars, and clothes don't matter at all.

SCORE [   ]

TOTAL SCORE [   ]

Name _____ Klasse _____ Datum _____

8 Mode? Ja oder nein?

Chapter Test

I. Listening

Maximum Score: 30 points

A. A student club is collecting used clothing to send to Romania. Some students are showing each other the things they brought from home. After listening to the conversation twice, choose the best answers from among the alternatives given. (10 points)

1. Anja brought all of the following things EXCEPT
   a. a Madonna-style skirt.
   b. a wool scarf.
   c. shoes with high heels.
   d. a knitted sweater.

2. Helmut brought all of the following things EXCEPT
   a. cutoff jeans.
   b. a leather cap.
   c. a silk tie.
   d. a wool cap.

3. Dieter's objection is that these clothes are not
   a. practical.
   b. fashionable.
   c. new enough.
   d. sportive enough.

4. The things that Dieter seems to think are all right to send include
   a. pants and sweat shirts.
   b. a camisole and lace skirt.
   c. cutoffs.
   d. a silk tie.

5. Helmut and Anja think that
   a. the people in Romania have more time to spend on washing things.
   b. if you're depending on others for help, you'd better take what you get and be glad.
   c. it's more blessed to give than to receive.
   d. people who don't have much would also like to have some nice things rather than only practical clothing.

SCORE _____

B. Lisa has just come back from shopping for shoes. Listen to her conversation with her father twice and mark each statement true (**a**) or false (**b**). (20 points)

_____ 6. Lisa is taking up basketball as a hobby.

_____ 7. She has her brother's wool shirt on.

Chapter Test

_____ 8. Boys and girls wear the same style of wool shirts at her school.

_____ 9. Her father thinks that "unisex" consists of girls and women wearing "men's" clothing.

_____ 10. Lisa thinks that high-heeled shoes are unhealthy as well as uncomfortable.

_____ 11. She thinks, however, that skirts und nylons look very sophisticated.

_____ 12. Her father thinks that men's ties are unnecessary.

_____ 13. Lisa and her friends are not interested in fashion.

_____ 14. Lisa and her friends follow the fashions dictated by film stars and Paris designers.

_____ 15. Lisa's father is basically pleased with her attitudes.

SCORE [   ]

II. Reading

Maximum Score: 24 points

C. Your time machine allows you to eavesdrop on people in various centuries. You overhear the following "intimate" conversations (printed here in modern German). When did they occur? Choose **a, b,** or **c** below. (14 points)

a. in 4th-century Germania
b. in 13th-century Burg Elznach, Duchy of Thuringia
c. in late 1990s Mittenwald

_____ 16.

FLAVIA	Was ziehst du heute Abend an?
CLAUDIA	Ich weiß nicht. Glaubst du, der junge Hermann kommt?
FLAVIA	Der mit dem Bärenfell-Mantel? Und den wilden, langen Haaren?
CLAUDIA	Ja. Vater hat ihn doch eingeladen. Gefällt er dir nicht? Ich finde ihn ja ganz nett — so einfach und natürlich.
FLAVIA	Das mag schon sein, aber ich ziehe den Tacitus vor. Der kämmt und rasiert sich wenigstens ordentlich.
CLAUDIA	Doch parfümiert sich der Tacitus so stark. Mir ist das echt unangenehm.

_____ 17.

PETER	Was ziehst du heute Abend an? Tracht?
INGE	Nein, lieber ein einfaches, schwarzes Kleid. Ein Dirndl ist zu altmodisch, meinst du nicht?
PETER	Aber der Albrecht trägt bestimmt wieder eine Lederhose.
INGE	Das ist mir egal. Ich finde, dass man nicht unbedingt auf dem Volksfest Tracht tragen muss. Außerdem hat der Albrecht doch nicht so schöne Beine!
PETER	Du, ein Sakko steht ihm aber auch nicht besser. Dazu sind seine Schultern zu breit!

_____ 18.

KUNIGUNDE	Was ziehst du heute Abend an?
HILDEGARD	Ich weiß nicht. Steht mir die blaue Robe besser als die grüne?
KUNIGUNDE	Beide stehen dir sehr gut. Aber, wenn der junge Engelbert kommt, dann solltest du lieber Grün tragen.
HILDEGARD	Wieso denn?
KUNIGUNDE	Na, Grün ist die Farbe der Hoffnung, aber Blau bedeutet Treue. Ich meine, du solltest dem Engelbert Hoffnung geben, aber noch nicht die Treue versprechen.
HILDEGARD	Hmm. Ja, erst mal sehen, ob er sich morgen bei dem Turnier auszeichnet, nicht wahr?

Below are three words used in the dialogues above. Using context as a clue, decide which is the best translation for each word:

a. man's jacket (dress jacket)
b. cloak or cape
c. woman's peasant costume
d. lady's gown

_____ 19. **Mantel** in paragraph 1

_____ 20. **Dirndl** in paragraph 2

_____ 21. **Robe** in paragraph 3

22. In the third dialogue, Hildegard and Kunigunde are discussing Engelbert. Kunigunde advises Hildegard: **Du solltest ihm Hoffnung geben, aber noch nicht die Treue versprechen.** If **versprechen** means *to promise*, what is Kunigunde advising Hildegard not to give?
   a. a dowry (her own)
   b. riches
   c. loyalty (as in commitment)
   d. a secret message

SCORE [   ]

D. Look at the questions on page 212 and then read the following passage twice. As you read, think about the questions. Choose the best answers from among the alternatives given. (10 points)

gerettet: *saved*
Pelz: *fur*
vertilgt: *wiped out*

Die Mode gefährdet

Im 19. Jahrhundert haben die „zivilisierten" Nationen den Seehund, den Walfisch, den Tiger, das Krokodil und Vögel wie den Strauß fast von unserem Planeten vertilgt. Und wozu? Straußenfedern brauchten Damen für ihre Fächer und als Kopfputz. Walfischbein stärkte ihre Korsetts. Walfisch-Ambra war ein nötiger Bestandteil von Parfüm. Die Haut von Krokodilen verarbeitete man zu Schuhen, Gürteln und

Chapter Test

Taschen für Damen und Herren. Aus den Seehund- und Tigerfellen wurden Pelzmäntel.

Heute trägt kein Mensch einen Zylinderhut aus gepresstem Biberpelz. Es war eigentlich nur die Entdeckung einer neuen, billigeren Methode, Hüte zu machen, nämlich aus Wollfilz, die den Biber gerettet hat. In Europa gibt es gar keine Biber mehr, und in Nordamerika existieren sie nur noch in Schutzgebieten, denn Biberpelze sind immer noch als luxuriöses Material für Jacken und Mäntel gefragt.

Nun müssen wir uns fragen: wie ist es mit den Handschuhen aus Kalbsleder oder der Jacke aus Wildleder? Wenn wir konsequent unsere Umwelt beschützen wollen, sollten wir denn nicht lieber all solche Modeartikel vermeiden?

23. The different species of animals mentioned in the first paragraph are endangered in part because
    a. people don't care about them.
    b. their fur or hide yields practical clothing.
    c. people are willing to spend lots of money on clothing.
    d. most people do not like animals.

24. Beavers are not killed as often anymore because
    a. felt hats are better and cheaper than hats made of beaver fur.
    b. people are more animal friendly today.
    c. no one wants a beaver coat anymore.
    d. they are extinct in Europe.

25. The best protection for an animal is that
    a. its fur or hide is rare and therefore very expensive.
    b. people think the animal is ugly or dangerous.
    c. there is no clothing article that could be made of its fur or hide that people would like.
    d. it is not considered edible.

26. Even animal lovers often wear clothing made from animal hides, for example,
    a. mink coats.
    b. leather jackets.
    c. crocodile purses.
    d. coral necklaces.

27. Which of the statements below would the author most likely have made to his wife?
    a. Kauf dir doch den Pelzmantel! Er steht dir prima.
    b. Ich freue mich, dass du dich so sehr für Mode interessierst.
    c. Kauf dir ja nichts aus Pelz oder Wildleder!
    d. Walfische sind mir doch egal!

SCORE

KAPITEL 8

Chapter Test

III. Culture
Maximum Score: 16 points

E. From reading and listening to what German teens think about fashion and its place in their lives, do you think their attitudes are typical for students at your school? Briefly explain using evidence about German teenagers from this chapter. (8 points)

_____

_____

_____

_____

_____

SCORE [   ]

F. After reading the results of the values survey from **Zum Lesen** in **Kapitel 8**, how do you think the values of German teens compare with your own? Give specific details about how they rank various "desirable" things in life. (8 points)

_____

_____

_____

_____

_____

SCORE [   ]

IV. Writing
Maximum Score: 30 points

G. Create a short conversation using the following elements:
  - your classmate, David, asks where you got your new jacket
  - you tell him you got it from a secondhand store
  - he says it looks good on you and goes really well with your pants
  - you respond to the compliment, but say that this jacket has to be dry cleaned
  - you tell him not to buy anything made of silk (15 points)

28.　　DAVID _____

29.　　　DU _____

KAPITEL 8

Chapter Test

30. DAVID _____

_____

_____

31. DU _____

_____

_____

32. _____

_____

_____

SCORE [   ]

H. You have designed the perfect three-piece outfit for yourself. Describe it in detail, including the style, colors, material, pockets, fasteners, and any accessories you will wear with it. Write at least five complete sentences. (15 points)

_____

_____

_____

_____

_____

_____

_____

_____

_____

_____

_____

SCORE [   ]

TOTAL SCORE [   ]

KAPITEL 8 Chapter Test Score Sheet

Circle the letter that matches the most appropriate response.

I. Listening   Maximum Score: 30 points

A. (10 points)   **B.** (20 points)

1. a b c d   6. a b   11. a b
2. a b c d   7. a b   12. a b
3. a b c d   8. a b   13. a b
4. a b c d   9. a b   14. a b
5. a b c d   10. a b   15. a b

SCORE [   ]   SCORE [   ]

II. Reading   Maximum Score: 24 points

C. (14 points)   **D.** (10 points)

16. a b c   21. a b c d   23. a b c d
17. a b c   22. a b c d   24. a b c d
18. a b c   25. a b c d
19. a b c d   26. a b c d
20. a b c d   27. a b c d

                     SCORE [   ]   SCORE [   ]

III. Culture   Maximum Score: 16 points

E. (8 points)

_____

_____

_____

_____

_____

                                    SCORE [   ]

K
A
P
I
T
E
L

8

F. (8 points)

_____

_____

_____

_____

_____

_____

SCORE [ ]

IV. Writing

Maximum Score: 30 points

G. (15 points)

_____

_____

_____

_____

_____

_____

_____

_____

_____

SCORE [ ]

H. (15 points)

_____

_____

_____

_____

_____

_____

_____

_____

SCORE [ ]

TOTAL SCORE [ ]

KAPITEL 8

Listening Scripts for Quizzes 8-1B, 8-2B, 8-3B

Quiz 8-1B Kapitel 8 Erste Stufe

I. Listening

A.

MUTTER	Bärbel, du hast ja deine Jacke nicht an. Die gefütterte. Wo ist die denn?
BÄRBEL	Zu Hause. Die Jacke passt nicht so richtig zu dieser Hose, Mutti.
MUTTER	Aber es ist doch richtig kalt heute. Und bei dem Wind! Was machen wir denn bloß? Ach, ich weiß was. Oma hat ihre Wolljacke gestern im Auto liegen gelassen. Die kannst du anziehen.
BÄRBEL	Oh Mutti! Omas Jacke? Die kann ich doch unmöglich zu meinem Outfit anziehen!
MUTTER	Doch, kannst du. Sonst erkältest du dich.
BÄRBEL	Aber die Jacke ist türkisblau und meine Hose ist olivgrün. Und mein Sweatshirt auch! Und außerdem ist so eine Jacke gar nicht mehr modern. Aus den siebziger Jahren ist sie!
MUTTER	Keine Ausreden, nun. Du ziehst dir jetzt die Jacke an! Hier ... So, jetzt ist's besser.
BÄRBEL	Mutti, da kommt gerade ein Junge aus meiner Klasse, der Max. Er hat mich schon gesehen — mit der Jacke. So ein Pech!
MUTTER	Das schadet doch nichts. Guten Tag, Max!
MAX	Guten Tag, Frau Holzmann! Tag, Bärbel! Wie siehst du aber heute fesch aus! So bunt und witzig habe ich dich noch nie gesehen. Passt dir doch prima. Wo hast du denn diese scharfe Jacke her?
BÄRBEL	Ja, diese Jacke? Hmm ...

Quiz 8-2B Kapitel 8 Zweite Stufe

I. Listening

A.

FRAU	Wenn Sie sich echt für Mode interessieren, dann wissen Sie bestimmt schon, welche Farben, Stoffe und Stoffmuster zusammenpassen und ein fesches Outfit machen. Heute aber beraten wir die jungen Herren, die weniger Interesse für Mode haben und trotzdem gut aussehen wollen.
	Wenn Sie zu einer konservativen Hose ein weißes oder hellblaues Hemd tragen, so sehen Sie monoton und uninteressant aus. Auch der konservative Herr soll heute ein gestreiftes oder kariertes Hemd in einer Kontrastfarbe dazu wählen. Darüber tragen Sie am besten eine gepunktete oder mehrfarbig bedruckte Krawatte. Die Socken dürfen auch nicht immer eintönig schwarz, dunkelblau oder grau sein, aber sie sollten doch zur Krawatte passen. Aber nicht unbedingt feuerrot oder knallgelb.

Quiz 8-3B Kapitel 8 Dritte Stufe

I. Listening

A.

ANNA	Wie findest du diesen Hosenanzug?
KATRIN	Steht dir gut! Ich finde ihn echt toll: viele Reißverschlüsse und mit Kapuze am Blouson. Kauf dir den Anzug doch!
ANNA	Ich weiß nicht. Eigentlich trage ich Steghosen lieber als diesen Stil. Was für Schuhe muss man bloß dazu tragen?
KATRIN	Am besten Stiefel mit hohen Absätzen, nicht wahr?
ANNA	Stiefel habe ich aber gar nicht. Hmm. Wie sieht die Hose von hinten aus? Ist sie mir nicht zu eng?
KATRIN	Nein, sie ist überhaupt nicht zu eng. Und die Gesäßtaschen sitzen genau richtig!
ANNA	Echt? Ja, ich glaube, die Hose passt gut. Aber das Hemd dazu ist aus Seide. Das muss man zur Reinigung bringen, oder? Was meinst du?
KATRIN	Oh je! Kauf dir ja nichts, was du nicht in die Waschmaschine tun kannst.
ANNA	Schade. Na ja, mir ist dieser Anzug auch ein bisschen zu teuer. Ich suche mir lieber was Preiswerteres aus.
KATRIN	Ja, suchen wir doch eine Kapuzenjacke aus Leinen oder Baumwolle. Naturfasern ziehe ich schon vor, aber echte Seide ist doch zu unpraktisch, oder?

ANSWERS Quiz 8-1A

A. (15 points; 3 points per item)
Answers will vary. Possible answers:
1. Schau mal! Diese Frau trägt einen coolen Blazer. Er ist konservativ, aber witzig.
2. Das stimmt! Aber ihre geblümten Hosen sehen furchtbar aus.
3. Und sieh mal! Sie trägt grüne Schuhe und ein blaues Käppi.
4. Das Käppi sieht sehr modisch aus and die Schuhe sehen sportlich aus.
5. He, schau, dieser junge Mann trägt einen gelben Parka und darunter ein rotes Hemd! Und seine Haare sind blau!

B. (12 points; 2 points per item)
6. Dieses gelbe
7. diesem gelben
8. Diese geblümte
9. diesem geblümten
10. dieses rote
11. diesem roten

C. (8 points; 2 points per item)
Answers will vary. Possible answers:
12. Petra will diese gelbe Winterjacke anprobieren.
13. Hans trägt eine grüne Hose zu dieser blauen Jacke.
14. Ulrike braucht ein weißes Hemd zur schwarzen Jeans.
15. Melanie sieht in dieser blauen Jeansweste fesch aus.

ANSWERS Quiz 8-1B

I. Listening

A. (10 points: 2 points per item)
1. T
2. F
3. F
4. T
5. T

II. Reading

B. (12 points: 2 points per item)
6. to protect oneself from the weather
7. a. age group
   b. sex (male/female)
   c. clique
8. a. interesting
   b. funny

III. Writing

C. (12 points: 4 points per sentence)
Answers will vary.

IV. Culture

D. (6 points: 3 points per item)
9. Teenagers in parts of southern Germany sometimes wear special costumes for special occasions; teens wear proper sports attire more often (for example: a white outfit to play tennis).
10. b

KAPITEL 8

Answers to Quizzes 8-2A, 8-2B

ANSWERS Quiz 8-2A

A. (15 points; 3 points per item)
Answers will vary. Possible answers:
1. Ich hab kein Interesse an Mode.
2. Wofür interessierst du dich?
3. Die weiße Bluse passt toll zur schwarzen Jeans.
4. Das steht dir prima!
5. Das ist ihm zu eng.

B. (8 points; 1 point per item)
6. dich
7. mich
8. euch
9. uns
10. sich
11. sich
12. sich
13. sich

C. (7 points; 1 point per item)
14. Lederjacke
15. ist
16. trägt
17. passt
18. darunter
19. interessieren
20. preiswert

ANSWERS Quiz 8-2B

I. Listening
A. (6 points: 2 points per item)
1. a
2. b
3. a

II. Reading
B. (12 points: 4 points per item)
4. b
5. c
6. a

III. Writing
C. (12 points: 4 points per item)
Answers will vary.

KAPITEL 8

Answers to Quizzes 8-3A, 8-3B

ANSWERS Quiz 8-3A

A. (10 points; 1 point per item)
1. dir
2. mir
3. mir
4. dich
5. mich
6. dir
7. dir
8. dir
9. mir
10. mir

B. (15 points; 3 points per item)
Answers will vary. Possible answers:
11. Kauf dir doch einen Anzug!
12. Trag ja nichts aus Seide!
13. Kauf dir ja keinen Sakko aus Wolle!
14. Trag doch mal einen Faltenrock aus Leinen.
15. Trag doch mal eine sportliche Jacke.

C. (10 points; 2 points per item)
Answers will vary. Possible answers:
16. Manuela kauft sich eine blaue Jacke mit Reißverschluss.
17. Dieser gelbe Blouson passt prima zur braunen Hose.
18. Warum kaufst du dir nicht dieses Wollhemd mit Druckknöpfen?
19. Ich kaufe gern fesche Klamotten, wenn ich Geld habe.
20. Diese karierte Hose ist dir viel zu weit.

ANSWERS Quiz 8-3B

I. Listening

A. (6 points: 2 points per item)
1. a
2. d
3. d

II. Reading

B. (8 points: 2 points per item)
4. a
5. a
6. c
7. c

III. Writing

C. (12 points: 4 points per item)
Answers will vary. Possible answers:
8. Kaufen Sie doch diese Bluse!
9. Gelb steht Ihnen sehr gut!
10. Nein, überhaupt nicht zu jung. Sie sehen sehr modisch aus.

IV. Culture

D. (4 points: 2 points per item)
11. T
12. F

Scripts for Chapter Test Kapitel 8

I. Listening

A.

DIETER   Tag, Anja! Was hast du mitgebracht?

ANJA   Guck, Dieter, ganz schöne Sachen: ein T-Shirt, das mir zu eng geworden ist, ein Sweatshirt mit Aufdruck, einen Pullover ...

DIETER   Schicker Pullover! Den willst du weggeben?

ANJA   Ja. Der ist halt aus reiner Wolle — mit der Hand gestrickt. Kannst du auch nur mit der Hand waschen. Das will ich eben nicht mehr.

DIETER   Und was hast du sonst noch?

ANJA   Ein Trägerhemd, fast neu ist das, und einen Spitzenrock. Madonna-Mode ist ja nicht mehr in. Dann ein Paar Sandalen mit hohen Absätzen. Und noch ein Paar Kniestrümpfe für den Winter.

DIETER   Und Helmut. Hast du was Schönes?

HELMUT   Jawohl! Bei mir habe ich diese Krawatte gefunden — steht mir gar nicht, ist aber aus echter Seide, und eine Badehose und zwei Jeanshosen, beide abgeschnitten. Und dieses Käppi aus Leder. Fesch, nicht?

DIETER   Mensch, aber, wo denkst du bloß hin? Wer in Rumänien soll denn dieses Zeug anziehen? Mindestens die Hälfte von euren Sachen ist ganz unmöglich!

HELMUT   Wie meinst du das?

ANJA   Ja. Wie?

DIETER   Die Leute drüben brauchen praktische, haltbare Kleidung. Was soll so ein armer Junge, der friert, mit diesen abgeschnitten Jeans, oder einer seidenen Krawatte? Und was kann ein armes Mädchen mit diesem Madonna-Outfit anfangen?

ANJA   Ich stimme dir zwar zu, Dieter, aber die Leute drüben wünschen sich doch auch schöne Klamotten, oder?

HELMUT   Außerdem ist mein Käppi doch sehr praktisch — und auch fesch. Ich finde, ein rumänischer Junge hat lieber dieses Käppi als so eine langweilige Wollmütze, wie du sie trägst, Dieter.

ANJA   Finde ich auch!

B.

LISA   Schau mal, Vati, was ich heute gekauft habe!

VATER   Schöne Schuhe, Lisa. Aber ich wusste gar nicht, dass du Basketball spielst. Ist das dein neustes Hobby?

LISA   Spiele ich doch nicht. Die Schuhe sind für den Alltag. Basketball-Schuhe sind jetzt große Mode. Und so schön bequem!

VATER   Ach so. Und das Wollhemd? Ist das auch neu? Oder hast du das von deinem Bruder?

LISA   Nein. Das ist mein Hemd. So karierte Wollhemden sind auch Mode — mit einem T-Shirt darunter — für Mädchen oder Jungen, ganz egal.

VATER   Hmm. Ich habe eine Frage, Lisa. Wie kommt es eigentlich, dass diese Unisex Mode daraus besteht, dass Mädchen in Herrensportkleidung rumlaufen? Von hinten siehst du fast aus wie dein Bruder, nur hat der längere Haare als du.

LISA   Ja, Vati, die Jugend von heute ist doch nicht so dumm. Röcke, Unterröcke, Strumpfhosen und Schuhe mit hohen Absätzen sind unbequem, unpraktisch und auch ungesund. Du siehst mich auch nicht im Sakko und mit einer Krawatte herumlaufen, nicht wahr?

VATER   Das stimmt schon. Und ich kann dir sagen, eine Krawatte ist der unbequemste Kleidungsartikel, den es für Männer gibt — und so völlig unnötig! Aber weißt du was? Die Marlene Dietrich hat Sakkos getragen, damals als dein Großvater noch jung war.

LISA   Nun, das ist schon fünfzig Jahre her, Vati! Die Schüler und Schülerinnen auf meiner Schule wollen ja keine verrückten oder extravaganten Klamotten anziehen. Uns ist die Mode nicht egal, aber wir lassen uns nicht von den Filmstars und von den Modeschöpfern in Paris sagen, was uns am besten passt.

VATER   Das freut mich eigentlich.

Answers to Chapter Test Kapitel 8

I. Listening Maximum Score: 30 points

A. (10 points: 2 points per item)   **B.** (20 points: 2 points per item)

1. b	6. b	11. b
2. d	7. b	12. a
3. a	8. a	13. b
4. a	9. a	14. b
5. d	10. a	15. a

II. Reading Maximum Score: 24 points

C. (14 points: 2 points per item)   **D.** (10 points: 2 points per item)

16. a	23. b
17. c	24. a
18. b	25. c
19. b	26. b
20. c	27. c
21. d	
22. c	

III. Culture Maximum Score: 16 points

E. (8 points)

Answers will vary. Answers should show students understand that trends in fashion are generally the same in Germany as in the United States. Some students are interested in fashion, some are not.

F. (8 points)

Answers will vary. Student responses should show familiarity with the results of the survey and the idea that both material and intangible items, such as contentment, are deemed desirable by German teens.

IV. Writing Maximum Score: 30 points

G. (15 points: 3 points per item)

28. Wo hast du dir die Jacke gekauft?
29. Ich habe sie mir in einem Secondhand-Laden gekauft.
30. Sie steht dir gut und passt auch zu deiner Hose.
31. Ehrlich? Aber ich muss die Jacke in die Reinigung bringen.
32. Kauf dir ja nichts aus Seide!

H. (15 points: 3 points per sentence)

Answers will vary.

Holt German 2 Komm mit!, Chapter 8

Wohin in die Ferien?

Quiz 9-1A

■ Erste Stufe

Maximum Score: 30

Grammar and Vocabulary

A. Where in the world are you and your friends going during summer vacation?
Write the correct grammar form in the blank in each sentence. (20 points)

Mein Freund Klaus fährt **1.** _____ Nordsee.

  a. nach   **b.** in die   **c.** ans   **d.** auf den   **e.** aufs   **f.** an die

Gertrude fährt mit ihrer Familie **2.** _____ Berge.

  a. nach   **b.** in die   **c.** ans   **d.** auf den   **e.** aufs   **f.** an die

Judith fliegt **3.** _____ Österreich, und Babsi bleibt zu Hause und arbeitet!

  a. nach   **b.** in die   **c.** ans   **d.** auf den   **e.** aufs   **f.** an die

Meine Familie plant eine lange Reise. Wir fahren zuerst **4.** _____ Schweiz.

  a. nach   **b.** in die   **c.** ans   **d.** auf den   **e.** aufs   **f.** an die

Dort werden wir **5.** _____ Brienzer Rothorn steigen.

  a. nach   **b.** in die   **c.** ans   **d.** auf den   **e.** aufs   **f.** an die

Dann fahren wir **6.** _____ Italien, **7.** _____ Meer .

  a. nach   **b.** in die   **c.** ans   **d.** auf den   **e.** aufs   **f.** an die

Danach fliegen wir **8.** _____ Vereinigten Staaten, wo wir **9.** _____

Pike's Peak steigen werden. (der Pike's Peak)

  a. nach   **b.** in die   **c.** ans   **d.** auf den   **e.** aufs   **f.** an die

Zuletzt werden wir zurück **10.** _____ Deutschland fliegen.

  a. nach   **b.** in die   **c.** ans   **d.** auf den   **e.** aufs   **f.** an die

SCORE ☐

Quiz 9-1A

B. Was machst du in den Ferien? Match the place with the correct grammar form used to talk about getting there. Choose the correct grammar form from the box and write it in the blank to the left of the place you want to go.
(10 points)

auf den	**in den**	**in die**	**auf die**
ins	**an den**	**nach**	

Ich will 11. _____ Tennisplatz gehen.

Ich will 12. _____ Hallenbad gehen.

Ich will 13. _____ Zugspitze steigen.

Ich will 14. _____ Berge fahren.

Ich will 15. _____ Bodensee fahren.

Ich will 16. _____ Rhein fahren.

Ich will 17. _____ Bayern fahren.

Ich will 18. _____ Alpen fahren.

Ich will 19. _____ Schwarzwald fahren.

Ich will 20. _____ Vereinigten Staaten fliegen.

SCORE [   ]

TOTAL SCORE [   ]

Holt German 2 Komm mit!, Chapter 9

Wohin in die Ferien?

Quiz 9-1B

■ Erste Stufe

Maximum Score: 40

I. Listening

A. Gesa and Ulf are at the breakfast table. Read the statements below. After you listen to their conversation twice, mark the statements true **(T)** or false **(F)**. (12 points)

_____ 1. Ulf has four weeks of vacation.

_____ 2. Ulf and Gesa usually stay in Germany or go to Austria for their vacation.

_____ 3. Gesa wants to go to Egypt and then take a Mediterranean cruise.

_____ 4. Ulf does not like Gesa's suggestion.

_____ 5. Ulf thinks it will be hot in Egypt in the summer.

_____ 6. Ulf doesn't think they should take Gesa's "dream trip."

SCORE

II. Reading

B. After reading this passage, choose the best answers from among the alternatives given. (6 points)

In der Bundesrepublik kann man mit den öffentlichen Verkehrsmitteln an tausende von schönen Ferienorten gelangen. Die Deutsche Bahn hat nicht nur Züge in Betrieb, sondern auch Busse, die in noch so kleine Dörfer fahren. Sollte kein Bummelzug oder Bus direkt an den Ort fahren, wo man sein Zelt aufschlagen will, so braucht man nicht die Strecke zu Fuß zu gehen, denn an vielen Bahnhöfen kann man für wenig Geld ein Fahrrad von der Bahn mieten. Oder man bringt das eigene Fahrrad von zu Hause mit. Das Rad wird sehr preiswert im Gepäckwagen befördert, und der Rucksack mit Zelt und Campingkocher auch.

Also, fragen Sie sich ja nicht „Was soll ich bloß in den Ferien machen, wenn ich kein Auto habe?" Fragen Sie lieber bei der DB Information, wo Sie überall hinfahren können. Mit der Bahn macht das Reisen Spaß!

7. This text most likely appeared in
   a. a letter from an American tourist to her parents.
   b. an ad for the German Railway (DB=Deutsche Bahn).
   c. an article on different transportation options in Germany.
   d. a travel guide.

8. What is the main point of this article?
   a. It's necessary to own a car in Germany in order to go on vacation.
   b. The German Railway makes vacation spots accessible to everyone via different forms of transportation.
   c. The German Railway only operates trains to major cities.
   d. You at least need to own a bike if you want to get to a nice vacation spot in Germany.

Quiz 9-1B

9. If you're planning to spend only one summer touring Germany, it would probably be cheapest to
   a. use the trains to get to major cities and then rent a car.
   b. buy a car there.
   c. rent a car and stay in hotels in major cities.
   d. take your backpacking equipment and rely on the **Deutsche Bahn** system.

SCORE [   ]

III. Writing

C. You and your friend have missed the last train back home. Use the following lines and directions to complete the conversation below. (12 points)

ER   Was willst du jetzt machen?

[Say you don't know. Ask what he suggests.]

10. DU _____

ER   Hmm ... Wir können eine Bushaltestelle suchen oder ein Taxi.

[Make a suggestion that will get the following response.]

11. DU _____

ER   Also, gut. Laufen wir ganz schnell zum Busbahnhof. Ich glaube aber, der letzte Bus ist auch schon weg.

[Ask what the two of you are supposed to do!]

12. DU _____

SCORE [   ]

IV. Culture

D. Based on the **Landeskunde** in **Kapitel 9**, mark each statement true (**T**) or false (**F**). (10 points)

_____ 13. It is impossible for students to have **Ferienjobs** because summer vacation is so short in Germany.

_____ 14. Students in Germany typically have about a total of twelve weeks off from school per year.

_____ 15. All **Bundesländer** have the same school vacation schedule.

_____ 16. Students in Germany attend school "year round."

_____ 17. Some students use their vacation time to attend schools in another country as exchange students.

SCORE [   ]

TOTAL SCORE [   ]

Name _____ Klasse _____ Datum _____

9 Wohin in die Ferien?

Quiz 9-2A

■ Zweite Stufe

Maximum Score: 40

Grammar and Vocabulary

A. Your friend is going on vacation to a hotel where you stayed several years ago, and he has some questions to ask about the facilities there. You don't remember the place all that well and give cautious answers. Using the cues given in German, formulate questions and answers. (20 points)

FREUND **1.** _____ ?
(Tennisplatz)

DU   Ja, ich glaube, dass **2.** _____ .

FREUND **3.** _____ ?
(Sauna)

DU   Nein, ich glaube nicht, dass **4.** _____ .

FREUND **5.** _____ ?
(tauchen)

DU   Ich glaube schon, dass **6.** _____ .

FREUND **7.** _____ ?
(Diskothek)

DU   Ich bin nicht ganz sicher, dass **8.** _____ .

FREUND **9.** _____ ?
(Liegewiese)

DU   Ich bezweifle, dass **10.** _____ .

SCORE ☐

B. You are telling your parents about the places where your friends went on vacation last year, and about the places they intend to go this year. Complete the sentences by filling in each blank with the correct preposition and article. (10 points)

Die Birgitte ist letztes Jahr in den großen Ferien 11. _____ Nordsee gewesen.

Dieses Jahr plant ihre Familie, 12. _____ Berge zu fahren.

Der Frank ist 13. _____ Vereinigten Staaten gewesen. Das hat viel gekostet.

Deswegen plant seine Familie dieses Jahr, nur 14. _____ Bodensee zu fahren.

Der Georg plant dieses Jahr eine Reise 15. _____ Italien.

SCORE [   ]

C. No matter what place your friend Katja mentions, you have already been there! Complete the following sentences by filling in the blanks with the correct preposition and definite article. Use contractions when possible. (10 points)

KATJA Fährst du 16. _____ Bayern?

DU Ich war schon mal 17. _____ Bayern.

KATJA Gehst du 18. _____ Golfplatz?

DU Ich war schon gestern 19. _____ Golfplatz.

KATJA Wir fahren morgen 20. _____ Berge.

DU Ich war letztes Jahr 21. _____ Bergen.

KATJA Gehst du heute Abend 22. _____ Disko?

DU Ich war vorgestern 23. _____ Disko.

KATJA Willst du 24. _____ Brienzer Rothorn fahren?

DU Nein, ich bin auch schon mal 25. _____ Brienzer Rothorn gewesen.

SCORE [   ]

TOTAL SCORE [   ]

KAPITEL 9

Wohin in die Ferien?

Quiz 9-2B

■ Zweite Stufe

Maximum Score: 30

I. Listening

A. Hugo, Hannah, and their son, Arndt, are trying to decide where to go on their vacation. Listen to the conversation twice and mark the statements below true (**T**) or false (**F**). (8 points)

_____ 1. Hannah suggests vacationing on the Mediterranean.

_____ 2. The Club Mediterranean™ resorts emphasize active sports and entertainment.

_____ 3. Hugo wants to know if there are golf courses at Club Med™.

_____ 4. Arndt would rather go to Sylt, because there would be more people his age there.

SCORE _____

II. Reading

B. Look at the questions on page 230 and then read the text twice. Choose the best answers from among the alternatives given. (6 points)

Ans Meer oder in die Berge? Wenn Sie nach British Columbien fahren, brauchen Sie sich gar nicht zu entscheiden, denn hier gibt es Berge, wo man im Juni noch Ski laufen kann. Es gibt hier auch tolle Strände und Küstenstriche.

Hier können Sie segeln, angeln, mit den Seelöwen schwimmen, and dann auf einen drei- bis viertausend Meter hohen Berg steigen — alles an <u>einem</u> Wochenende! Sicherlich wollen Sie auch die charmante alte Stadt Victoria und das moderne Vancouver besuchen. Und wenn Sie das ursprüngliche *(unspoiled)* Hinterland sehen wollen, so buchen *(to book)* Sie leicht von Vancouver aus eine Busfahrt nach Prince George und Dawson Creek.

Wenn Sie uns erst einmal besuchen, werden Sie gerne wiederkommen. Das können Sie uns glauben!

Und wie kommen Sie zu uns? Je nach Wunsch können Sie

• täglich (mit Lufthansa) von Frankfurt nach Vancouver fliegen.

• mit der Fähre *(ferry)* von Seattle nach Victoria oder Vancouver fahren.

• von Montreal oder Toronto eine 3-tägige, wunderschöne Reise durch ganz Kanada mit Canadian National Railways machen.

• mit Auto oder Reisebus auf dem kanadischen National Highway von Calgary über Banff National Park und die kanadischen Rockies fahren.

Quiz 9-2B

5. This passage is probably
   a. a news item from a paper.
   b. advertising put out by an airline company.
   c. an article from the culture section of a German newspaper.
   d. advertising given out by the Office of Tourism for British Columbia.

6. According to the article,
   a. you can see all of the province in one weekend.
   b. you can enjoy both the beach and the mountains in a single weekend.
   c. you probably will want to skip Victoria.
   d. Vancouver and Victoria are the only things you'll really want to see.

7. How many different modes of transportation (vehicles) are mentioned in the last section?
   a. four
   b. five
   c. six
   d. seven

SCORE [   ]

III. Writing

C. Your German pen pal has written and invited you to go on a bicycle tour of Austria this summer. You doubt that you can do that. Write and express your doubts, and explain why you probably can't go. You accept the fact that there is nothing you can do about it this summer, but you're certain you'll go to visit someday. Write at least four sentences. (16 points)

_____

_____

_____

_____

_____

_____

_____

_____

_____

_____

SCORE [   ]

TOTAL SCORE [   ]

9 Wohin in die Ferien?

Quiz 9-3A

Dritte Stufe

Maximum Score: 30

Grammar and Vocabulary

A. You live in the **Innenstadt** of Vienna and tourists are constantly asking you questions. Complete their questions by filling in the blanks with the correct dative preposition and the correct article. Make contractions whenever possible. (10 points)

Ist das Rathaus (from the) **1.** _____ 19. Jahrhundert? Finde ich einen Parkplatz

(near the) **2.** _____ Post? Gibt es eine U-Bahn Station nicht weit (from the)

3. _____ Schottentor? Wo finde ich ein Schreibwarengeschäft, (across from the)

4. _____ Rathaus? Wie komme ich am besten (to the) **5.** _____

Schloss? Wie komme ich am besten (to the) **6.** _____ Universitätskirche? Ist die

beste Bäckerei in der Stadt (near the) **7.** _____ Alten Rathaus? Wo ist bitte die

nächste Apotheke, (in front of the) **8.** _____ Stephansdom? Wo ist bitte die

Stadtsinformation, (next to the) **9.** _____ Karlskirche? Ich habe gehört, dass die

beste Konditorei der Stadt nur 100 Meter (away from the) **10.** _____ Staatsoper

entfernt ist. Aber in welcher Richtung?

SCORE _____

B. The tourists are out in large numbers during the summer in Vienna. Many ask you questions and you patiently give answers. Complete the sentences by filling in each blank with the correct preposition and the correct article. Use contractions whenever possible. (20 points)

TOURIST Ist das Denkmal Maria Theresias (between the) **11.** _____ Naturhis-

torischen Museum und (the) **12.** _____ Kunsthistorischen Museum?

DU Ja, wenn Sie (between the) **13.** _____ Naturhistorische Museum und

(the) **14.** _____ Kunsthistorische Museum gehen, finden Sie dieses

Denkmal.

TOURIST Wo finde ich das Strauss Denkmal, (in the) **15.** _____ Stadtpark?

DU Ja, von der Ringstraße biegen Sie nach rechts (into the) **16.** _____

Stadtpark.

TOURIST Gibt es immer noch Kanonenbälle ([embedded] in the) **17.** _____

alten Stadtmauer?

DU Ja, natürlich! Gehen Sie nur (into the) **18.** _____ Restaurant unter

dem Schild vom lieben Augustin und schauen Sie nach!

TOURIST Ist die älteste Gegend von Wien (next to the) **19.** _____ Rotenturm-

straße?

DU Ja, gehen Sie (through the) **20.** _____ kleine Tor hier, und Sie wer-

den sie sehen.

SCORE

TOTAL SCORE

Name _____ Klasse _____ Datum _____

Wohin in die Ferien?

Quiz 9-3B

■ Dritte Stufe

Maximum Score: 30

I. Listening

A. You are at the **Marktplatz** (number 7 on the map below.) You get directions to two different places: a café and the travel bureau. Mark the locations of these places on the map below. (6 points)

1. a café
2. the travel bureau

1. Parkplatz
2. Stadttor
3. Backhaus
4. Bürgerhaus
5. Kachelsches Haus
6. Posthalterei
7. Marktbrunnen
8. Rathaus
9. Hormoldhaus
10. Evangelische Stadtkirche
11. Kleines Bürgerhaus
12. Bietigheimer Schloss

SCORE [ ]

II. Reading

B. After reading the following passage, answer the questions on page 234. (4 points)

„Ein Platz — place, plaza, piazza — ist eine freie Stelle innerhalb (within) einer Stadt, meistens dort, wo sich mehrere Straßen kreuzen (cross); ein Ort, wo sich Einwohner und Besucher versammeln (gather)." So steht es im Wörterbuch geschrieben. Das Wort kommt von dem lateinischen *platea*. Die Idee kommt von den Römern. Auch die Form eines Platzes — meistens viereckig — entspricht dem römischen Stadtbild. In den alten germanischen Dörfern waren die Plätze wahrscheinlich rund oder halbrund.

Holt German 2 Komm mit!, Chapter 9

Testing Program **233**

Quiz 9-3B

In einem typischen Dorf gruppieren sich die „besseren" Häuser um den Platz vor der Kirche. Im Mittelalter hat man das Rathaus oft neben der Kirche oder gegenüber der Kirche gebaut. Dieser Platz wurde Marktplatz genannt. Hier haben Bauern *(peasants)* Gemüse, Obst, Brot, Fleisch und Wurst verkauft. Jeder Markt- platz hat einen Brunnen gehabt, von dem die Einwohner Wasser geholt haben und an dem sie ihre Wäsche gewaschen haben.

3. The idea of a square or plaza comes from
   a. the Romans.
   b. the ancient Germanic tribes.
   c. the medieval peasants.
   d. the modern Italians.

4. According to the text, all of the following could be found on or at a typical **Marktplatz** during the Middle Ages EXCEPT
   a. a fountain.
   b. the homes of wealthy citizens.
   c. the stores of the rich merchants.
   d. the market.

SCORE [   ]

III. Writing

C. Look at the map of Bietigheim on the first page of this quiz. Answer the following questions in German. (20 points)

5. Wo liegt die Stadt? (**Die Metter** is the name of the river.)

_____

6. Wo ist der Brunnen? (Use the verb **stehen**.)

_____

7. Wo ist das Kachelsche Haus?

_____

8. Wo ist die Kirche? (What is it across from?)

_____

9. Gibt es hier einen Parkplatz? (Use the verb **sich befinden**.)

_____

SCORE [   ]

TOTAL SCORE [   ]

Holt German 2 Komm mit!, Chapter 9

KAPITEL **9**

Wohin in die Ferien?

I. Listening

Maximum Score: 30 points

A. Hilda is planning to attend the International Bach Festival in Eugene, Oregon, for one week this summer. Listen to the conversation twice. As you listen, mark the statements true (**a**) or false (**b**). (16 points)

_____ 1. Hilda has two weeks to spend touring the Pacific Northwest.

_____ 2. Her first activity in the U.S. will be the music festival.

_____ 3. She's really not interested in seeing any of Canada.

_____ 4. Mike doesn't know the area very well, actually.

_____ 5. He does suggest going to the Pacific Ocean.

_____ 6. Mike also suggests a park where Hilda can do some mountain climbing.

_____ 7. Mike is not really sure that Hilda will enjoy the trip.

_____ 8. The northern coast of Germany looks very different, in Mike's opinion, from the Oregon coast.

SCORE _____

B. Regina and Klaus are having trouble getting reservations for their vacation. Listen to the conversation twice and mark the statements true (**a**) or false (**b**). (14 points)

_____ 9. They're planning to go to a beach resort.

_____ 10. Their vacation is in late June this year.

_____ 11. A travel agent recommended a hotel that still has vacancies.

_____ 12. The hotel has everything except a sauna.

_____ 13. Klaus thinks it sounds like a good place for active young people.

_____ 14. Regina doubts that the hotel has tennis or swimming.

_____ 15. Regina is ready to give up.

SCORE _____

Chapter Test

II. Reading
Maximum Score: 30 points

C. After you read the letter below twice, choose the best answers from among the alternatives given. (15 points)

Berlin, den 27. Mai

Liebe Christa!

Heute ist deine Postkarte angekommen! Herzlichen Dank dafür!
Bitte verzeih, dass ich erst heute schreibe, aber ich hatte
Schwierigkeiten, einen Flug zu bekommen. Im Sommer sind nicht
nur die Ferien, sondern auch die Fußballweltmeisterschaften in den
USA. So war ich zuerst bei zwei Fluglinien auf der Warteliste. Dann
hat mir eine ehemalige *(former)* Klassenkameradin geholfen — sie
arbeitet in einem Reisebüro.

Wenn alles gut geht, werde ich am 22. Juli von Berlin nach New
York fliegen, von dort nach Salt Lake City, dann weiter nach Los
Angeles, wo ich um 22.25 Uhr ankomme. Ist es zu dieser späten
Tageszeit noch möglich, zu euch zu fahren? Mit dem Taxi? Oder soll
ich ein Zimmer im Flughafenhotel nehmen? Der Rückflug ist am
10. August und geht über Cincinnati und New York nach Berlin.

Unser Onkel Max ist gerade mit Oma und Derrik auf der Insel
Bornholm (Dänemark). Sie machen dort 14 Tage Urlaub. Onkel Max
muss ab Juni wieder in Köln arbeiten. Sie drehen dort eine
Fernsehserie. Dann kommt er erst im Herbst wieder nach Berlin,
meint er.

Also, bis zum nächsten Brief! Hoffentlich kannst du alles lesen,
ich habe so schnell geschrieben, da ich noch zum Arzt muss.

Lass dich umarmen,

deine Alexandra

P.S. Hast du einen Brief von Tante Ursula aus Cincinnati bekommen? Sie wollte uns beide eigentlich für August einladen. Was
meinst du?

16. Christa and Alexandra are most likely
    a. former classmates from high school.
    b. sisters.
    c. acquaintances.
    d. business colleagues.

17. Christa's postcard to Alexandra must have included
    a. an invitation to meet her in Cincinnati.
    b. questions about Alexandra's travel plans and dates.
    c. an invitation to come visit her someday.
    d. just family news.

18. In the second paragraph, Alexandra is worried because
    a. she's still on the waiting list for a flight.
    b. she's not sure if Christa wants her to come visit this summer.
    c. she's afraid that her flight won't arrive on time.
    d. she doesn't know about late-night transportation from the airport to Christa's house.

19. According to her flight schedule, Alexandra will be
    a. taking different routes to and from Los Angeles.
    b. flying directly from Berlin to Los Angeles and back.
    c. arriving in the early afternoon in Los Angeles.
    d. stopping for a few days in Cologne to visit her aunt.

20. One could infer from Alexandra's letter that Uncle Max
    a. usually resides in Berlin.
    b. usually resides in Denmark.
    c. is a very private person and does not share his plans with his niece.
    d. has no contact with members of his extended family.

SCORE [   ]

D. For each set below, choose the one response that is NOT an appropriate reply. (15 points)

21. Warst du schon in Spanien, an der Costa Brava?
    a. Ja, wir fahren jedes Jahr ans Mittelmeer.
    b. Ja, dort gibt es herrliche Sandstrände, nicht wahr?
    c. Ich schlage vor, wir fahren an die Ostsee.
    d. Ja, wir fahren gern ans Mittelmeer.

22. Was schlägst du vor?
    a. Ich bin dafür, dass wir mit der Bahn fahren.
    b. Fahren wir mal mit dem Bus!
    c. Ich habe gar keine Idee. Vielleicht hat Markus eine gute Idee.
    d. Was soll ich bloß machen?

![Chapter Test]

23. Verzeihung! Wissen Sie vielleicht, wie ich zum Golfplatz komme?
    a. Gehen wir mal auf den Golfplatz!
    b. Ich bezweifle, dass es hier einen Golfplatz gibt.
    c. Tut mir Leid. Ich bin nicht von hier.
    d. Ja, der ist gleich um die Ecke.

24. Fahren wir mal in die Vereinigten Staaten!
    a. Ich bezweifle, dass wir die Reise noch buchen können.
    b. Ich bin nicht sicher, ob ich so viel Geld ausgeben möchte.
    c. Aber wir waren letztes Jahr in den Staaten.
    d. Das ist gerade passiert.

25. Hier darf man gar nicht angeln. Schade!
    a. Ja, ich fahre gern ans Meer.
    b. Ja, das ist nun leider so.
    c. Ja, aber da kann man nichts machen.
    d. Aber ich bin sicher, dass man hier angeln darf!

SCORE [   ]

III. Culture

Maximum Score: 10 points

E. Based on your cultural knowledge of Germany, mark the following statements true (**a**) or false (**b**). (10 points)

_____ 26. Generally, German students expect to travel somewhere during their summer vacation, although some do get a **Ferienjob.**

_____ 27. Summer vacation dates for the **Bundesländer** are staggered.

_____ 28. The beach is a popular vacation spot.

_____ 29. About 80% of German teenagers travel to another country for vacation.

_____ 30. Spain and France are extremely popular vacation spots.

_____ 31. Visiting grandparents or other relatives for vacation is very uncommon.

_____ 32. According to **Zum Lesen** in **Kapitel 9** most <u>younger</u> teens would like to visit a farm if they had their choice.

_____ 33. Younger teens are more interested in amusement parks than in any other vacation goal.

_____ 34. Most teens prefer to travel by themselves and meet new people, rather than go with family or friends from school.

_____ 35. Summer vacation for students is six weeks long.

SCORE ☐

IV. Writing

Maximum Score: 30 points

F. Your pen pal wonders whether you would rather go on a vacation with your family or with your friends. Explain the advantages and/or disadvantages of the vacation you prefer. (You might think about the types of transportation, activities, and places to stay, and what the differences are, depending on whom you go with.) Write at least five sentences. (15 points)

_____

_____

_____

_____

_____

_____

_____

_____

_____

_____

_____

_____

_____

SCORE ☐

KAPITEL 9

Chapter Test

G. Which part of your town or city do you like and know well? Choose five specific locations (buildings, parks, monuments, famous landmarks, etc.) and write a short walking-tour guide for a visitor from Germany. Write at least five sentences. (Using imperative forms such as **Geh!** is acceptable.) (15 points)

_____

_____

_____

_____

_____

_____

_____

_____

_____

_____

_____

_____

_____

_____

SCORE ☐

TOTAL SCORE ☐

KAPITEL 9 Chapter Test Score Sheet

Circle the letter that matches the most appropriate response.

I. Listening
Maximum Score: 30 points

A. (16 points)

1. a b	5. a b
2. a b	6. a b
3. a b	7. a b
4. a b	8. a b

SCORE [ ]

B. (14 points)

9. a b	13. a b
10. a b	14. a b
11. a b	15. a b
12. a b	

SCORE [ ]

II. Reading
Maximum Score: 30 points

C. (15 points)

16. a b c d
17. a b c d
18. a b c d
19. a b c d
20. a b c d

SCORE [ ]

D. (15 points)

21. a b c d
22. a b c d
23. a b c d
24. a b c d
25. a b c d

SCORE [ ]

III. Culture
Maximum Score: 10 points

E. (10 points)

26. a b	31. a b
27. a b	32. a b
28. a b	33. a b
29. a b	34. a b
30. a b	35. a b

SCORE [ ]

KAPITEL 9

IV. Writing

Maximum Score: 30 points

G. (15 points)

_____
_____
_____
_____
_____
_____
_____
_____
_____
_____
_____
_____

SCORE [   ]

H. (15 points)

_____
_____
_____
_____
_____
_____
_____
_____
_____
_____
_____
_____
_____
_____

SCORE [   ]

TOTAL SCORE [   ]

Holt German 2 Komm mit!, Chapter 9

Listening Scripts for Quizzes 9-1B, 9-2B, 9-3B

Quiz 9-1B Kapitel 9 Erste Stufe

I. Listening

A.   GESA   Wie lange hast du dieses Jahr Urlaub?

     ULF   Leider nur drei Wochen. Eigentlich zwanzig Tage. Warum fragst du? Willst du was vorschlagen?

     GESA   Ja, schon. Ich bin dafür, dass wir dieses Jahr mal nicht an die Nordsee oder nach Österreich in die Berge fahren. Dieses Jahr möchte ich etwas ganz anderes machen.

     ULF   Na, und was schlägst du denn vor?

     GESA   Ich möchte was ganz Einmaliges unternehmen, am liebsten nach Ägypten fliegen und mir die Pyramiden und den Nil einmal ansehen. Weißt du, das habe ich mir schon immer gewünscht.

     ULF   Dann machen wir das doch mal. Keine schlechte Idee, finde ich.

     GESA   Dann könnten wir von Alexandrien aus eine kleine Schiffsreise auf dem Mittelmeer machen — ein paar Tage auf einer griechischen Insel verbringen — und dann von Malta nach Frankfurt zurückfliegen.

     ULF   Wahrscheinlich ist es aber im Sommer heiß. Immerhin, ich bin dafür, dass wir dieses Jahr deine Traumreise machen. Doch möchte ich nächstes Jahr wieder nach Tirol.

Quiz 9-2B Kapitel 9 Zweite Stufe

I. Listening

A.   HUGO   Also, wohin fahren wir dieses Jahr? Wieder nach Sylt? Oder lieber an die Ostsee? Hannah, was schlägst du vor?

     HANNAH   Ich fahre zwar sehr gern an die Nordsee, aber vielleicht doch dieses Jahr lieber ans Mittelmeer. Ich habe einen Reiseprospekt vom Club Mediterranean™ bekommen — die haben eine tolle Auswahl von Resorts im Süden — in Tunesien, Algerien und Marokko und auch auf Sardinien, Kreta und einigen anderen Inseln.

     ARNDT   Und was gibt's dort zu tun? Ich möchte eigentlich mal Tauchen lernen oder Schnorcheln.

     HANNAH   Ja, Arndt, kannst du. Und Windsurfen auch. Und die Hotels haben fast alle auch Saunas und Fitnessräume — und Diskotheken. Also wird sich keiner von uns langweilen, meine ich.

     HUGO   Ich bezweifle, dass ich meine Ferien in Diskotheken verbringen werde, aber Golfplätze — gibt es dort welche?

     HANNAH   Das weiß ich nicht, aber ich kann mich bei dem Club Med™ in Paris erkundigen, wenn ihr dafür seid, dass wir so ein Resort besuchen.

     ARNDT   Ich bin auf jeden Fall dafür. Auf Sylt gibt es fast keine Leute in meinem Alter. Die reisen ja alle in den Süden hin, nach Spanien oder Portugal.

     HANNAH   Eben.

Quiz 9-3B Kapitel 9 Dritte Stufe

I. Listening

A. 1.   STUDENTIN   Entschuldigen Sie, bitte, können Sie mir sagen, ob es hier in der Nähe ein Café gibt?

     PASSANT   Klar doch. Sehen Sie das Rathaus? Wenn Sie hier die Farbstraße ein Stück weitergehen, kommen Sie an das Hormoldhaus. Gehen Sie daran vorbei, und dann sehen Sie gleich rechts das Café. Es liegt zwischen dem Hormoldhaus und dem Schloss.

     STUDENTIN   Danke schön!

     PASSANT   Bitte, bitte.

   2.   STUDENTIN   Entschuldige, bitte! Kannst du mir sagen, wie ich von hier zum Reisebüro komme?

     STUDENT   Ja. Also, geh hier die Hauptstraße bis zur Pfarrstraße entlang. Dann biegst du in die Pfarrstraße ein und gehst zwei Straßen weiter. Da siehst du rechts so ein altes Fachwerkhaus. Das ist das Kleine Bürgerhaus. Das Reisebüro liegt auf der linken Seite, gegenüber vom Bürgerhaus.

     STUDENTIN   Vielen Dank!

     STUDENT   Bitte. Nichts zu danken.

ANSWERS Quiz 9-1A

A. (20 points; 2 points per item)
1. **f.** an die
2. **b.** in die
3. **a.** nach
4. **b.** in die
5. **e.** aufs
6. **a.** nach
7. **c.** ans
8. **b.** in die
9. **d.** auf den
10. **a.** nach

B. (10 points; 1 point per item)
11. auf den
12. ins
13. auf die
14. in die
15. an den
16. an den
17. nach
18. in die
19. in den
20. in die

ANSWERS Quiz 9-1B

I. Listening

A. (12 points: 2 points per item)
1. F
2. T
3. T
4. F
5. T
6. F

II. Reading

B. (6 points: 2 points per item)
7. b
8. b
9. d

III. Writing

C. (12 points: 4 points per item)
Answers will vary. Possible answers:
10. Ich weiß nicht. Was schlägst du vor?
11. Ich bin dafür, dass wir zum Busbahnhof laufen.
12. Was machen wir bloß?

IV. Culture

D. (10 points: 2 points per item)
13. F
14. T
15. F
16. T
17. T

ANSWERS Quiz 9-2A

A. (20 points; 2 points per item)
Answers will vary. Possible answers:
1. Gibt es dort einen Tennisplatz
2. es dort einen Tennisplatz gibt
3. Gibt es dort eine Sauna
4. es dort eine Sauna gibt
5. Kann man dort tauchen
6. man dort tauchen kann
7. Gibt es dort eine Diskothek
8. es dort eine Diskothek gibt
9. Gibt es dort eine Liegewiese
10. es dort eine Liegewiese gibt

B. (10 points; 2 points per item)
11. an der
12. in die
13. in den
14. an den
15. nach

C. (10 points; 1 point per item)
16. nach
17. in
18. auf den
19. auf dem
20. in die
21. in den
22. in die
23. in der
24. aufs
25. auf dem

ANSWERS Quiz 9-2B

I. Listening

A. (8 points: 2 points per item)
1. T
2. T
3. T
4. F

II. Reading

B. (6 points: 2 points per item)
5. d
6. b
7. b

III. Writing

C. (16 points: 4 points per sentence)
Answers will vary.

ANSWERS Quiz 9-3A

A. (10 points; 1 point per item)
1. aus dem
2. bei der
3. vom
4. gegenüber vom
5. zum
6. zur
7. beim
8. vor dem
9. neben der
10. von der

B. (20 points; 2 points per item)
11. zwischen dem
12. dem
13. zwischen das
14. das
15. im
16. in den
17. in der
18. ins
19. neben der
20. durchs

ANSWERS Quiz 9-3B

I. Listening

A. (6 points: 3 points per item)

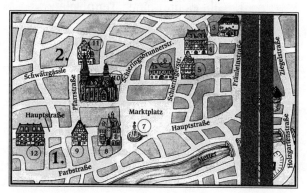

II. Reading

B. (4 points: 2 points per item)
3. a
4. c

III. Writing

C. (20 points: 4 points per item)
5. Bietigheim liegt an der Metter.
6. Der Brunnen steht auf dem Markt-platz.
7. Das Kachelsche Haus ist in der Schieringerstraße.
8. Die Kirche ist gegenüber vom Kleinen Bürgerhaus.
9. Der Parkplatz befindet sich in der Holzgartenstraße.

Scripts for Chapter Test Kapitel 9

I. Listening

A.

HILDA   Wir freuen uns schon sehr auf das Bach Fest, aber wir wissen noch nicht, was wir sonst noch machen sollen. Was schlägst du vor?

MIKE   In Oregon? Ja, also ich komme aus Oregon. Da kannst du den ganzen Sommer verbringen und noch immer nicht alles gesehen haben. Wie lange bleibt ihr eigentlich?

HILDA   Wir landen am 26. Juni in Portland und fliegen am 17. Juli von Banff in Kanada zurück. Wir wollen nämlich die Staaten und Kanada in 3 Wochen bereisen und so viel wie möglich sehen.

MIKE   Die Zeit ist wahnsinnig knapp. Aber, wenn das so ist, dann schlage ich als Erstes vor, ihr mietet euch ein Auto und nehmt eure Campingsachen mit. Doch am besten bucht ihr die Campingplätze schon im Voraus, denn ich glaube nicht, dass zu der Jahreszeit noch viele Plätze frei sind.

HILDA   Und hast du eine Idee wo?

MIKE   Ich habe ganz viele Ideen. Von Eugene aus sollt ihr unbedingt an den Pazifischen Ozean fahren.

HILDA   Ich fahre gern ans Meer. Kann man in Oregon surfen? Ich habe das noch nie gemacht.

MIKE   Das schon, aber ich bezweifle, dass du so schnell surfen lernst. Doch ihr könnt eine Tagesfahrt mit einem Fischerei-Boot machen und angeln und auch am Sandstrand nach Muscheln suchen.

HILDA   Und was sonst noch?

MIKE   Na, ihr fahrt eben die Küste entlang bis in den nördlichen Teil vom Staate Washington, und dann durch den Olympic National Park. Dort könnt ihr ein bisschen bergsteigen — auf den Mount Olympus, macht euch bestimmt Spaß. Und weiter nach Port Townsend, dann mit der Autofähre nach Victoria in Kanada.

HILDA   Und die Fahrt lohnt sich? Macht Spaß?

MIKE   Das könnt ihr mir glauben! Vergesst ja nicht die Kamera! Diese Küste ist ganz anders als die Nordsee oder die Ostsee in Deutschland.

B.

KLAUS   Hast du das Hotel heute angerufen?

REGINA   Ja, aber leider sind sie schon die erste Julihälfte ausgebucht. Der Manager hat mir ein anderes Hotel im Ort vorgeschlagen, das noch Zimmer frei hat ... heißt La Paloma, und kostet ungefähr dasselbe.

KLAUS   Liegt es auch gleich am Strand?

REGINA   Ja, mit Blick aufs Meer. Das Hotel hat einen Fernsehraum, eine Liegewiese, Zimmertelefon und Lift.

KLAUS   Na. Fernsehraum und Liegewiese interessieren mich so gut wie gar nicht. Hat das Hotel einen Pool? Oder einen Tennisplatz?

REGINA   Das bezweifle ich sehr. Aber es liegt gleich neben dem Minigolfplatz, sagt der Manager.

KLAUS   Für ältere Leute ist das bestimmt ganz schön, aber ich glaube nicht, dass ich meinen Urlaub mit Faulenzen vertun möchte. Ich bin dafür, dass wir es erst mit ein paar anderen Hotels versuchen.

REGINA   Aber, was soll ich bloß machen? Der Ort ist bekannt für seine Segel- und Windsurfmöglichkeiten, und die Touristen buchen schon Monate im Voraus. Das ist nun leider so, Klaus.

Answers to Chapter Test Kapitel 9

I. Listening Maximum Score: 30 points

A. (16 points: 2 points per item) **B.** (14 points: 2 points per item)

1. b	9. a
2. a	10. b
3. b	11. a
4. b	12. b
5. a	13. b
6. a	14. a
7. b	15. a
8. a	

II. Reading Maximum Score: 30 points

C. (15 points: 3 points per item) **D.** (15 points: 3 points per item)

16. b	21. c
17. b	22. d
18. d	23. a
19. a	24. d
20. a	25. a

III. Culture Maximum Score: 10 points

E. (10 points: 1 point per item)

26. a
27. a
28. a
29. a
30. a
31. b
32. a
33. b
34. b
35. a

IV. Writing Maximum Score: 30 points

F. (15 points: 3 points per item)
Answers will vary.

G. (15 points: 3 points per item)
Answers will vary.

Viele Interessen!

■ Erste Stufe

Maximum Score: 40

Grammar and Vocabulary

A. Match the following descriptions of shows with the names of the types of show they represent. Write the correct German words in the blanks to the left of the descriptions. (10 points)

Kultursendung	Wetterbericht	Nachrichten	Sportübertragung
Natursendung	Diskussion über Politik
Werbung	Ratesendung	Krimi	Abenteuerfilm

1. _____ a show which encourages you to buy a certain product

2. _____ a show in which someone wins a lot of money

3. _____ a show where the police force catches the bad guy

4. _____ a show about staging an opera production

5. _____ a show about brown bears in the wilderness

6. _____ a show where a hero rescues someone

7. _____ a show which tells you that it will be sunny tomorrow

8. _____ a show which tells you news about the world

9. _____ a show where three politicians talk about their platforms

10. _____ a show televising the German national soccer match

SCORE [_____]

Quiz 10-1A

B. The **ORF (Österreichischer Rundfunk)** is conducting an on-air survey to find out what shows teenagers are interested in seeing. Complete the following questions and replies by filling in the blanks with the correct reflexive pronouns, indefinite articles, prepositions, and **wo-** or **da-**compounds. (30 points)

ORF SPRECHER   11. _____ interessierst du dich?

JUNGE   Ich interessiere 12. _____ 13. _____ Sportsendungen.

ORF SPRECHER   Interessierst du 14. _____ auch 15. _____ ?

zweiter JUNGE   Wie bitte? Ich habe leider Ihre Frage nicht gehört. 16. _____ sprechen Sie?

ORF SPRECHER   Wir sprechen 17. _____ Sportsendungen.

zweiter JUNGE   Ach, ja! Ich interessiere 18. _____ auch

19. _____ ! Ich freue 20. _____ auch

21. _____ 22. _____ Krimi.

ORF SPRECHER   Und 23. _____ interessieren 24. _____ die Mädchen?

erstes MÄDCHEN   Ich interessiere 25. _____ 26. _____ Spielshows und Komödien.

zweites MÄDCHEN   Aber ich interessiere 27. _____ nur

28. _____ Krimis! Du und deine Freundinnen, freut ihr

29. _____ nicht auch 30. _____ ?

erstes MÄDCHEN   Ganz und gar nicht! Unsere Eltern interessieren 31. _____

32. _____ !

ORF SPRECHER   Meine Damen und Herren, Sie haben es gehört. Jungen interessieren

33. _____ 34. _____ Sportsendungen und

Krimis. Einige Mädchen freuen 35. _____

36. _____ Krimis, andere interessieren

37. _____ 38. _____ Spielshows und Komö-

dien. 39. _____ freuen 40. _____ ihre

Eltern? Auch auf Krimis!

SCORE _____

TOTAL SCORE _____

KAPITEL 10

Name _____ Klasse _____ Datum _____

10 Viele Interessen!

■ Erste Stufe

Maximum Score: 40

I. Listening

A. Herr and Frau Wegli are working at an institute near Washington, DC. An interviewer conducting a survey asks Herr Wegli about TV programs. As you listen to their conversation, think about the following questions. Then answer the questions briefly in English. (10 points)

1. What do Herr und Frau Wegli watch? _____

   _____

2. Which channel do they prefer? _____

3. Why do they prefer this channel? _____

   _____

4. What does Udo watch? _____

5. Who watches more TV on average, Udo or the Weglis? _____

SCORE [   ]

II. Reading

B. After reading the following passage, choose the best answer from among the alternatives given. (8 points)

Was tun deutsche Jugendliche, um zu relaxen?

Wir haben einhundert deutsche Jugendliche gefragt, was sie tun, um zu relaxen. Die meisten Jugendlichen haben geantwortet, dass sie zur Entspannung fernsehen. Viele haben auch geantwortet, dass sie CDs oder Radio hören. Zwanzig Jugendliche sagten, dass sie sich gern mit Freunden oder Eltern und Geschwistern unterhalten (converse). Wichtig ist hierbei die Tatsache (fact), dass sie sich unterhalten und nicht worüber sie sich unterhalten. Zehn Jugendliche spielen gern auf dem Computer. Einige Jugendliche haben gesagt, dass sie zur Entspannung gern Bücher oder Zeitschriften lesen. Aber nur zwei der Befragten lesen gern Tageszeitungen. Wir waren etwas überrascht, dass nur drei Jugendliche im Internet surfen, um zu relaxen.

6. Was tun nicht viele Jugendliche, um zu relaxen?
   a. fernsehen
   b. CDs hören
   c. im Internet surfen
   d. auf dem Computer spielen

Quiz 10-1B

7. Worüber unterhalten sich Jugendliche, um zu entspannen?
   a. über die Schule
   b. Das Thema spielt keine Rolle.
   c. über die Eltern und Geschwister
   d. über Bücher und Zeitschriften

SCORE

III. Writing

C. Write at least three complete sentences to include in a letter to your pen pal explaining what kinds of TV shows you do and don't like to watch and why. (12 points)

_____

_____

_____

_____

_____

_____

SCORE

IV. Culture

D. Choose the best answers from among the alternatives given. (8 points)

8. Public television in Germany is paid for by
   a. contributions from various foundations and corporations.
   b. voluntary contributions from the viewing public.
   c. manufacturers of televisions.
   d. a tax or license collected from the owners of every TV set in use.

9. The television industry's oversight agency is
   a. mostly controlled by the corporate sponsors.
   b. mostly controlled by private TV stations.
   c. federally regulated to represent the various taxpayers.
   d. regulated by the people who produce the shows.

E. Mark the following statement true (**T**) or false (**F**). (2 points)

_____ 10. On non-cable German channels, commercials appear about every
            ten minutes, as in the United States.

SCORE

TOTAL SCORE

Holt German 2 Komm mit!, Chapter 10

Viele Interessen!

■ Zweite Stufe

Grammar and Vocabulary

A. Write the correct words from the box below in the blanks in the conversation. Capitalize words when necessary. (10 points)

lassen	**laufen**	**lass**	**lasst**	**lassen**
lässt	**laufe**	**läuft**	**lauft**	**lauf**

DU   Frau Schneider, **1.** _____ Sie mich bitte meine

Hausaufgaben erst morgen machen, denn ein spannender Abenteuerfilm

2. _____ heute Abend im Fernsehen.

FRAU SCHNEIDER   Nein, nein, mein Junge, **3.** _____ das Programm ohne dich

4. _____ !

DU   Aber, bitte, Frau Schneider, alle wollen das Programm sehen!

FRAU SCHNEIDER   Mein Junge, du weißt, dass wir montags immer viele Hausaufgaben

haben. **5.** _____ schnell nach Hause und mach deine

Hausaufgaben.

DU   Vielleicht **6.** _____ meine Mutter mich die Hausaufgaben

morgen früh machen. Also gut, ich **7.** _____ schnell nach

Hause, mache einen Teil der Hausaufgaben, und sehe mir das Programm an.

FRAU SCHNEIDER   Babsi und Klaus, würden euere Eltern euch die Hausaufgaben morgen

früh machen **8.** _____ ?

BABSI u. KLAUS   Natürlich nicht, Frau Schneider, niemals! Wenn wir unsere Eltern fragen

würden, „Mutti und Vati, **9.** _____ ihr uns unsere

Haufgaben nach dem Fernsehen machen?" würden sie nur lachen und

dann zu uns sagen: „**10.** _____ schnell in eure Zimmer und

macht sofort die Hausaufgaben!"

SCORE ☐

Quiz 10-2A

B. Make your own television survey, using the following cues to write the questions.
(10 points)

     haben / was für / Fernsehgerät / ihr

11. _____

     ihr / Kabelfernsehen / oder / Zimmerantenne / haben

12. _____

     es / im Haus / Fernseh- und Videowagen / geben

13. _____

     wie / ihr / euer / einschalten / Fernsehgerät

14. _____

     wann / gebrauchen / du / Kopfhörer / ein

15. _____

SCORE ☐

C. Write answers to the questions you have created. Use complete sentences.
(10 points)

16. _____

17. _____

18. _____

19. _____

20. _____

SCORE ☐

TOTAL SCORE ☐

KAPITEL 10

10 Viele Interessen!

Name _____ Klasse _____ Datum _____

■ Zweite Stufe

Maximum Score: 30

I. Listening

A. Lotte is trying to run a computer program she wrote. Her brother Willie is helping her. Before you listen to their conversation, read the following statements. After you listen, mark the statements true (**T**) or false (**F**). (6 points)

_____ 1. Lotte is working on a math program.

_____ 2. Willie knows very little about how to run their computer.

_____ 3. Lotte is going to let Willie fix her program.

SCORE _____

II. Reading

B. Read the conversation and then answer the questions that follow. (12 points)

HEIKE   Was läuft im Fernsehen? Es ist Viertel nach acht. Da kommt bestimmt eine gute Sendung.

BETTINA   Lass mich mal im Fernsehmagazin nachsehen. Also, Montag, 20:15. Im ZDF kommt ein Fernsehfilm, „Die Rache der Carola Waas".

HEIKE   Worum geht's in diesem Film?

BETTINA   Ein Mann fährt in das Auto von Carola Waas und ihrer Familie. Er begeht Fahrerflucht *(hit-and-run)*. Carola verbringt den Rest ihres Lebens damit, ihn zu suchen. Sie will Rache *(revenge)* nehmen.

HEIKE   Hmm ... Was kommt im ARD?

BETTINA   „Die Schlagerparade der Volkmusik" mit Jantje Smit und dem Alpentrio Tirol. Im RTL kommt „Quiz Einundzwanzig". Sat1 zeigt einen Krimi, „Wolffs Revier", und Pro7 zeigt „Akte X — Die unheimlichen Fälle des FBI".

HEIKE   Ich glaube, dass montags immer „Hör mal, wer da hämmert" mit Tim Allen kommt. Vielleicht im Super RTL?

BETTINA   Ja, stimmt! Ich finde, dass der Allen ein lustiger Schauspieler ist.

4. Welcher Sender zeigt eine Ratesendung?
   a. ZDF   **b.** RTL   **c.** Super RTL   **d.** ARD

5. Was für Lieder singt das Alpentrio Tirol?
   a. Volkslieder   **b.** Operetten   **c.** Chansons   **d.** Liebeslieder

6. Welche Sendung sehen sich Heike und Bettina wahrscheinlich an?
   a. „Hör mal, wer da hämmert"   **c.** „Quiz Einundzwanzig"
   b. „Die Rache der Carola Waas"   **d.** „Wolffs Revier"

SCORE _____

Quiz 10-2B

III. Writing

C. You are with your German host family in their living room. Write the following sentences as indicated. (12 points)

7. Ask the parents (politely) if you may watch the news on TV.

   _____

   _____

8. Ask your host sibling if you can have the remote control.

   _____

   _____

9. Tell your host sibling to let you turn the set on. (Use the separable-prefix verb **einschalten.**)

   _____

   _____

SCORE [   ]

TOTAL SCORE [   ]

Viele Interessen!

■ Dritte Stufe

Maximum Score: 30

Grammar and Vocabulary

A. You and your friends are all planning to own and do certain things in the future. Write the German equivalents of the following sentences about future plans, using the verb **werden**. (18 points)

I am going to have a great car.

1. _____

Bettina and Barbara are going to have a car with air conditioning.

2. _____

Johann, do you want to have a car with a sunroof?

3. _____

Ludwig is going to get a driver's license next year.

4. _____

We are going to have a car with an alarm system.

5. _____

My parents are going to sell their color television.

6. _____

SCORE ☐

B. Fill in the blanks with the correct form of **kein**. (7 points)

Ich finde es komisch, dass du dir **7.** _____ Auto mit Klimaanlage kaufst.

Kauf dieses Auto nicht, denn es hat **8.** _____ Scheibenwischer! Schau!

Du brauchst doch **9.** _____ Schiebedach. Das kostet zu viel.

Kauf dir doch **10.** _____ Auto ohne Alarmanlage!

Kauf dir dieses gebrauchte Auto nicht, weil es **11.** _____ Scheinwerfer hat.

Der Markus hat doch **12.** _____ Führerschein.

Ich habe jetzt **13.** _____ Zeit mehr!

SCORE ☐

Quiz 10-3A

C. Give two ways to express surprise, two ways to express agreement, and one way to express disagreement in German. (5 points)

Hier ist mein neues Auto! (surprise)

14. _____

Dieses Auto hat kein Radio! (surprise)

15. _____

Aufkleber sehen scheußlich aus. (agreement)

16. _____

Ein Schiebedach ist sehr praktisch. (agreement)

17. _____

Man soll das Fernsehen abschaffen. Jetzt wird ja nur noch geglotzt. (disagreement)

18. _____

SCORE [ ]

TOTAL SCORE [ ]

Name _____ Klasse _____ Datum _____

Viele Interessen!

■ Dritte Stufe

Maximum Score: 30

I. Listening

A. An interviewer for a teen magazine is talking to Heike, Rolf, and Julia. The question is: What do you expect to be doing in your 20s? Read the statements before you listen to the conversation. As you listen, decide whether the statements are true **(T)** or false **(F)**. (10 points)

_____ 1. Heike thinks she'll study and then get a job.

_____ 2. She says that she'll marry before she's 30.

_____ 3. Rolf thinks he'll marry in his late twenties.

_____ 4. Both Rolf and Heike are interested in traveling.

_____ 5. Julia does not plan to go to a university.

SCORE [   ]

II. Reading

B. Read the ad for a BMW below and then decide if the statements that follow are true (T) or false (F). (8 points)

Das neue BMW 3er Cabrio

Fahren Sie gern unter freiem Himmel? Das neue BMW Cabrio bietet Ihnen Fahrspaß, Komfort und Sicherheit. Elektrisch verstellbare Sitze, ein großer Innenraum und gute Akustik sorgen für Freude am Fahren. Ein Bordcomputer hilft Ihnen beim Navigieren. Zur Innenausstattung (*interior equipment*) gehören auch eine Digitaluhr, eine Klimaanlage und ein HiFi-Lautsprechersystem.

Zusätzliche Karosserieverstärkungen und sitzintegrierte Sicherheitsgurte machen dieses offene Auto sicher. Fahrer- und Beifahrer-Airbags und Seiten-Airbags gehören zur Serienausstattung. Das neue BMW 3er Cabrio hat eine Alarmanlage, ein Anti-Blockier-System, eine Servolenkung und eine Zentralverriegelung. In Sachen Sicherheit setzt dieses Cabrio einen neuen Standard.

Das Cabrio hat einen 2,5-Liter-Motor mit Vierventiltechnik. Die Höchstgeschwindigkeit ist 222 km/h. Das Cabrio braucht in der Stadt 12,8 l/km und auf der Autobahn 7,4 l/km.

Das BMW 3er Cabrio gibt Ihnen Spaß am Fahren. Überzeugen Sie sich selbst!

_____ 6. Das Cabrio braucht mehr Benzin *(gasoline)* auf der Autobahn als in der Stadt.

_____ 7. Dieser BMW hat ein großes Schiebedach.

Quiz 10-3B

_____ **8.** Die Ausstattung dieses Autos sorgt für Freude am Fahren, aber nicht für Sicherheit.

_____ **9.** Dieses Auto hat eine bequeme Innenausstattung.

SCORE [   ]

III. Writing

C. You and your pen pal have been corresponding for quite some time. Now he or she wants to know what you plan to do after you graduate from high school. He or she also asks about one of your friends whom you have often mentioned in your letters. Write at least 3 complete sentences using the future tense with **werden.**
(12 points)

_____

_____

_____

_____

_____

_____

SCORE [   ]

TOTAL SCORE [   ]

Holt German 2 Komm mit!, Chapter 10

KAPITEL 10

KAPITEL 10

Viele Interessen!

I. Listening

Maximum Score: 30 points

A. Hans Reiner has built up a career as a film director (**Regisseur**) for the East German television studios in Babelsberg. We interviewed him in **Köln**, where he's now working temporarily for an independent studio. After you listen to the interview, choose the best answers from among the alternatives given. (15 points)

1. From the interview with Reiner, it is clear that he is
   a. married with older children.
   b. a bachelor.
   c. no longer married.
   d. married with young children.

2. Reiner's reaction to the fall of the Berlin Wall was:
   a. It had no effect on him or his life.
   b. He was sorry to hear about it.
   c. He was very excited about it and almost immediately traveled to the West, to Hamburg.
   d. He was very excited, but decided never to leave East Germany.

3. Compared to the studios in West Germany, TV studios in East Germany were
   a. extremely modern.
   b. not as modern.
   c. practically nonexistent.
   d. technically more advanced.

4. The main difference for Reiner between East German and West German TV studios is:
   a. He can now choose his own scripts for shows.
   b. He's supposed to follow the script that the studio gives him.
   c. There's no difference at all.
   d. There's not much difference except that in the West business interests determine what will be produced.

5. When he was working for the East German studio, Reiner
   a. was only allowed to direct romance films.
   b. often directed romance films, but occasionally got a script that he thought was interesting.
   c. never directed romance films.
   d. had constant trouble with the censors.

SCORE [ ]

Chapter Test

B. Jack has saved some money and is set on buying a car. He's explaining this to Gisela, the new exchange student from Germany. Read the following statements before you listen to their conversation. After you listen, mark the statements true (**a**) or false (**b**). (15 points)

_____ 6. Jack is already 16 years old.

_____ 7. He's planning to buy a car.

_____ 8. Gisela isn't surprised that he's going to buy a car.

_____ 9. He has money for the car from his parents.

_____ 10. Gisela guesses that he'll want a Ford™.

_____ 11. He wants a Volkswagen™ "bug".

_____ 12. He's planning to buy a used car and fix it up himself.

_____ 13. He's hoping to get a custom paint job for his car one of these days.

_____ 14. Gisela says that in Germany, one can get an older model VW™ pretty easily.

_____ 15. Repair costs in Germany for old cars are very low.

SCORE [   ]

II. Reading

Maximum Score: 30 points

C. For each of the numbered sets below, choose the one response that is NOT an appropriate reply. (15 points)

16. Worüber habt ihr gesprochen?
    a. Über Politik eigentlich.
    b. Wir haben vieles diskutiert.
    c. Ich freue mich auf die Diskussion.
    d. Eigentlich über gar nichts.

17. Ich interessiere mich nicht dafür.
    a. Findest du das denn langweilig?
    b. Für wen interessierst du dich denn?
    c. Wofür interessierst du dich denn?
    d. Ich interessiere mich auch nicht dafür.

18. Weißt du, ob die Serie *Raumschiff Enterprise* noch im Fernsehen läuft?
    a. Ich meine, die gibt's nicht mehr.
    b. Lass mich im Fernsehprogramm nachschauen.
    c. Ich glaube schon, dass sie noch im Kabelkanal läuft.
    d. Das stimmt überhaupt nicht.

KAPITEL 10

Chapter Test

19. Ich habe im Lotto gewonnen!
    a. Das gibt's doch nicht!
    b. Das ist ja unglaublich!
    c. Ja, natürlich.
    d. Mensch, das ist doch nicht möglich!

20. Ich werde nach der Uni einen tollen Job finden.
    a. Wie willst du das machen?
    b. Was wirst du dann machen?
    c. Wie hast du das bloß gemacht?
    d. Was für einen Beruf willst du haben?

SCORE

D. Read the article and then answer the questions that follow. (15 points)

Viele Deutsche beklagen sich über (*complain about*) die vielen Filmen, die aus den USA kommen. In jeder deutschen Kleinstadt läuft mindestens ein Film aus den Vereinigten Staaten. Die Jugend zieht die englische Version mit deutschen Untertiteln vor, weil sie dann den neusten Slang sowie die Filmmusik „original" zu hören bekommt. Deutsche Kinder lernen Märchen (*fairy tales*) nicht mehr von den Gebrüdern Grimm, sondern vom Walt Disney® Studio.

Im deutschen Fernsehen sind viele Unterhaltungssendungen „amerikanisiert"; viele haben sogar Werbespots. Diese Werbung will Kinder zum Kauf von Computerspielen anregen (*entice*). Die Kinder wollen oft Sachen, die sie in den Werbespots sehen.

Ist es möglich, dass die deutsche Kultur von der amerikanischen Kultur verdrängt wird (*will be replaced*)? Ist es möglich, Kinder gleichzeitig (*at the same time*) für regionale, nationale und europäische Sendungen zu interessieren?

Die Redaktion (*editors*) vom Elternkreis hört gerne von unseren Lesern. Was schlagen Sie vor? Schreiben Sie uns doch bitte!
Postfach 1078, D-10115 Berlin.

21. This article is probably
    a. a report of a news event.
    b. an editorial.
    c. a humor column.
    d. an article about the German movie industry.

22. The article says that many Germans complain about all of the following EXCEPT
    a. the effect of American-made movies on German culture.
    b. the Americanization of entertainment programs.
    c. the loss of German culture.
    d. the effect of Sesame Street® on German children.

KAPITEL 10

Chapter Test

23. German teens prefer
    a. American films with the original English soundtrack and German subtitles.
    b. German- or French-made films.
    c. American films with the soundtrack dubbed in German.
    d. none of the above.

24. According to the author, what may be happening to German children?
    a. They may no longer be interested in fairy tales.
    b. They watch too much TV.
    c. They may no longer learn German cultural values.
    d. They may no longer be interested in playing chess or card games.

25. The main concern for German parents is
    a. to balance regional cultural input with that of imported American media.
    b. to find new ways to tell old fairy tales.
    c. how to manipulate their children without their noticing it.
    d. to earn more money to spend on their kids.

SCORE [   ]

III. Culture

Maximum Score: 10 points

E. Choose the best answers from among the alternatives given. (10 points)

26. According to the statistics on television viewing in Germany given in this chapter,
    a. situation comedies are the most popular television shows.
    b. the largest percentage of the viewing public watches news.
    c. **Krimis** aren't very popular on German TV.
    d. talk shows and political discussions aren't even mentioned in the statistics.

27. The 1997 Hitparade revealed that young viewers most often watch
    a. the cable channels.
    b. the public channels (ARD and ZDF).
    c. only American cable channels.
    d. sports events.

28. The German ratings are taken
    a. by telephone surveys of representative households.
    b. by polling the advertising sponsors.
    c. by the watchdog agency called **Rundfunk- und Fernsehrat**.
    d. by computerized devices attached to people's television sets.

29. In order to get a driver's license in Germany, you need all of the following EXCEPT
    a. proof that you are 18 years old or older.
    b. at least 30 hours of driving practice.
    c. proof that you know at least basic first aid.
    d. at least 15 hours of classroom instruction.

30. According to the **Landeskunde** section of this chapter, you could say about the younger generation of Germans that
    a. they are interested in many of the same types of free-time activities as American teens.
    b. in-line skating and tandem jumping are unknown in Germany.
    c. they are not interested in trends which are popular in the United States.
    d. they have no time during the week to relax or pursue hobbies.

SCORE _____

IV. Writing

Maximum Score: 30 points

F. You have some money and intend to buy something really nice, like a TV or a car. Write 5 or more complete sentences to your pen pal, describing the TV or car and its various capabilities and features. What are the advantages of some of them? (15 points)

_____

_____

_____

_____

_____

_____

_____

_____

_____

_____

SCORE _____

KAPITEL 10

Chapter Test

G. Write a conversation using the directions below. (15 points)

Your German friend thinks that sixteen-year-olds (**Sechzehnjährige**) shouldn't be allowed to drive a car. State his opinion and your reaction (either agreement or disagreement).

31. ER _____

_____

_____

32. DU _____

_____

_____

Your friend intends to buy a motorcycle when he is 18. State his intent. Then express your surprise and whether or not you think that's a good idea.

33. ER _____

_____

_____

34. DU _____

_____

_____

State whether or not you are also interested in motorcycles.

35. DU _____

_____

_____

SCORE ☐

TOTAL SCORE ☐

KAPITEL 10

Name _____ Klasse _____ Datum _____

Circle the letter that matches the most appropriate response.

I. Listening
Maximum Score: 30 points

A. (15 points)

1. a b c d
2. a b c d
3. a b c d
4. a b c d
5. a b c d

SCORE ☐

B. (15 points)

6. a b
7. a b
8. a b
9. a b
10. a b

11. a b
12. a b
13. a b
14. a b
15. a b

SCORE ☐

II. Reading
Maximum Score: 30 points

C. (15 points)

16. a b c d
17. a b c d
18. a b c d
19. a b c d
20. a b c d

SCORE ☐

D. (15 points)

21. a b c d
22. a b c d
23. a b c d
24. a b c d
25. a b c d

SCORE ☐

III. Culture
Maximum Score: 10 points

E. (10 points)

31. a b c d
32. a b c d
33. a b c d
34. a b c d
35. a b c d

SCORE ☐

K A P I T E L 1 0

IV. Writing

Maximum Score: 30 points

F. (15 points)

_____

_____

_____

_____

_____

_____

_____

_____

_____

SCORE ☐

G. (15 points)

31. ER _____

_____

_____

32. DU _____

_____

_____

33. ER _____

_____

_____

34. DU _____

_____

_____

35. DU _____

_____

_____

SCORE ☐

TOTAL SCORE ☐

Listening Scripts for Quizzes 10-1B, 10-2B, 10-3B

Quiz 10-1B Kapitel 10 Erste Stufe

I. Listening

INTERVIEWER	Ich möchte Sie nun für unsere Umfrage zur Hilfe ziehen. Darf ich Sie fragen, was Sie im Fernsehen schauen?
HERR WEGLI	So, was wir schauen? ... Nachrichten, natürlich, und sonst so einiges im Dritten Programm. Wir mögen es nicht, wenn alle 15 Minuten Werbung kommt, wissen Sie?
FRAU WEGLI	Das stimmt. Die mögen wir gar nicht, die Werbung.
HERR WEGLI	Und meine Frau hier, sie schaut gerne Spielshows, nicht wahr?
FRAU WEGLI	Ja, die sind manchmal ganz lustig.
INTERVIEWER	Also, was meinen Sie, wie viele Stunden läuft bei Ihnen normalerweise der Fernseher pro Tag? eine Stunde? zwei Stunden? drei oder mehr?
HERR WEGLI	Das weiß ich nicht. Hast du eine Ahnung?
FRAU WEGLI	Normalerweise? Nun, vielleicht zwei Stunden. Mehr nicht.
INTERVIEWER	Und der Junge? Was schaut er am liebsten?
HERR WEGLI	Dies ist der Udo. Udo ist unser Enkelsohn. Der ist jetzt bei uns zu Besuch. Freut uns doch immer, wenn er kommt.
INTERVIEWER	Tag, Udo. Schaust du auch gern Spielshows?
UDO	Ach, nein! Ich schaue Sportsendungen — eigentlich finde ich Eurosport ganz gut. Und MTV™ finde ich toll. Bei mir läuft der Fernseher drei Stunden oder mehr. Das können Sie mir glauben!
INTERVIEWER	Also, herzlichen Dank allerseits.

Quiz 10-2B Kapitel 10 Zweite Stufe

I. Listening

LOTTE	Mensch! Schon wieder Pech! Das gibt es doch nicht!
WILLIE	Kann ich dir helfen? Ich kenne doch diesen Computer. Was willst du eigentlich damit machen?
LOTTE	Na, irgendwie habe ich etwas Falsches gemacht, und jetzt hänge ich fest. Ich will einfach raus.
WILLIE	Also, zuerst Control-break drücken. Hier, lass mich das machen! Also, jetzt haben wir den Fehler gefunden. Nun, weißt du, ob du am Anfang F1 eingeschaltet hast?
LOTTE	Ja, natürlich. Ich meine doch, dass ich jetzt auf mein Printout schauen soll. Da kann ich wahrscheinlich den Fehler sehen.
WILLIE	Nein, gucken wir lieber auf den Monitor. Zeig mal! So, was hast du hier gemacht? Was soll das?
LOTTE	Ich muss eine Kalkulation machen.
WILLIE	Du bist in Mathe schon so weit? Und wofür steht dieses X?
LOTTE	Für die Nummer, die ich hier unten angegeben habe.
WILLIE	Ich meine nicht, dass das logisch ist. Der Computer versteht das bestimmt nicht so.
LOTTE	Doch, soll er. Lass mich mal ins Buch schauen. Gibst du es mir bitte?
WILLIE	Hier, bitte.
LOTTE	Nun, guck doch. Hier ist die Aufgabe und dort das Rechenbeispiel.
WILLIE	Hmm ... das ist doch alles ziemlich kompliziert. Wofür steht dieses Y?
LOTTE	Das verstehst du auch nicht? Dann lässt du es mich lieber alleine versuchen, denn Mathe verstehe ich wenigstens schon.

Quiz 10-3B Kapitel 10 Dritte Stufe

I. Listening

INTERVIEWER	Ja, und jetzt werde ich dich etwas Persönliches fragen: Was willst du alles machen, wenn du in deinen Zwanzigern bist?
HEIKE	Hmm ... Also, ich werde zuerst studieren, glaube ich, und dann einen guten Job bei einer soliden Firma finden. Dann werde ich mir wohl einen Sportwagen und fesche Klamotten kaufen.
INTERVIEWER	Und sonst noch etwas?
HEIKE	Ja, ich werde mein Leben ganz groß genießen. Reisen werde ich auch — nach New York und San Francisco, und nach Hawaii, da habe ich einen Brieffreund. Ich werde ihn besuchen und dort surfen.
INTERVIEWER	Und wie steht's mit dir, Rolf? Was wirst du wohl machen?
ROLF	Ich möchte gerne eine Reise um die Welt machen und vielleicht ein oder zwei Jahre in den USA studieren. Ich glaube, dass ich heiraten werde, aber erst mit 27 oder 28.
INTERVIEWER	Und du, Julia, was wirst du wohl machen?
JULIA	Ich werde an der Uni Medizin studieren, denn ich möchte Ärztin werden.

ANSWERS Quiz 10-1A

A. (10 points; 1 point per item)
1. Werbung
2. Ratesendung
3. Krimi
4. Kultursendung
5. Natursendung
6. Abenteuerfilm
7. Wetterbericht
8. Nachrichten
9. Diskussion über Politik
10. Sportübertragung

B. (30 points; 1 point per item)
11. Wofür
12. mich
13. für
14. dich
15. dafür
16. Worüber
17. über
18. mich
19. dafür
20. mich
21. auf
22. einen
23. wofür
24. sich
25. mich
26. für
27. mich
28. für
29. euch
30. darauf
31. sich
32. dafür
33. sich
34. für
35. sich
36. auf
37. sich
38. für
39. Worauf
40. sich

ANSWERS Quiz 10-1B

I. Listening

A. (10 points: 2 points per item)
1. news and game shows
2. public TV / **Drittes Programm**
3. less advertising
4. sports and MTV
5. Udo

II. Reading

B. (8 points: 4 points per item)
6. c
7. b

III. Writing

C. (12 points: 4 points per sentence)
Answers will vary.

IV. Culture

D. (8 points: 4 points per item)
8. d
9. c

E. (2 points)
10. F

KAPITEL 10

ANSWERS Quiz 10-2A

A. (10 points; 1 point per item)
1. lassen
2. läuft
3. lass
4. laufen
5. Lauf
6. lässt
7. laufe
8. lassen
9. lasst
10. Lauft

B. (10 points; 2 points per item)
Answers will vary. Possible answers:
11. Was für ein Fernsehgerät habt ihr?
12. Habt ihr Kabelfernsehen oder eine Zimmerantenne?
13. Gibt es im Haus einen Fernseh- und Videowagen?
14. Wie schaltet ihr euer Fernsehgerät ein?
15. Wann gebrauchst du einen Kopfhörer?

C. (10 points; 2 points per item)
Answers will vary. Possible answers:
16. Wir haben einen Farbfernseher.
17. Wir haben Kabelfernsehen/eine Zimmerantenne.
18. Ja, im Haus gibt es einen Fernseh- und Videowagen.
19. Wir gebrauchen eine Fernbedienung.
20. Ich gebrauche einen Kopfhörer, wenn andere Leute die Sendung nicht hören wollen.

ANSWERS Quiz 10-2B

I. Listening

A. (6 points: 2 points per item)
1. T
2. F
3. F

II. Reading

B. (12 points: 4 points per item)
4. b
5. a
6. a

III. Writing

C. (12 points: 4 points per item)
Answers will vary. Possible answers:
7. Darf ich bitte die Nachrichten im Fernsehen schauen?
8. Kann ich bitte die Fernbedienung haben?
9. Lass mich den Fernseher einschalten.

ANSWERS Quiz 10-3A

A. (18 points; 3 points per item)
Answers will vary. Possible answers:
1. Ich werde ein tolles Auto haben.
2. Bettina und Barbara werden ein Auto mit einer Klimaanlage haben.
3. Johann, willst du ein Auto mit einem Schiebedach haben?
4. Ludwig wird nächstes Jahr den Führerschein machen.
5. Wir werden ein Auto mit einer Alarmanlage haben.
6. Meine Eltern werden ihren Farbfernseher verkaufen.

B. (7 points; 1 point per item)
7. kein
8. keine
9. kein
10. kein
11. keine
12. keinen
13. keine

C. (5 points; 1 point per item)
Answers will vary. Possible answers:
14. Das ist ja unglaublich!/Das ist nicht möglich!
15. Das gibt's doch nicht!
16. Da stimm ich dir zu!
17. Da hast du (bestimmt) Recht!/Einverstanden!
18. Das finde ich nicht./Das stimmt (überhaupt) nicht.

ANSWERS Quiz 10-3B

I. Listening

A. (10 points: 2 points per item)
1. T
2. F
3. T
4. T
5. F

II. Reading

B. (8 points: 2 points per item)
6. F
7. F
8. F
9. T

III. Writing

C. (12 points: 4 points per sentence)
Answers will vary. Possible answers:
Nach der Schule werde ich an der Uni studieren. Danach werde ich einen Job mit einem guten Einkommen suchen. Aber meine Freundin Anja wird nach der Schule erst eine Reise in die USA machen.

KAPITEL 10

Scripts for Chapter Test Kapitel 10

I. Listening

A.

INTERVIEWER   Als im November 1989 die Berliner Mauer fiel, ging das Echo rund um den ganzen Erdball. Aber wie hat es Sie persönlich getroffen?

REINER   Wir — meine Frau, meine Kinder und ich — wir waren außer uns vor Freude. Zuerst haben wir es kaum glauben können, aber schon im Dezember haben wir zu Weihnachten eine Reise in den Westen — nach Hamburg — gemacht. Das war das erste Mal, dass unsere Kinder, sie waren damals 18 und 20, überhaupt im Westen waren. Ich muss sagen, meine Frau und ich haben geweint, so schön war es!

INTERVIEWER   Ist es aber beruflich nicht schwierig für Sie gewesen?

REINER   Na, klar. Man hatte nämlich alles in der Fernsehindustrie doppelt eingerichtet — einmal in der BRD und noch einmal in der DDR — und unsre Studios im Osten waren natürlich nicht so modern und technisch hoch entwickelt. Jetzt legen wir die Studios zusammen, und das bedeutet, dass manche Kollegen, also Freunde von mir, dadurch arbeitslos sind — und ich jetzt zeitweise auch.

INTERVIEWER   Sie drehen jetzt hier in Köln einen Film, nicht wahr? Finden Sie, dass Sie hier im Westen freier arbeiten können?

REINER   Zum Teil schon, aber wissen Sie, für einen Fernsehregisseur ist es nicht so ganz anders als es im Osten war. Auch hier bekomme ich das Drehbuch vom Studio und habe mich ziemlich daran zu halten. Nur sind es hier mehr die kommerziellen Interessen, die entscheiden, ob ein Film produziert wird oder nicht. Das ist für das Studio sehr wichtig.

INTERVIEWER   Ist Ihnen der Stoff, ich meine, also sind die gegebenen Themen Ihnen nicht sympathischer als die, die in der DDR bevorzugt wurden?

REINER   Na ja, meistens haben wir so harmlose Themen behandeln müssen, wissen Sie, so Liebes- oder Heimatfilme. Aber ab und zu haben wir Filme gemacht, die mir außerordentlich gut gefallen haben — Filme mit interessanten und auch wichtigen Themen.

B.

GISELA   Ein Auto wirst du kaufen? Bist du schon achtzehn? Und wo hast du so viel Geld her, wenn ich fragen darf?

JACK   Wir dürfen schon ab 16 fahren. Ich habe den Führerschein schon seit Monaten, und ich habe durch meinen Sommerjob eine ganze Menge Geld gespart.

GISELA   Und was für ein Auto wirst du dir kaufen? Einen Ford™? Der ist aber auch teuer, oder?

JACK   Nein, nein. Ich werde mir einen ganz alten VW™ kaufen, einen Käfer.

GISELA   Ich meine aber, dass es die gar nicht mehr gibt. VW™ produziert seit Jahren keine Käfer mehr, und sie sind nach und nach alle alt geworden, also nicht mehr verkehrsfähig.

JACK   Hier bei uns sind die Käfer, also VWs™, zu Oldtimern geworden. Man repariert sie selbst, baut vielleicht einen neuen Motor ein, kauft sich neue Sitzschoner und ein paar bunte Aufkleber, und schon hat man ein tolles Auto, das noch jahrelang hält.

GISELA   Und Fahrvergnügen abgibt, nicht wahr?

JACK   Eben. Und sobald ich mehr Geld habe, werde ich mein Auto schön lackieren lassen — in ganz witzigen Farben — und es auf Oldtimer-Autoausstellungen zeigen.

GISELA   Bei uns in Deutschland könntest du so was nicht machen.

JACK   Warum denn nicht?

GISELA   Weil der Gebrauchtwagenmarkt solche alten Autos nicht anbieten darf. Das ist einfach so. Wir müssen unsere Autos regelmäßig vom TÜV überprüfen lassen, und der ist wahnsinnig streng. Alles, was nicht hundertprozentig in Ordnung ist, muss sofort zur Reparatur. Sonst darfst du das Auto nicht mehr fahren. Also werden die Reparaturkosten schon bei sechs- oder acht Jahre alten Autos sehr hoch.

JACK   Wie schade! Mein Käfer macht mir noch viel Spaß, besonders wenn er beim Anfahren so laut dröhnt.

GISELA   Hoffentlich hat eure Polizei einen Sinn für Humor!

Answers to Chapter Test Kapitel 10

I. Listening Maximum Score: 30 points

A. (15 points: 3 points per item)   **B.** (15 points: 1 ½ points per item)

1. a	6. a	11. a
2. c	7. a	12. a
3. b	8. b	13. a
4. d	9. b	14. b
5. b	10. a	15. b

II. Reading Maximum Score: 30 points

C. (15 points: 3 points per item)   **D.** (15 points: 3 points per item)

16. c	21. b
17. b	22. d
18. d	23. a
19. c	24. c
20. c	25. a

III. Culture Maximum Score: 10 points

E. (10 points: 2 points per item)

26. b
27. a
28. d
29. c
30. a

IV. Writing Maximum Score: 30 points

F. (15 points: 3 points per sentence)
Answers will vary.

G. (15 points: 3 points per sentence)
Answers will vary. Possible answers:
31. Sechzehnjährige sollen nicht Auto fahren.
32. Ich stimme dir zu! / Das finde ich nicht.
33. Ich werde ein Motorrad kaufen, wenn ich achtzehn bin.
34. Wirklich? Das finde ich toll! / Das finde ich nicht so gut.
35. Ich interessiere mich auch/nicht für Motorräder.

Holt German 2 Komm mit!, Chapter 10

KAPITEL 11

Mit Oma ins Restaurant

■ Erste Stufe

Maximum Score: 35

Grammar and Vocabulary

A. What would you like to do if you and your friends were in Berlin? Complete the conversation by filling in the blanks with the correct **würde**-form, and the correct article and noun. (23 points)

DU   Du, ich **1.** _____ am liebsten **2.** _____

3. _____ (the cathedral) besichtigen!

JANUS   Aber wir **4.** _____ zuerst **5.** _____

6. _____ (tour of the city) mit dem Bus machen.

DU   Das kann man immer tun! Was **7.** _____ du tun, Heiko?

HEIKO   Ich bin gar nicht sicher, wo man in Berlin anfangen soll. Anna und Imke, was

8. _____ ihr machen?

ANNA u. IMKE   Wir denken auch, dass man zuerst einen Überblick über die ganze Stadt

haben sollte. Die Katrina hat gesagt, sie **9.** _____ am liebsten

auch eine Stadtrundfahrt machen. Danach können wir etwas anderes

unternehmen.

DU   Also gut, dann stimme ich auch zu. Was **10.** _____ ihr alles

danach machen?

ALLE   Ich **11.** _____ gern **12.** _____

13. _____ (a symphony) hören. Wir **14.** _____

gern **15.** _____ **16.** _____ (an excursion)

machen. Jana und Klaus **17.** _____ gern

18. _____ **19.** _____ (a play) sehen. Der Lehrer

20. _____ gern **21.** _____

22. _____ (a monument) oder eine **23.** _____

(synagogue) sehen.

SCORE [   ]

KAPITEL 11

Quiz 11-1A

B. In talking about all the sightseeing possibilities, some of your friends show real preferences. Give the German equivalents of the following English sentences. (12 points)

I am for visiting Sanssouci Palace.

24. _____

Wouldn't you like to go to a typical German restaurant?

25. _____

No, I would rather see an operetta.

26. _____

That wouldn't be bad.

27. _____

SCORE [   ]

TOTAL SCORE [   ]

11 Mit Oma ins Restaurant

Quiz 11-1B

■ Erste Stufe

Maximum Score: 40

I. Listening

A. Henning is from Cincinnati. He is touring Germany after finishing college and this is his first visit to Berlin. His cousin, Jens, meets him at the **Bahnhof Friedrichstraße**. (16 points)

1. Right now, Henning would rather
   a. take a tour of the city.
   b. drive out to see the palace Sanssouci.
   c. walk around somewhere.
   d. have something to eat and drink.

2. "**Ku'damm**" is slang for
   a. the zoo.
   b. a famous boulevard in (former West) Berlin.
   c. a well-known café.
   d. a river that runs through Berlin.

3. Henning had heard that **Berliner** speak a dialect and have no sense of humor. Jens' response is that
   a. Henning is right.
   b. the **Berliner** speak like everyone else.
   c. the **Berliner** speak very fast, but they do have a sense of humor.
   d. the **Berliner** speak fast and have no sense of humor.

4. True (**T**) of false (**F**)?

   _____ Henning cannot expect to meet any real **Berliner** because Jens doesn't know any himself.

SCORE [____]

II. Reading

B. Read about the rise and fall of the Berlin Wall and then decide if the statements that follow are true (T) or false (F). (8 points)

Die Berliner Mauer

Aufgrund der schlechten wirtschaftlichen und politischen Verhältnisse haben mehr und mehr Menschen die DDR verlassen. Von Januar bis Anfang August 1961 haben 160.000 Menschen die DDR verlassen. Um den Massenexodus zu beenden, wurde in den frühen Morgenstunden des 13.8.1961 Ost-Berlin und die DDR mit Panzern (*tanks*) und Stacheldraht (*barbed wire*) abgeriegelt (*sealed off*). Dann wurde eine 107 km lange Mauer gebaut. Es gab etwa hundert Tote an der Berliner Mauer.

Quiz 11-1B

Ein Massenexodus von DDR-Bürgern nach Ungarn *(Hungary)* in 1989 und die Leipziger Montagsdemonstration führten zur Öffnung der Grenzen *(borders)*. Am 12. November wurde die Mauer am Potsdamer Platz geöffnet und am 22. Dezember erfolgte die Öffnung am Brandenburger Tor für Fußgänger. Stücke der Mauer wurden als Souvenirs verkauft. Man findet heute kaum mehr Reste der Mauer.

_____ 5. The Berlin Wall was built to keep West Germans out of East Germany.

_____ 6. The Berlin Wall was built to replace tanks and barbed wire.

_____ 7. Events in 1989 led to the opening of borders between East and West Germany.

_____ 8. Most of the wall was left standing as a reminder of the Cold War.

SCORE _____

III. Writing

C. You want to offer your friend a choice of 2 things to do on your night out in Berlin. Ask what he or she would rather do, using two different verbs. (Write two sentences, or one sentence with the clauses joined by **oder**.) (6 points)

_____

_____

_____

SCORE _____

IV. Culture

D. Based on what you learned in the **Erste Stufe** of **Kapitel 11** about German culture, mark the following statements true (**T**) or false (**F**). (10 points)

_____ 9. Teenagers never attend art exhibits or see plays.

_____ 10. The city doesn't have a resident symphony orchestra.

_____ 11. Sanssouci is not actually in Berlin itself.

_____ 12. You can take a tour of Berlin by boat.

_____ 13. There are fewer cultural events taking place in Berlin than in a **Kleinstadt** like Wedel.

SCORE _____

TOTAL SCORE _____

Mit Oma ins Restaurant

■ Zweite Stufe

Maximum Score: 35

Grammar and Vocabulary

A. You took part in an international cooking class while you were in Germany, and now you are telling your German class at home about all the interesting dishes which were prepared. Complete the following report by filling in the blanks with the correct adjective endings. (15 points)

Der Koch hat viel **1.** _____ ausländisch **2.** _____ Köstlichkeiten zubereitet. Es

gab französisch **3.** _____ Käse, ägyptisch **4.** _____ Schisch-Kebab, italienisch

5. _____ Nudelgerichte, ungarisch **6.** _____ Rotkohl, hausgemacht **7.** _____

italienisch **8.** _____ Eis, norwegisch **9.** _____ Lachs und deftig **10.** _____

Wurst. Ich habe besonders gern gemischt **11.** _____ grün **12.** _____ Salat aus

Deutschland, scharf **13.** _____ würzig **14.** _____ Spezialitäten aus Mexiko, und

geräuchert **15.** _____ Fisch aus Dänemark gegessen.

SCORE _____

B. Classmates ask you questions about your report and you respond. Complete the following questions and replies by filling in the blanks with the correct articles and the correct adjective endings where necessary. (14 points)

KLASSENKAMERAD   Hat dir **16.** _____ deftig **17.** _____ Wurst gut geschmeckt?

DU   Ja, dies **18.** _____ Wurst war Spitze!

KLASSENKAMERAD   Hat dir **19.** _____ geräuchert **20.** _____ Fisch gut geschmeckt?

DU   Und wie! Ich mag **21.** _____ geräuchert **22.** _____ Fisch
besonders gern.

KLASSENKAMERAD   Hast du auch **23.** _____ kalt **24.** _____ Braten gegessen?

DU   Nein, **25.** _____ habe ich nicht probiert.

KLASSENKAMERAD   Hast du roh **26.** _____ oder mariniert **27.** _____ Fisch
gegessen?

DU   Beide, aber nur ein einziges Mal. Sie waren scheußlich!

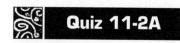

Quiz 11-2A

KLASSENKAMERAD	Hast du roh **28.** _____ Schinken oder die Klöße probiert?
DU	Beides habe ich gegessen, und mehr als einmal! Sie schmecken gut.
KLASSENKAMERAD	Hat dir **29.** _____ Rotkohl auch gut geschmeckt?
DU	Nein, der war mir zu sauer.

SCORE [ ]

C. Give the German equivalents of the following sentences. (6 points)

I heard that the fried fish is good here.

30. _____

Someone told me that the fattened duck is good here.

31. _____

The lobster is supposed to be great.

32. _____

SCORE [ ]

TOTAL SCORE [ ]

KAPITEL 11

Name _____ Klasse _____ Datum _____

11 Mit Oma ins Restaurant

■ Zweite Stufe

Maximum Score: 30

I. Listening

A. Bärbel and Udo are from a small town in Schleswig-Holstein. After you listen to their conversation, choose the best answer from among the alternatives given. (6 points)

1. Udo and Bärbel have been visiting Berlin and Udo is tired because
   a. he's been sick recently.
   b. they've been trying to see and do everything in Berlin.
   c. he's been eating too much rich food this week.
   d. he's very old.

2. They have not yet tried
   a. Indian food.
   b. Russian food.
   c. Egyptian lamb with rice.
   d. Bulgarian food.

3. This evening, they'll probably eat
   a. fish and boiled potatoes.
   b. an Indian curry dish.
   c. something American.
   d. Berlin specialties.

SCORE ☐

II. Reading

B. After reading the passage, choose the best answers from among the alternatives given. (12 points)

> Ein englischer Humorist sagte einmal: „Wenn ich reise, so würde ich am liebsten in Frankreich essen, in Deutschland in die Symphonie gehen und in der Schweiz schlafen, denn die Schweizer Hotels sind sehr sauber und die Städte nachts ab zehn Uhr ganz ruhig".
>
> Leider ist unsere Stadt Zürich nicht mehr so ruhig, aber, was das Essen betrifft, so meinen wir, würde man hier genauso gut — und viel preiswerter — essen wie in Paris! Die Schweizer Küche ist nämlich eine Mischung aus der französischen, der italienischen und der deutschen Küche.
>
> Zu Hause kochen wir gern Spaghetti oder Risotto, natürlich mit recht viel Käse. Wir gehen natürlich gern Käsefondue essen, oder in eine Raclettestube, wo man ein herrliches Gericht aus Kartoffeln und Käse bekommt. Das sind so unsere gemütlichen Abende unter uns. Aber wenn wir vornehm sein wollen, bestellen wir im Zunfthausrestaurant Fondue Bourguignonne (aus Rindfleisch) oder Homard (Hummer) à la nage. Beliebte hors d'oeuvre sind Nordseelachs, Tartar oder Escargot (Weinbergschnecken). Also, bitte!

Quiz 11-2B

4. The writer objects to the Englishman's joke because
   a. Swiss cities aren't all that "dead" at night.
   b. she thinks the Swiss can compete with the Parisians in the area of cooking.
   c. Germany's symphonies aren't all that great.
   d. the food in France isn't what it used to be.

5. In the writer's opinion,
   a. the majority of Swiss eat Italian food at restaurants.
   b. cheese fondu and raclette are what people go out to eat with their close friends or family.
   c. Swiss people should eat more salad.
   d. snails and lobster are not eaten in Switzerland.

6. Popular dishes at home include all of the following EXCEPT
   a. Italian dishes.
   b. risotto.
   c. cheese.
   d. frog legs and other French delicacies.

SCORE ☐

III. Writing

C. You're writing to your pen pal, doing some checking on the things you've heard about German food. Tell him what you've heard (at least 2 things) and ask him what he thinks. (12 points)

_____

_____

_____

_____

_____

_____

_____

_____

_____

_____

SCORE ☐

TOTAL SCORE ☐

KAPITEL 11

Mit Oma ins Restaurant

■ Dritte Stufe

Maximum Score: 30

Grammar and Vocabulary

A. You and your classmates have gone out to dinner in Berlin and you are asking about what everyone is going to order. Complete the following conversation by filling in the blanks with the correct **hätte**-forms. (12 points)

DU   Ich **1.** _____ gern den kalten Braten. Was

2. _____ ihr gern?

HANS u. PETER   Wir **3.** _____ gern das Schweinerückensteak mit Kroketten.

DU   Und du, Ilse, was **4.** _____ du gern?

ILSE   Ich nehme den Lachs. Die Sonja kommt erst später, aber sie

5. _____ gern die Mastente. Wir sollen sie für sie bestellen.

DU   Und Sie, Frau Schneider, was **6.** _____ Sie gern?

FRAU SCHNEIDER   Ich glaube, ich nehme das Wiener Schnitzel.

SCORE [   ]

B. The waiter comes to take your order and each person at the table orders. Some students have questions about the food, while others decide to change their orders. Complete the following conversations by filling in the blanks with the German equivalent of the foods listed in parentheses. (10 points)

KELLNER   Guten Abend. Haben Sie schon gewählt?

DU   Als (appetizer) **7.** _____ nehme ich (deviled egg)

8. _____ . Als (main dish)

9. _____ nehme ich das (fillet of perch)

10. _____ . Was für (side dishes)

11. _____ gibt es?

KELLNER   Es gibt heute Abend (fried potatoes) **12.** _____ ,

Möhren und grüne Erbsen.

DU   Also gut. Dann nehme ich die Kartoffeln und die Erbsen.

HANS   Können Sie mir sagen, was für Suppen es gibt?

Quiz 11-3A

KELLNER   Scharfe mexikanische Tomatensuppe und Kartoffelsuppe haben wir.

HANS   Also, dann bringen Sie mir bitte die Tomatensuppe und dann das (pan-cooked

entree) **13.** _____ .

PETER   Bringen Sie mir bitte ein Wiener Schnitzel. Als (dessert)

14. _____ möchte ich (red berry dessert)

15. _____ .

ILSE   Für mich den Lachs bitte. Als (drink) **16.** _____

nehme ich ein Spezi.

SCORE [   ]

C. Give the German equivalents of the following English sentences and phrases.
(8 points)

To your health!

17. _____

Cheers!

18. _____

Bon appétit!

19. _____

Thank you, the same to you!

20. _____

SCORE [   ]

TOTAL SCORE [   ]

KAPITEL

11 Mit Oma ins Restaurant

■ Dritte Stufe

Maximum Score: 30

I. Listening

A. Magda and Thomas are exchange students living in the United States. Recently, they have begun to miss German food. Listen to their conversation, and then choose the best answers from among the alternatives given. (6 points)

1. Magda would most like to have
   a. a real German roll.
   b. something nice and healthy.
   c. a good hearty soup.
   d. a smoked German sausage.

2. Thomas wants all of the following EXCEPT
   a. pork roast with gravy.
   b. coconut pie.
   c. marinated herring.
   d. sauerkraut.

3. They both agree that
   a. you shouldn't mix German and American food in the same menu.
   b. dumplings are better when they're homemade.
   c. coconut pie fits well with German food.
   d. roasted rabbit is not edible.

SCORE ☐

II. Reading

B. After reading the passage, mark the following statements true (**T**) or false (**F**). (8 points)

Gibt es ein typisch deutsches Essen? Wir meinen, es gibt Speisen und Gerichte, die in ganz Deutschland beliebt sind — zum Beispiel Brotsuppe, Arme Ritter und Semmelknödel, alle aus altbackenem Brot. Aber als Deutsche denken wir auch an die bayerische, die schlesische oder die hessische Küche, denn jede Region von Deutschland hat ein anderes Klima, einen anderen Boden, und infolgedessen andere Möglichkeiten, Gemüse, Getreide, Fleisch oder Fisch, Eier oder Milchprodukte zu produzieren.

Machen wir eine kulinarische Rundreise durch das Kochbuch von dem beliebten Dr. Oetker, so finden wir Rezepte wie:

• westfälisches blindes Huhn, ein Eintopfgericht aus Bohnen (aber gar kein Huhn);

• Kasseler Rippchen, ein hessisches Gericht aus geräucherten Schweinerippen;

KAPITEL 11

Quiz 11-3B

- Wiener Krauteintopf, ein Gericht aus Grünkohl und Kartoffeln mit Schweinefleisch;
- Thüringer Kartoffelklöße, aus rohen Kartoffeln und mit Backpflaumen serviert;
- bayerische Zwetschgenklöße, aus gekochten Kartoffeln und frischen Pflaumen und noch vieles mehr.

_____ 4. **Brotsuppe** and **Semmelknödel** are mentioned as popular dishes all over Germany.

_____ 5. Germans generally think there are many different kinds of "German" cuisines.

_____ 6. Climate is one reason why different regions of Germany have different specialties.

_____ 7. However, there is only one kind of potato dumpling that is the same all over Germany.

SCORE [   ]

III. Writing

C. Your German pen pal is curious as to what kinds of foods you would or would not eat. He asks about a number of items including: rabbit (**der Hase**), venison (**das Rehfleisch**), as well as beef liver (**die Rindsleber**), and tongue or kidney hash (**das Zungen-** or **Nierenragout**). Tell him at least one thing you would like to try and two that you would rather not eat. Give a reason why not. (16 points)

_____

_____

_____

_____

_____

_____

SCORE [   ]

TOTAL SCORE [   ]

KAPITEL 11

Name _____ Klasse _____ Datum _____

11 Mit Oma ins Restaurant

I. Listening
Maximum Score: 30 points

A. Agnes and Henry are getting married, and they plan to have the wedding banquet at a nice restaurant. Before you listen to their conversation, read the statements below. Then listen again and mark the statements as true (**a**) or false (**b**). (15 points)

_____ 1. Agnes wants to serve melon with ham as appetizer.

_____ 2. Henry wants to change the first course to smoked salmon.

_____ 3. Henry wants to serve bouillon soup.

_____ 4. They decided on a fish soup.

_____ 5. They agree on steak with mushrooms for the main course.

_____ 6. The restaurant's speciality, **Jägersteak,** is served with French fries.

_____ 7. Henry suggests a different kind of salad dressing.

_____ 8. They have not yet decided on a dessert.

_____ 9. Henry admits that he doesn't know much about choosing wines.

_____ 10. In their future life together, Henry is probably going to be very accepting of whatever Agnes decides to cook.

SCORE [   ]

B. Gerd calls his grandmother for advice, because his mother is away for the afternoon. After you listen to their conversation, choose the best answers from among the alternatives given. (15 points)

11. Gerd needs help
    a. figuring out the menus for a party this weekend.
    b. figuring out the quantities of each food to buy.
    c. getting the best buys at the supermarket.
    d. choosing the ripest, best-tasting fruit for dessert.

12. The grandmother recommends ... per person of pork steak.
    a. one hundred grams
    b. at least a quarter of a German pound
    c. 250 grams
    d. half a German pound

Chapter Test

13. Gerd's grandmother advises him to
    a. buy enough for about one liter of soup per person.
    b. serve the soup as an appetizer before the cold cuts.
    c. buy enough for about a half liter of soup per person.
    d. throw any leftover soup away after supper.

14. The usual quantity of green beans per person is
    a. 250 grams.
    b. one hundred grams.
    c. two hundred grams.
    d. a little more than for potatoes.

15. For dessert, Gerd needs
    a. to decide which type of fruit he wants in order to know the quantity he needs.
    b. about 125 grams of fruit.
    c. at least one plum per person.
    d. about half an apple or pear per person.

SCORE [   ]

II. Reading

Maximum Score: 30 points

C. For each of the numbered sets below, choose the one response that is NOT an appropriate reply. (10 points)

16. Was wünschen Sie als Beilage?
    a. Ich möchte einen Kloß.
    b. Nein danke! Ich möchte keins mehr.
    c. Bringen Sie mir bitte den Reis.
    d. Nudeln hätte ich gern.

17. Was würde dich interessieren?
    a. Ich bin dafür, dass wir ins Pergamonmuseum gehen.
    b. Ich habe gehört, dass die Staatsoper heute Abend ein Ballett zeigt.
    c. Potsdam würde ich gern sehen.
    d. Das wird sicherlich interessant sein.

18. Ich habe gehört, dass das Kabarett am Brenauerplatz ganz toll ist.
    a. Das Kabarett in der Lausitzstraße soll doch besser sein.
    b. Mir hat man gesagt, dass es nicht so gut ist.
    c. Das stimmt doch nicht. Wer hat dir das gesagt?
    d. Wer hat das gehört?

19. Prost, allerseits!
    a. Auf dein Wohl!
    b. Zum Wohl!
    c. Mahlzeit!
    d. Prost!

20. Wie wär's mit einer Nachspeise?
    a. Ich hätte gern das Jägersteak.
    b. Danke, für mich nichts mehr.
    c. Ein bisschen Obst wäre nicht schlecht.
    d. Bestellst du auch etwas?

SCORE [   ]

D. Read the passage below and then answer the questions that follow. (20 points)

   In der Literatur des 15. bis 17. Jahrhunderts spricht man oft vom Schlaraffenland —
dem Paradies auf Erden (*earth*). Im Schlaraffenland ist das Wetter immer schön. Dort gibt
es keinen Regen und keine Kälte. Im Schlaraffenland gibt es auch genug zu essen. Täglich
isst man fette Braten, Honigkuchen und Schokolade und trinkt so viele süße Getränke, wie
man will. Im Schlaraffenland braucht kein Mensch zu arbeiten. Die Kühe (*cows*) melken
sich selbst, und die Äpfel fallen vom Baum, wenn man vorbeikommt. Und das Getreide
(*grain*) erntet (*harvests*) sich und wird zu schönen Weißbroten gebacken, alles von selbst.
In diesem Land, das irgendwo in Europa ist, vielleicht mitten in Nordrhein-Westfalen, gibt
es keine Kriege, keine Pestilenzen und keine Straßenbanditen. Die Armeen haben kein
Schießpulver (*gunpowder*) und keine Kanonenkugeln, um Städte und Dörfer zu zerstören
(*to destroy*). Niemand stirbt (*dies*) an Hunger, weil die Ernte (*crops*) zerstört wurde.

   Das wäre schön, nicht wahr? Frieden auf Erden und Gesundheit. Nur hat diese Fantasie
auch seine Nachteile. Wenn wir keinen Regen hätten, so würde auch nichts wachsen
(*grow*), also hätten wir keine Äpfel und kein Getreide, und nichts, was die Schweine und
die Kühe fressen könnten. Wenn es im Winter nicht kalt wäre, so würden uns die Insekten
bald über den Kopf wachsen. Und wenn wir nur von fetten Braten und Süßigkeiten leben
würden, wären wir alle bald krank. Ja, und was mit unserem Körper (*body*) passiert, wenn
wir nicht arbeiten und keinen Sport machen, sehen wir schon jetzt.

21. As described in the paragraph, **Schlaraffenland** is closest to
    a. the best of all possible worlds.
    b. a fool's paradise.
    c. life in a typical medieval town.
    d. a perfectly planned economy.

22. One of the more appealing elements of **Schlaraffenland** for people in the late Middle
    Ages was:
    a. Honest work was easy to find.
    b. There would be no hunger, hard work, or sickness.
    c. Everyone could afford to buy chocolate.
    d. It was located in Westphalia.

23. The author says that if **Schlaraffenland** were a reality,
    a. we would have trouble thinking of ways to entertain ourselves.
    b. we would not need pesticides and chemicals anymore.
    c. we would get sick from an unhealthy diet and lack of exercise.
    d. we would somehow have enough irrigation water without rain.

KAPITEL 11

Chapter Test

24. A "visitor" from late medieval Germany to the twenty-first century might think he was in
    Schlaraffenland if he
    a. heard about world hunger today.
    b. went to a modern German supermarket.
    c. read today's newspaper headlines.
    d. observed the progress we have made in controlling the weather.

25. According to the author, what would happen if it were not cold in winter?
    a. Crops would not grow.
    b. Insects would become a real problem.
    c. Pigs and cows would have nothing to eat.
    d. People would not catch cold.

26. If we assume that myths and legends tell something about the people who made them up,
    Schlaraffenland could mean that in the Middle Ages
    a. people were basically lazy.
    b. people were just idealistic dreamers.
    c. most people worked very hard and life was strenuous.
    d. most people ate extremely well, because harvests were so abundant.

27. One of the major changes that occurred in Europe during the period from the 15th to the
    17th century was that
    a. religious tolerance spread throughout most countries.
    b. modern rulers were able to exterminate bands of highway robbers.
    c. the civilian population was increasingly affected by wars.
    d. the discovery of the germ theory of disease helped bring epidemics under control.

28. During the period from the 15th to the 17th century, people were concerned about having
    enough food because
    a. wars and pestilence did not leave enough people to harvest the crops.
    b. wars and armies destroyed the crops and many people starved to death.
    c. pests destroyed most of the crops.
    d. the aristocracy hoarded most of the food in big warehouses.

SCORE

III. Culture

Maximum Score: 10 points

E. Mark the following statements true (**a**) or false (**b**). (10 points)

_____ 29. Germans don't expect a **Kleinstadt** to be much of a "cultural center."

_____ 30. Since reunification, Berlin has lost many of its cultural attractions.

_____ 31. Berlin can't actually be said to have a cuisine of its own, due to the influx of foreign restaurants.

_____ 32. An authentic Greek restaurant in Frankfurt or Düsseldorf might look like a "typical German" restaurant on the outside.

_____ 33. **Danke, gleichfalls!** is another way to say **Ich danke Ihnen auch.**

SCORE [   ]

IV. Writing

Maximum Score: 30 points

F. You have invited your friend out to dinner for her birthday. The waiter brings your meal and pours the beverage. Write a conversation following the directions below. (14 points)

You toast your friend and she responds.

34. DU _____

35. SIE _____

You say, "Enjoy your meal!" and your friend responds.

36. DU _____

37. SIE _____

You suggest that she have a dessert and offer a choice of at least two things that would be appropriate in a German restaurant. She responds.

38. DU _____

39. DU _____

40. SIE _____

SCORE [   ]

KAPITEL 11

Chapter Test

G. You're going to visit an elderly relative in Berlin. She is planning to book you on city tours and excursions. You appreciate her kindness, but think there are lots of things you'd rather do on your own. Write a polite note explaining this and mentioning the things you would prefer to do. (Write five complete sentences and an appropriate greeting and closing.) (16 points)

_____

_____

_____

_____

_____

_____

_____

_____

_____

                                              _____

SCORE [   ]

TOTAL SCORE [   ]

KAPITEL 11

KAPITEL 11 Chapter Test Score Sheet

Circle the letter that matches the most appropriate response.

I. Listening
Maximum Score: 30 points

A. (15 points)

1. a b
2. a b
3. a b
4. a b
5. a b

6. a b
7. a b
8. a b
9. a b
10. a b

SCORE ☐

B. (15 points)

11. a b c d
12. a b c d
13. a b c d
14. a b c d
15. a b c d

SCORE ☐

II. Reading
Maximum Score: 30 points

C. (10 points)

16. a b c d
17. a b c d
18. a b c d
19. a b c d
20. a b c d

SCORE ☐

D. (20 points)

21. a b c d
22. a b c d
23. a b c d
24. a b c d
25. a b c d

26. a b c d
27. a b c d
28. a b c d

SCORE ☐

III. Culture
Maximum Score: 10 points

E. (10 points)

29. a b
30. a b
31. a b
32. a b
33. a b

SCORE ☐

IV. Writing

Maximum Score: 30 points

F. (14 points)

34. DU _____

35. SIE _____

36. DU _____

37. SIE _____

38. DU _____

39. DU _____

40. SIE _____

SCORE [＿＿＿]

G. (16 points)

_____

_____

_____

_____

_____

_____

_____

_____

_____

_____

_____

_____

SCORE [＿＿＿]

TOTAL SCORE [＿＿＿]

Listening Scripts for Quizzes 11-1B, 11-2B, 11-3B

Quiz 11-1B Kapitel 11 Erste Stufe

I. Listening

A.

JENS	Nun bist du also in Berlin, atmest die berühmte Berliner Luft! Was machen wir zuerst? Würdest du gern eine Stadtrundfahrt machen — dir die Denkmäler und bekannte Gebäude ansehen? Oder würdest du lieber gleich nach Potsdam hinausfahren und dir Schloss Sanssouci angucken?
HENNING	Am liebsten würde ich jetzt ein bisschen zu Fuß gehen.
JENS	Na, wie wär's denn, wenn wir mit der U-Bahn ein paar Stationen weiterfahren, bis zum Zoo? Dann können wir am Ku'damm entlangspazieren.
HENNING	Meinst du den Kurfürstendamm, den eleganten Boulevard im Westen von Berlin?
JENS	Ja, eben. Dort ist es immer ganz lebhaft. Später können wir uns in ein Straßencafé setzen und Passanten anschauen, wie in Paris — ganz amüsant ist das.
HENNING	Das wäre nicht schlecht. Aber wie ist das mit dem Dialekt hier? Oma hat mir erzählt, die Berliner haben einen komischen Dialekt, den ich kaum verstehen werde, und dass sie auch keinen Humor haben.
JENS	Na ja, die haben schon die berühmte Berliner Schnauze — reden ganz schnell und etwas frech und lassen sich nichts gefallen! Aber Humor haben sie doch.
HENNING	Ich würde ganz gern ein paar echte Berliner kennen lernen.
JENS	Daran habe ich schon gedacht. Heute Abend gehen wir in eine Diskothek und treffen einige Freunde von mir.

Quiz 11-2B Kapitel 11 Zweite Stufe

I. Listening

A.

UDO	Ach du, mir tun die Füße weh! Ich bin ja ziemlich robust, aber so vieles an einem Tag besichtigen, das schaffe ich in meinem Alter nicht mehr.
BÄRBEL	Ach was! Du bist doch erst 41, und wir müssen das alles schaffen, denn übermorgen geht's wieder nach Hause. Nun sag mal, was würdest du heute Abend gern essen? Wie wär's mit etwas Indischem? Das haben wir noch nicht versucht. Oder möchtest du lieber noch mal mexikanisch essen?
UDO	Nein, lieber nicht! Diese scharf gewürzten Speisen verderben mir doch den Magen, du!
BÄRBEL	Hmmm. Bulgarisch haben wir schon probiert, russisch auch. Und gestern Abend ägyptisches Essen ... das würde ich gern mal kochen lernen: dieses gegrillte Lamm mit Reis vielleicht. Chinesisch können wir bei uns in der Nähe bekommen.
UDO	Ich bin dafür, dass wir heute Abend etwas Einheimisches essen. Ich habe gehört, dass das Restaurant hier um die Ecke guten Fisch hat. Fisch würde mir schmecken, mit Pellkartoffeln.
BÄRBEL	Wir sind aber nicht an der See hier. Der Fisch wird bestimmt nicht so frisch sein wie bei uns.
UDO	Na, dann gehen wir einfach in ein gutbürgerliches Restaurant und bestellen einen Braten, oder meinetwegen ein Eintopfgericht, irgendwas Herzhaftes.
BÄRBEL	Ja, warte mal. Es soll hier in der Gegend ein Restaurant für Berliner Spezialitäten geben. Lass mich doch mal in den Reiseführer schauen!

Quiz 11-3B Kapitel 11 Dritte Stufe

I. Listening

A.

THOMAS	Was würdest du eigentlich für ein deutsches Brötchen geben, so eine richtig frische Semmel, noch warm von der Bäckerei?
MAGDA	Hör doch auf, Mensch! Lass mal! Das Essen hier schmeckt mir ganz gut. Meine Gastmutter gibt sich viel Mühe mit dem Kochen und macht leckere Gerichte. Nur würde ich doch gern mal eine richtig deftige Suppe essen, wie meine Großmutter sie immer kocht!
THOMAS	Du, wir spielen ein Fantasiespiel. Wir bestellen uns in Gedanken unser Lieblingsessen von zu Hause. Also, was würdest du zuerst nehmen?
MAGDA	Zuerst die Suppe — Linsensuppe mit Karotten drin und Zwiebeln und kleinen Stücken geräucherter Wurst.
THOMAS	Und ich möchte als Vorspeise irgendein Fischgericht — vielleicht Lachs oder geräuchertes Forellenfilet. Nun, als Hauptspeise?
MAGDA	Mmm ... weißt du, für mich einfach ein Jägerschnitzel mit frischen Champignons und Zwiebeln — und dazu Spätzle oder Bratkartoffeln und einen knackigen, gemischten Salat!
THOMAS	Lecker! Mir läuft das Wasser im Munde zusammen, wenn ich das höre. Also, was würde ich nehmen? Schweinebraten mit Rotkohl und Kartoffelklößen — und ganz viel Soße. Aber richtige Thüringer Klöße müssen das sein, aus rohen Kartoffeln. Nicht aus gekochten Kartoffeln und bestimmt nicht aus der Packung!
MAGDA	Nein, fertig aus der Packung schmeckt das Essen gar nicht.
THOMAS	Nun, was würdest du zum Nachtisch nehmen?
MAGDA	Ach, ich weiß nicht. Schlag was vor!
THOMAS	Wie wär's mit einem Stück Coconut Pie?
MAGDA	Nach dem großen Essen? Und ich dachte, du willst deutsches Essen haben?
THOMAS	Ja, schon, aber darf ich mir nicht das aussuchen, was mir von jedem Land am besten schmeckt?

ANSWERS Quiz 11-1A

A. (23 points; 1 point per item)
1. würde
2. den
3. Dom
4. würden
5. eine
6. Stadtrundfahrt
7. würdest
8. würdet
9. würde
10. würdet
11. würde
12. ein
13. Symphoniekonzert
14. würden
15. einen
16. Ausflug
17. würden
18. ein
19. Theaterstück/Schauspiel
20. würde
21. ein
22. Baudenkmal
23. Synagoge

B. (12 points; 3 points per item)
Answers will vary. Possible answers:
24. Ich bin dafür, dass wir Schloss Sanssouci besichtigen.
25. Würdest du gern mal in ein typisches deutsches Lokal gehen?
26. Nein, ich würde lieber eine Operette sehen.
27. Das wäre nicht schlecht.

ANSWERS Quiz 11-1B

I. Listening

A. (16 points: 4 points per item)
1. c
2. b
3. c
4. F

II. Reading

B. (8 points: 2 points per item)
5. F
6. T
7. T
8. F

III. Writing

C. (6 points)
Answers will vary. Possible answer:
Würdest du gern ins Restaurant gehen, oder würdest du lieber einen Film sehen?

IV. Culture

D. (10 points: 2 points per item)
9. F
10. F
11. T
12. T
13. F

Answers to Quizzes 11-2A, 11-2B

ANSWERS Quiz 11-2A

A. (15 points; 1 point per item)
1. e
2. e
3. en
4. es
5. e
6. en
7. es
8. es
9. en
10. e
11. en
12. en
13. e
14. e
15. en

B. (14 points; 1 point per item)
16. die
17. e
18. e
19. der
20. e
21. den
22. en
23. den
24. en
25. den/ihn
26. en
27. en
28. en
29. der

C. (6 points; 2 points per item)
Answers will vary. Possible answers:
30. Ich habe gehört, dass der gebratene Fisch hier gut ist.
31. Man hat mir gesagt, dass die Mast-ente hier gut ist.
32. Der Hummer soll prima sein.

ANSWERS Quiz 11-2B

I. Listening
A. (6 points: 2 points per item)
1. b
2. a
3. d

II. Reading
B. (12 points: 4 points per item)
4. b
5. b
6. d

III. Writing
C. (12 points: 4 points per item)
Answers will vary.

ANSWERS Quiz 11-3A

A. (12 points; 2 points per item)
1. hätte
2. hättet
3. hätten
4. hättest
5. hätte
6. hätten

B. (10 points; 1 point per item)
7. Vorspeise
8. das gefüllte Ei
9. Hauptgericht
10. Seebarschfilet
11. Beilagen
12. Bratkartoffeln
13. das Pfannengericht
14. Nachspeise (Nachtisch)
15. Rote Grütze
16. Getränk

C. (8 points; 2 points per item)
17. Zum Wohl! / Auf dein/Ihr/euer Wohl!
18. Prost!
19. Guten Appetit! / Mahlzeit!
20. Danke, gleichfalls! / Danke, ebenfalls! / Danke! Dir/Ihnen auch!

ANSWERS Quiz 11-3B

I. Listening

A. (6 points: 2 points per item)
1. c
2. d
3. b

II. Reading

B. (8 points: 2 points per item)
4. T
5. T
6. T
7. F

III. Writing

C. (16 points: 4 points per sentence)
Answers will vary.

KAPITEL 11

Scripts for Chapter Test Kapitel 11

I. Listening

A.

AGNES   Also, wir sprechen gleich mit dem Koch. Wir müssen uns jetzt entscheiden, wie das Hochzeitsessen aussehen soll. Ich denke mir das Menü eigentlich so: als Vorspeise Melone mit rohem Schinken ...

HENRY   Rohen Schinken — ungekochtes Schweinefleisch?? Nein, das würde ich nicht machen. Meine Gäste würden überhaupt kein rohes Fleisch essen! Wie wär's mit geräuchertem Lachs mit sauren Gurken?

AGNES   Also gut. Zuerst geräucherten Lachs mit Gurken. Dann die Suppe. Da hätte ich gern eine Fischsuppe gehabt, da wir aber jetzt den Fisch als Vorspeise servieren ...

HENRY   Ja, also ich würde sagen, lieber eine leichte Hühnersuppe.

AGNES   Einfach eine Bouillon?

HENRY   Schon, aber mit Kräutern und Ereinlage, bitte!

AGNES   Das ist mir recht. Als Hauptgericht müssen wir unbedingt die Spezialität des Hauses bestellen: Jägersteak mit Champignons in Rotweinsoße. Das schmeckt wirklich köstlich und wird auch sehr schön angerichtet, weißt du?

HENRY   Meinst du? Und was wird als Beilage serviert?

AGNES   Röstkartoffeln, denke ich, und grüner Salat mit Sauerrahmsoße.

HENRY   Röstkartoffeln passen gut zum Jägersteak mit Champignons, aber ich bezweifle, dass man die Sauerrahm-Salatsoße dazu nehmen sollte.

AGNES   Warum denn nicht?

HENRY   Na ja, du hast gesagt, sie würden das Steak in Rotweinsoße servieren. Also, Rotweinsoße und Sauerrahmsoße passen nicht gut zusammen! Am besten soll uns der Koch eine leichte Salatsoße machen aus Öl und Zitronensaft.

AGNES   Vielleicht wäre es besser, wenn du selbst hingehen würdest, um mit dem Koch zu sprechen.

HENRY   Warum denn? Du hast doch alles ganz gut geplant, meine ich, mit ein paar Ände-rungen wird das ein ausgezeichnetes Essen.

AGNES   Es gibt aber auch noch Obst und Käse als Nachtisch und die ganzen Getränke! Mit den Weinen kennst du dich wohl besser aus als ich, nicht wahr?

HENRY   Hmm ... du hast vielleicht Recht. Also, gut. Ich fahre schon morgen früh zum Restau-rant hin. Ich werde das schon in allen Details mit dem Koch besprechen können.

B.

GERD   Hallo, Omi! Ich soll jetzt fürs Wochenende einkaufen gehen, aber Mutti hat keine Liste gemacht, und ich weiß nicht so recht, wie viel ich von den verschiedenen Lebensmitteln einkaufen soll.

GROSSMUTTER   Also, was will denn die Mutti alles kochen?

GERD   Heute Abend belegte Brote natürlich und eine Suppe, sagte sie.

GROSSMUTTER   Bei Aufschnitt würde ich pro Person hundert Gramm Wurst rechnen — ebenso viel Käse. Und Suppe als Hauptgericht, hmm ... da rechnet man so einen halben Liter pro Person.

GERD   Okay. Und für morgen? Da soll es Schweinerückensteak geben — das ist heute im Sonderangebot, ganz preiswert — und Salzkartoffeln natürlich und grüne Bohnen — ja, und zum Nachtisch frisches Obst.

GROSSMUTTER   Vom Schweinerückensteak bring bitte 125 Gramm pro Person. Und als Beilage bring bitte ein halbes Pfund, also 250 Gramm Kartoffeln pro Person. Und von den Bohnen ein bisschen weniger, so 200 Gramm für jeden sollten reichen.

GERD   Und wie viel Obst?

GROSSMUTTER   Na, das kannst du dir schon denken, Kind, dass es darauf ankommt, was für Obst du kaufst. Bei Weintrauben oder Pflaumen reichen 125 Gramm pro Person schon aus, aber wir brauchen für jeden mindestens einen Apfel oder eine Birne.

GERD   Ja, klar.

GROSSMUTTER   Sag mal, wie wär's, wenn wir zusammen einkaufen gehen? Ich hätte auch gern ein Schweinerückensteak für Sonntag.

GERD   Klar, Omi! Ich komme gleich vorbei.

Answers to Chapter Test Kapitel 11

I. Listening Maximum Score: 30 points

A. (15 points: 1½ points per item)

1. a	6. b		
2. a	7. a		
3. b	8. a		
4. b	9. b		
5. a	10. b		

B. (15 points: 3 points per item)

11. b
12. b
13. c
14. c
15. a

II. Reading Maximum Score: 30 points

C. (10 points: 2 points per item)

16. b
17. d
18. d
19. c
20. a

D. (20 points: 2½ points per item)

21. b
22. b
23. c
24. b
25. b

26. c
27. c
28. b

III. Culture Maximum Score: 10 points

E. (10 points: 2 points per item)

29. a
30. b
31. b
32. a
33. a

IV. Writing Maximum Score: 30 points

F. (14 points: 2 points per item)

34. Auf dein Wohl!
35. Zum Wohl!
36. Guten Appetit!
37. Danke! Dir auch!
38. Ich schlage vor, dass wir noch einen Nachtisch essen.
39. Würdest du lieber ... oder ... essen?
40. Am liebsten würde ich ... essen.

G. (16 points: 3 points per sentence; 1 point for salutation and closing)
Answers will vary.

12 Die Reinickendorfer Clique

Quiz 12-1A

■ Erste Stufe

Maximum Score: 35

Grammar and Vocabulary

A. Match the German words with their English equivalents. Write the German words in the blanks to the left of their matches. (14 points)

1. _____	decathlete	der Fortgeschrittene
2. _____	secret tip	die Bucht
3. _____	varied	zahlreich
4. _____	beginner	die Küste
5. _____	to be bored	die Klippe
6. _____	numerous	die Anlage
7. _____	bicycle shed	die Insel
8. _____	cliff	der Anfänger
9. _____	experienced (person)	abwechslungsreich
10. _____	advanced (person)	sich langweilen
11. _____	grounds, site	der Geheimtipp
12. _____	bay	der Zehnkämpfer
13. _____	coast	das Fahrrad-Depot
14. _____	island	der Erfahrene

SCORE [   ]

Holt German 2 Komm mit!, Chapter 12

Testing Program **301**

Name _____ Klasse _____ Datum _____

B. Everyone is back from summer vacation. You are all talking about where you went and what you did. Complete the sentences by filling in the blanks with the correct helping verb and past participle. (14 points)

Ich 15. _____ mit einem Freund nach Griechenland 16. _____

(fliegen). Wir 17. _____ drei Wochen auf einer griechischen Insel

18. _____ (verbringen). Es 19. _____ viel Spaß

20. _____ (machen). Wir 21. _____ Tennis

22. _____ (spielen). Dort 23. _____ wir auch im Mittelmeer

24. _____ (schwimmen). Wir 25. _____ oft

26. _____ (wandern), aber wir 27. _____ auch viel in die

Diskotheken 28. _____ (gehen)!

SCORE _____

C. Where were your friends during their vacation? Complete the following conversations by filling in the blanks with the correct past tense form of the verb **sein**. (7 points)

Weiß jemand, wo die Monika und die Renate 29. _____ ?

Ja, in den Vereinigten Staaten.

Und Heiko, wo 30. _____ er?

Ich glaube in Schottland.

Wo 31. _____ du, Manfred?

Ich 32. _____ in der Schweiz.

Boris und Katrin, wo 33. _____ ihr?

Wir 34. _____ in Italien. Und die Birgitt 35. _____ auch dort.

SCORE _____

TOTAL SCORE _____

12 Die Reinickendorfer Clique

Quiz 12-1B

■ Erste Stufe

Maximum Score: 40

I. Listening

A. Agnes and Henry are planning their wedding trip. They have only a week's holiday. Look at the questions below before you listen to their conversation. After you listen, answer the questions by filling in the blanks. (8 points)

1. What 3 destinations are suggested and by whom?

   a. _____ by _____

   b. _____ by _____

   c. _____ by _____

2. Listen to the conversation again. What objection is raised to the second (b) suggestion?

   _____

SCORE ☐

II. Reading

B. Read the passage below, and then decide whether the statements that follow are true (T) or false (F). (10 points)

Eine Frau erzählt:

Die schönsten Ferien in meinem Leben habe ich erlebt, als ich ein kleines Mädchen war. Da bin ich jeden Sommer ganz alleine mit der Bahn zu den Großeltern gefahren, die in einer kleinen Stadt an der Ostsee wohnten. Mein Großvater hatte ein kleines Geschäft, und meine Großmutter hat im Geschäft mitgeholfen. Beide hatten also tagsüber für mich wenig Zeit. Aber das war mir egal, denn ich hatte viel zu tun. Vormittags bin ich mit dem Hund meines Großvaters spazieren gegangen. Manchmal habe ich auch die verschiedenen Geschäfte und Läden in der Stadt besucht. Nachmittags habe ich meiner Großmutter im Laden „geholfen". Oft war ich nachmittags auch im Café und hab mir Eis oder Saft bestellt. Meine Großmutter hat später dafür bezahlt.

An den Strand durfte ich nicht alleine. Wir sind aber abends nach Ladenschluss oft zu dritt in dem alten Wagen an den Strand gefahren. Ich bin geschwommen, aber das Wasser war sehr kalt. Meine Großmutter hat sich Schuhe und Strümpfe ausgezogen und ist auch ins Wasser gegangen. Mein Großvater hat manchmal Muscheln gesammelt und sie mir geschenkt. Bis heute habe ich eine kleine Zigarrenkiste voller Muscheln, die er gesammelt hat.

Quiz 12-1B

_____ 3. Die Großeltern der Frau haben in einer Stadt an der Ostsee gewohnt.

_____ 4. Die Frau hat sich bei ihren Großeltern sehr gelangweilt.

_____ 5. Die Frau hat ihren Großeltern oft vormittags im Laden geholfen.

_____ 6. Die Frau hat jeden Nachmittag am Strand verbracht.

_____ 7. Die Frau hat immer noch die Muscheln, die ihr der Großvater geschenkt hat.

SCORE [ ]

III. Writing

C. Write a short paragraph to your pen pal about the best vacation you've ever had. What made it so special? Write three or more complete sentences. (12 points)

_____

_____

_____

_____

_____

_____

SCORE [ ]

IV. Culture

D. Answer the following questions briefly in English. (10 points)

8. Describe and define a **Gaststätte**: _____

_____

9. Describe and define a **Biergarten**. How is it different from most American establishments?

_____

10. What do Germans think of when they talk about "American food"? _____

_____

SCORE [ ]

TOTAL SCORE [ ]

12 Die Reinickendorfer Clique

Name _____ Klasse _____ Datum _____

Quiz 12-2A

■ Zweite Stufe

Maximum Score: 30

Grammar and Vocabulary

A. How many international foods can you identify? Match the dishes in the box with the descriptions that follow. Place the name of the food in the blank to the left of its description. (10 points)

> Moussaka   Schisch-Kebab   Fettucine   Crêpes Suzette
>   Steak
> Wiener Schnitzel   Tacos   Paella   Gulasch   Couscous

1. _____   a Spanish rice dish

2. _____   an Italian pasta dish

3. _____   a French pancake dish

4. _____   a spicy Mexican food

5. _____   grilled Egyptian meat dish

6. _____   Greek dish with eggplant and lamb

7. _____   a Moroccan grain dish

8. _____   a piece of beef

9. _____   an Austrian meat dish

10. _____   a spicy Hungarian meat dish

SCORE [   ]

Quiz 12-2A

B. You are in charge of a dinner party being held to raise funds for the German club, and you have to tell everyone what to do. Complete the following commands by filling in the blanks with the correct form of the verb given in parentheses. (20 points)

Jana, **11.** _____ (machen) eine Liste! **12.** _____

(vergessen) die Liste nicht, wenn du einkaufen gehst!

Claudia, **13.** _____ (nehmen) doch die Kochbücher mit!

Franziska, **14.** _____ (gehen) doch und **15.** _____

(holen) das Brot! **16.** _____ (trinken) das Spezi nicht! Unsere Gäste

brauchen was zum Trinken.

Heidi, **17.** _____ (kaufen) noch ein Kilo Kartoffelsalat.

Hans, **18.** _____ (bringen) mir bitte die Speisekarten.

Franzi, **19.** _____ (machen) einen Anschlag. **20.** _____

(schreiben) doch die Speisen und die Preise darauf.

SCORE [ ]

TOTAL SCORE [ ]

KAPITEL 12

Die Reinickendorfer Clique

Quiz 12-2B

Zweite Stufe

Maximum Score: 30

I. Listening

A. Herr and Frau Strom and their 13-year-old son, Udo, are vacationing in Italy. Herr Strom has ordered a meal in a nice restaurant in Milan. Before you listen to their conversation, look at the outline below. After you listen, complete the outline by filling in the blanks. (8 points)

During the discussion between Udo and his parents,

1. Udo says he's not eating his pasta because _____
   _____

2. Udo says he'd prefer _____ and that the main dish looks just like ordinary
   _____

3. The waiter explains that the main dish is made of _____
   _____

4. The waiter speaks German very well because _____
   _____

SCORE [   ]

II. Reading

B. Tom received a letter from his German pen pal, Markus. Before you read the passage, look at the questions that follow. After you read, answer the questions briefly in English. (6 points)

Lieber Tom!

Vielen Dank für deinen schönen, ausführlichen Brief! Es freut mich sehr, dass du im Sommer nach Hawaii fliegen wirst. Schön, dass du dort auf einer kleineren Insel wohnst und die vielen Touristen dadurch vermeiden kannst.

Ich habe gehört, dass das Essen auf Hawaii eine ganz eigenartige Mischung aus einheimischen Gerichten, Chinesischem, Japanischem und Amerikanischem sein soll. Du musst dich unbedingt auf eine Luau-Party einladen lassen. Aber iss keinen rohen Fisch! Der soll gefährlich sein. Übrigens, wusstest du, dass Poi aus einer Art Wurzel besteht, die gegärt wird? Das klingt nicht sehr appetitlich, nicht wahr?

Quiz 12-2B

Wir waren vorigen Sonntag in einem arabischen Restaurant und haben Tagine mit Couscous gegessen. Couscous besteht eigentlich aus zerstampftem Weizen, der nicht direkt in Wasser gekocht wird, sondern in einem besonderen Topf über kochendem Wasser gedämpft wird.

...

5. Where is Tom going to stay and what is he avoiding? _____

_____

6. What advice does Markus give Tom about the food there? _____

_____

7. Markus says couscous is prepared by _____

_____

SCORE ☐

III. Writing

C. A particular ethnic restaurant has been recommended to you. You heard that one of the dishes was especially good, but you also heard one should avoid eating the steak. You advise your friend about what to eat and then order for yourself. Write the exchange using the lines below. (16 points)

8.   DU _____

9.   DU _____

10. KELLNER _____

11.   DU _____

SCORE ☐

TOTAL SCORE ☐

KAPITEL 12

Die Reinickendorfer Clique

Quiz 12-3A

■ Dritte Stufe

Maximum Score: 35

Grammar and Vocabulary

A. Your German club is giving a fashion show and you are responsible for writing the commentary. Complete the following clothing descriptions by filling in the blanks with the correct adjective and article endings, where necessary. (20 points)

Das Ehepaar ist für einen Ball angezogen. Die junge Dame trägt ein 1. _____ elegant

2. _____ Abendkleid. Der Rock hat ein 3. _____ schön 4. _____ Karomuster und

ein 5. _____ lang 6. _____ Schleife. Der junge Mann trägt ein 7. _____ schwarz

8. _____ Smoking mit rot 9. _____ Kummerbund, weiß 10. _____ Hemd und

schwarz 11. _____ Lackschuhe.

Das nächste Mädchen trägt salopp 12. _____ Jeans, ein 13. _____ weit 14. _____

Weste und eine braun 15. _____ Wildlederjacke. Ihr Freund trägt ein 16. _____

gestreift 17. _____ Pulli, ein 18. _____ grau 19. _____ Hose und schwarz

20. _____ Turnschuhe.

SCORE ☐

B. Your friend Gerhard is trying to work a crossword puzzle and doesn't remember the German equivalent for some comparatives. Finish the crossword puzzle by filling in the blanks with the correct comparative form of the word in parentheses. (5 points)

(gut)   Dieses Modell ist 21. _____ als dein Modell.

(alt)   Dieses Haus im Dorf ist 22. _____ als mein Haus.

(teuer)   Dein Auto ist 23. _____ als mein Auto.

(neu)   Dieser schwarze Anzug ist 24. _____ als der braune Anzug.

(viel)   Dieses elegante Kleid kostet 25. _____ als das einfache Kleid.

SCORE ☐

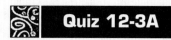

C. Your friend Katrina has definite ideas about what clothing she thinks you should buy. Complete her statements by filling in the blanks with the correct endings. (10 points)

Kauf doch dies 26. _____ geblümt 27. _____ Krawatte!

Nimm doch dies 28. _____ Anzug!

Zieh doch dies 29. _____ elegant 30. _____ Smoking an!

Warum kaufst du dies 31. _____ Pulli mit Ringelmuster nicht?

Nimm doch dies 32. _____ gelb 33. _____ T-Shirt!

Kauf dies 34. _____ rot 35. _____ Fliege nicht!

SCORE _____

TOTAL SCORE _____

Die Reinickendorfer Clique

Quiz 12-3B

Maximum Score: 30

■ Dritte Stufe

I. Listening

A. Helga and Bertram have received an invitation from the Heinemanns. Listen to their conversation and answer the questions that follow. (10 points)

1. Helga mentions two different styles of clothes. Describe one.

   _____

2. Where is the party being held?

   _____

3. What does Helga decide to wear to the party?

   _____

4. What are the men wearing?

   _____

5. What has Bertram heard about the place where the party will be held?

   _____

SCORE ☐

II. Reading

B. Before you read the passage, look at the questions that follow. After you read, answer the questions briefly in English. (8 points)

Wie werden sich die Menschen des 22. oder des 44. Jahrhunderts anziehen? Manche Sciencefictionautoren geben sich Mühe, diese Frage logisch zu beantworten. Was für Stoffe wird man vorziehen? Würde es noch Unterschiede geben zwischen weiblicher und männlicher Kleidung? Würde sich jeder frei nach Fantasie und Wunsch anders anziehen? Oder würde die Gesellschaft Uniformen vorziehen — mit oder ohne Abzeichen für die verschiedenen sozialen Klassen?

Was die Stoffe betrifft, so lautet die Antwort fast immer: Kunststoffe, die auf einer uns noch ungeahnten Weise produziert werden. Die Optimisten unter den Autoren

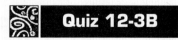

Quiz 12-3B

entscheiden sich fast immer für schöne und äußerst bequeme Kleidung — und meistens für einen individuellen und variationsreichen Look. Die Pessimisten sind eher für Uniformen, die den Leuten aufgezwungen werden — also auch in der Mode keine freie Wahl — aber doch verhältnismäßig bequem sind. Krawatten und Schuhe mit hohen Absätzen kommen selten vor.

6. What kind of materials do science fiction writers usually choose for the clothing of the future?

   _____

   What two basic styles are mentioned? What kinds of people choose each?

Style	**Who chooses it?**
7. _____	_____
8. _____	_____

9. What characteristic do both styles of clothing have in common?

   _____

   SCORE [   ]

III. Writing

C. You are thinking about Utopia — the perfect world. What would you suggest that people wear? Write three or more complete sentences. (12 points)

_____

_____

_____

_____

_____

_____

SCORE [   ]

TOTAL SCORE [   ]

KAPITEL **12**

Die Reinickendorfer Clique

I. Listening

Maximum Score: 30 points

A. Max, an exchange student from Germany, and his American host Fred are thinking about summer vacation. After you listen to their conversation, choose the best answers from among the alternatives given. (15 points)

1. Fred's idea is to
   a. fly to Mexico City.
   b. fly to Acapulco.
   c. drive all around Mexico.
   d. rent a car and drive to Mexico City.

2. Fred would like to
   a. see the pyramids.
   b. explore ruins.
   c. go to museums in different cities.
   d. live on the beach in a hut.

3. Max is hesitant for all of the following reasons EXCEPT:
   a. He's nervous about speaking Spanish.
   b. He's heard there are a lot of insects in Mexico.
   c. He thinks it would be very hot.
   d. He's heard that one shouldn't drink the water there.

4. Fred thinks there will be no problem because
   a. he speaks Spanish fluently.
   b. they'll take plenty of things for sun protection.
   c. there aren't any insects or poisonous snakes.
   d. they'll catch their own fish in the ocean.

5. Max seems to be more interested in
   a. camping out.
   b. swimming and surfing.
   c. the ancient culture and historical sites.
   d. learning to speak Spanish.

SCORE

B. Pat is getting ready to take a trip with her German classmates. Her friend, Luise, is helping her pack. Read the following statements before you listen to their conversation. After you listen, mark the statements as true (**a**) or false (**b**). (15 points)

_____ 6. Pat is wondering whether her suitcase is big enough.

_____ 7. Luise advises her to take just a carry-on bag.

Chapter Test

_____ 8. All the students will check their luggage at each train station.

_____ 9. The other students will probably put their luggage in the overhead racks on the train.

_____ 10. The students will take taxis to the youth hostel.

_____ 11. Pat had planned to take a dress and a nice pair of shoes.

_____ 12. Luise agrees that Pat needs a jogging suit and two sweaters.

_____ 13. The students are going away just for the weekend.

_____ 14. Luise tells Pat to bring T-shirts and a pair of jeans and not too much else.

_____ 15. One thing Pat will need is a container for her sandwich.

SCORE [   ]

II. Reading

Maximum Score: 30 points

C. Ulrike is a student in Berlin. The following is an excerpt from a letter she wrote to her best friend from her hometown. Read the questions first and then read the letter. Choose the best answers from among the alternatives given. (15 points)

Wie du weißt, bleibe ich in den Osterferien hier in Berlin, weil ich eine Seminararbeit schreibe. Mutti und Vati haben mich aber schon besucht. Gleich am ersten Abend wollten sie in ein schönes Restaurant gehen. Ich habe Verschiedenes vorgeschlagen, was natürlich ein Fehler war, meinerseits, denn Mutti hat sich für ein türkisches Lokal entschieden (*decided*), aber Vati wollte lieber typisch deutsch essen.

Wir sind doch ins türkische Restaurant gegangen. Aber sobald wir die Speisekarte bekommen haben, hat mein Vater angefangen, sich richtig kindisch zu benehmen. Er hat die Namen der Gerichte ganz laut buchstabiert und mich bei jedem Gericht gefragt, was das bloß sein sollte. Bei den Vorspeisen hat er sich sehr laut gegen Meeresfrüchte erklärt, weil sie „hier nicht frisch wären". Da Mutti und ich in der Tat allergisch gegen Krabben und Muscheln sind, habe ich das ignoriert, und wir haben uns für einen Salat entschieden.

Als Hauptgericht habe ich die Moussaka vorgeschlagen, weil ich gehört habe, dass sie dort sehr lecker ist — das ist so ein Gericht aus Auberginen und Hammelfleisch. Aber am Ende haben wir uns auf eine türkische Art von Schisch–Kebab geeinigt. Aber, als wir bestellen wollten, sagte der Kellner, das Gericht wäre schon alle.

Dann haben sich der Kellner und mein Vater in ein endloses Gespräch über die Speisekarte verwickelt. Und so ging das weiter den ganzen Abend.

Als wir endlich mit dem Essen fertig waren — wir haben Kalbsschnitzel gegessen — hat mein Vater ...

Holt German 2 Komm mit!, Chapter 12

16. Ulrike's parents
   a. are from Berlin.
   b. came to see her in Berlin during her school holidays.
   c. insisted that she come back home for the holidays.
   d. took her on a trip to Berlin during the Easter holidays.
   e. All of the above are true.

17. They went to a Turkish restaurant because
   a. Ulrike insisted that her parents try Turkish food.
   b. her father loves to try new and different foods.
   c. her mother selected it from among the places that Ulrike suggested.
   d. one of her mother's friends had recommended it.
   e. All of the above are true.

18. They ordered a salad as an appetizer mainly because
   a. the seafood appetizers didn't look very fresh.
   b. Ulrike and her mother are allergic to different kinds of fish.
   c. Ulrike's father was suspicious of the restaurant's seafood.
   d. Both a and b are true.
   e. Both b and c are true.

19. For a main dish, they had
   a. veal cutlets.
   b. shish kebab.
   c. moussaka.
   d. an eggplant (**Aubergine**) and mutton dish.
   e. Both c and d.

20. You could infer from Ulrike's letter that at the restaurant she felt
   a. embarrassed.
   b. happy her parents were with her.
   c. unsure about the food.
   d. proud of her father.
   e. sentimental about her parents.

SCORE [ ]

D. Look at the questions on page 316 and then read the passage twice. As you read, think about the questions and choose the best answers from among the alternatives given. (15 points)

DER MITGIFTJÄGER

Es war einmal ein Prinz, dessen Vater ganz ganz arm war. Der einzige Schatz, der dem Vater geblieben war, war sein äußerst gut aussehender Sohn — eben unser Prinz. Eines Tages rief der arme König seinen Sohn zu sich und sagte: „Mein lieber Sohn, es ist jetzt Zeit, dass du in die Welt hinausgehst, um dein Glück zu suchen. Ich kann dir aber gar nichts mitgeben — so gern ich dich schön und reichlich ausrüsten möchte — als diesen Rat: mach bloß eine reiche Partie!" Der Prinz, der nicht besonders clever aber doch ein ehrlicher Mensch war, fragte entrüstet: „Aber Vater, soll ich denn Mitgiftjäger werden? Das wäre mir ja peinlich und würde

Chapter Test

meine zartesten Gefühle verletzen!" „Egal", sagte der König, „eine reiche Braut (*bride*) wirst du schon finden. Adieu!"

Der arme Prinz machte sich also auf den Weg, und in jeder Stadt stieg er in den besten Hotels ab und stellte sich beim Tanztee den Damen vor: „Ich bin der Prinz von Dingsbums, und wenn Sie Geld haben, würde ich Sie gerne heiraten (*marry*)." Aber alle Debutantinnen waren schon längst von ihren Eltern vor Mitgiftjägern gewarnt, und sie wiesen ihn unbarmherzig ab.

Aber eines Tages, als er endlich ganz traurig und allein auf dem Platz vor dem American Express Büro in Paris saß, kam ihm ein wunderschönes Mädchen in abgeschnittener Jeanshose und T-Shirt entgegen, und er sagte, „Guten Tag. Ich bin der Prinz von Dingsbums, und wenn Sie Geld hätten, würde ich Sie gern heiraten!"

„Schon gut", sagte das Mädchen, „ich bin ja eine selbst gemachte Millionärin. Hätten Sie morgen um zehn Uhr Zeit? Ich sammle nämlich Ehemänner mit Adelstiteln. Wenn Sie mich morgen heiraten wollen, können Sie mein dritter Mann werden."

21. From reading this story, you can guess that a **Mitgiftjäger** is
    a. a bum.
    b. a jetsetter.
    c. a fortune hunter.
    d. usually handsome but stupid.

22. Before the prince set out, the king in the story gave his son
    a. a parting bit of advice.
    b. all the riches the prince could want.
    c. introductions to a number of debutantes.
    d. a magic good-luck charm.

23. The debutantes in every city he visited
    a. gave the prince a hearty welcome.
    b. were pleased to dance with him.
    c. helped him out financially, so he could continue his quest.
    d. had been warned about people like him.

24. In Paris, he met someone who was NOT
    a. beautiful.
    b. dressed very well.
    c. wealthy.
    d. single.

25. The story implies that the person he met in Paris was
    a. a sweet, trusting young girl.
    b. a French girl who adored aristocratic titles.
    c. a casting director for films.
    d. an American divorcee.

SCORE [ ]

Chapter Test

III. Culture

Maximum Score: 10 points

E. Based on the information in **Kapitel 12**, mark each statement below true (**a**) or false (**b**). (10 points)

_____ **26.** Germans spend more money on travel than other Europeans.

_____ **27.** The Austrians and the Swiss are right behind the Germans in money spent on foreign travel.

_____ **28.** Germans usually take fairly short annual vacations.

_____ **29.** If you go to a **Lokal** in Germany, it's all right to seat yourself at the **Stammtisch** without being invited.

_____ **30.** If you go to a **Lokal** in Germany, it's all right to ask another person or group if you can share their table.

_____ **31.** If you see someone taking their dog into a **Lokal** with them, it's probably not a very clean place to eat.

_____ **32.** Italian food is very popular among German teenagers.

_____ **33.** The fast food outlets in Germany are all franchises of American-owned chains.

_____ **34.** Some Germans think of American food as just hamburgers and other fast foods.

_____ **35.** "Franzi" is a well-known personality due to her Olympic success.

SCORE _____

Chapter Test

IV. Writing

Maximum Score: 30 points

F. You're planning to spend the summer in Germany. Your mother has some suggestions about what kinds of clothes you should take, but you are not sure. Write and discuss this with your pen pal in detail and be sure to ask for his or her suggestions. Write five or more complete sentences. (15 points)

_____

_____

_____

_____

_____

_____

_____

_____

SCORE [   ]

G. Pretend that you spent your vacation at La Santa. Write to your pen pal and tell him all about it — what you did and how you liked it. Write five or more complete sentences. (15 points)

_____

_____

_____

_____

_____

_____

_____

_____

_____

SCORE [   ]

TOTAL SCORE [   ]

Holt German 2 Komm mit!, Chapter 12

KAPITEL 12 Chapter Test Score Sheet

Circle the letter that matches the most appropriate response.

I. Listening
Maximum Score: 30 points

A. (15 points)

1. a b c d
2. a b c d
3. a b c d
4. a b c d
5. a b c d

SCORE [ ]

B. (15 points)

6. a b
7. a b
8. a b
9. a b
10. a b

11. a b
12. a b
13. a b
14. a b
15. a b

SCORE [ ]

II. Reading
Maximum Score: 30 points

C. (15 points)

16. a b c d e
17. a b c d e
18. a b c d e
19. a b c d e
20. a b c d e

SCORE [ ]

D. (15 points)

21. a b c d
22. a b c d
23. a b c d
24. a b c d
25. a b c d

SCORE [ ]

III. Culture
Maximum Score: 10 points

E. (10 points)

26. a b
27. a b
28. a b
29. a b
30. a b

31. a b
32. a b
33. a b
34. a b
35. a b

SCORE [ ]

KAPITEL 12

IV. **Writing**

F. (15 points)

_____
_____
_____
_____
_____
_____
_____
_____
_____
_____

SCORE [   ]

G. (15 points)

_____
_____
_____
_____
_____
_____
_____
_____
_____
_____

SCORE [   ]

TOTAL SCORE [   ]

Listening Scripts for Quizzes 12-1B, 12-2B, 12-3B

Quiz 12-1B Kapitel 12 Erste Stufe

I. Listening

A.
HENRY Wohin möchtest du am liebsten reisen?

AGNES Ich würde gern mal an die Küste der Normandie fahren. Das soll sehr schön sein — und romantisch. Wir könnten an den Klippen entlang wandern, vielleicht mit einer Fähre auf eine Insel hinausfahren. Und die Küche in der Normandie ist natürlich etwas ganz Besonderes.

HENRY Hmm. Und wie ist dein Französisch?

AGNES Es geht schon. Als Schülerin war ich ein Jahr auf einem Internat in der Schweiz, bei Lausanne.

HENRY Ich spreche nicht so gern Französisch. Eigentlich würde ich Skandinavien vorziehen, sagen wir mal Norwegen. Da würdest du auch schöne Klippen bewundern können, und die Bedienung kann meistens Englisch.

AGNES Aber in Norwegen warst du schon mehrere Male, nicht wahr?

HENRY Eben. Da kenne ich mich aus. In einer stillen Bucht dort segeln oder schwimmen ist herrlich, sag ich dir. Wenn du willst, können wir meinetwegen auf einer Insel wohnen.

AGNES Ist Norwegen im Juni nicht noch ziemlich kalt?

HENRY Das kann sein — das weiß ich nicht genau. Ich schlage vor, wir fliegen nach Marokko und suchen uns ein schönes Hotel mit einem Swimmingpool. Da habe ich einen Geheimtipp vom Reiseclub Mediterranean™ — eine ganz preiswerte Pauschalreise, inklusive Bedienung. Und das Personal soll Französisch und Englisch sprechen.

AGNES So geheim ist dieser Marokko-Reisetipp gewiss nicht, Henry. Das ist eben so eine Massenreise mit überbuchten Flügen und überfüllten Hotel-Restaurants, wo du Schlange stehen musst, wenn du bloß eine Tasse Kaffee trinken willst. Ich will doch lieber alleine mit dir mit dem Auto fahren — ans Meer!

Quiz 12-2B Kapitel 12 Zweite Stufe

I. Listening

A.
VATER Udo, iss doch deine Pasta! Das Hauptgericht kommt bald.

UDO Ich warte auf die Soße. Spaghetti ohne Soße schmeckt mir nicht.

VATER Das sind keine Spaghetti. Das sind Fettucine. Und die Soße ist schon drauf: Olivenöl mit Champignons, Anschovis und Parmesan Käse. Und nimm den Ellbogen bitte vom Tisch, Udo!

UDO Eigentlich hätte ich lieber eine Pizza.

VATER Pizza ist süditalienisch. Wir sind hier in Mailand, im Norden von Italien.

UDO Trotzdem. Ich habe von einer aus meiner Klasse gehört, dass es ein sehr gutes Pizza-Lokal hier gleich beim Bahnhof gibt. Die Pizza soll ausgezeichnet sein.

VATER Na, sieh mal. Jetzt bringt uns der Ober die Teller mit dem Hauptgericht. Grazie, Signore. Bellissimo!

UDO Das sieht doch aus wie ein ganz gewöhnliches Wiener Schnitzel.

VATER Schmeckt aber ganz anders. Das ist Scalloppini a la Milanese. Das wird dir bestimmt besser schmecken als Pizza.

UDO Woraus besteht das denn?

VATER Udo, ich bezweifle, dass der Herr deine Frage versteht.

BEDIENUNG Doch. Das ist Kalbfleisch — ein Kotelett mit Semmelbröseln und Käse in Butter überbacken. Aber wenn du lieber eine Pizza essen würdest, darf ich dir unsere Hauspizza vorschlagen?

VATER Sie sprechen aber ausgezeichnet Deutsch!

BEDIENUNG Ich studiere in München und komme nur in den Ferien hierher zu meinen Verwandten, um bei dem Ansturm von deutschen Touristen auszuhelfen. Ja, wie wär's nun mit der Pizza?

UDO Danke — aber ich glaube, ich probiere die Scalloppini — sieht doch lecker aus!

MUTTER Das ist toll, Udo. Und übrigens, nimm den Ellbogen bitte vom Tisch!

Quiz 12-3B Kapitel 12 Dritte Stufe

I. Listening

A.
BERTRAM Heinemanns haben uns auf eine Fete eingeladen. Was ziehst du an?

HELGA Es kommt darauf an, was für eine Fete es ist. Soll ich mich lieber salopp oder elegant anziehen? Ziehst du den sportlichen Look vor?

BERTRAM Also, Heinemanns feiern ihre Silberhochzeit, 25 Jahre! Da die meisten Gäste etwas älter sind, werden sie sich höchstwahrscheinlich gut anziehen. Die Fete findet in einem Hotel-Restaurant statt — im Hotel Adler.

HELGA Das hättest du mir doch gleich sagen können! Trägst du denn Fliege oder Krawatte?

BERTRAM Nur Sakko und Krawatte.

HELGA In diesem Fall brauche ich kein langes Abendkleid tragen. Also, ich könnte den schwarzen Faltenrock anziehen, den ich sonst trage, wenn ich im Orchester Flöte spiele, und dazu kaufe ich mir eine neue Bluse, in einer hellen Farbe, vielleicht eine seidene Bluse mit kurzen Ärmeln. Was meinst du?

BERTRAM Prima! Es wird bestimmt eine tolle Fete, denn im Hotel Adler gibt's immer gutes Essen.

Answers to Quizzes 12-1A, 12-1B

ANSWERS Quiz 12-1A

A. (14 points; 1 point per item)
1. der Zehnkämpfer
2. der Geheimtip
3. abwechslungsreich
4. der Anfänger
5. sich langweilen
6. zahlreich
7. das Fahrrad-Depot
8. die Klippe
9. der Erfahrene
10. der Fortgeschrittene
11. die Anlage
12. die Bucht
13. die Küste
14. die Insel

B. (14 points; 1 point per item)
15. bin
16. geflogen
17. haben
18. verbracht
19. hat
20. gemacht
21. haben
22. gespielt
23. sind
24. geschwommen
25. sind
26. gewandert
27. sind
28. gegangen

C. (7 points; 1 point per item)
29. waren
30. war
31. warst
32. war
33. wart
34. waren
35. war

ANSWERS Quiz 12-1B

I. Listening

A. (8 points: 2 points per item)
1. a. coast (of Normandy) / Agnes
   b. Norway / Henry
   c. Morocco / Henry
2. the weather / too cold

II. Reading

B. (10 points: 2 points per item)
3. T
4. F
5. F
6. F
7. T

III. Writing

C. (12 points: 4 points per sentence)
Answers will vary.

IV. Culture

D. (10 points)
8. a restaurant serving local or regional specialties (4 points)
9. a restaurant with an outdoor eating area; you can bring your own food (4 points)
10. hot dogs, hamburgers, fast food (2 points)

ANSWERS Quiz 12-2A

A. (10 points; 1 point per item)
1. Paella
2. Fettucine
3. Crêpes Suzette
4. Tacos
5. Schisch-Kebab
6. Moussaka
7. Couscous
8. Steak
9. Wiener Schnitzel
10. Gulasch

B. (20 points; 2 points per item)
11. mach
12. Vergiss
13. nimm
14. geh
15. hol
16. Trink
17. kauf
18. bring
19. mach
20. Schreib

ANSWERS Quiz 12-2B

I. Listening

A. (8 points: 2 points per item)
1. because there is no sauce
2. pizza / Wiener Schnitzel
3. veal
4. he studies in Munich

II. Reading

B. (6 points: 2 points per item)
5. a small island of Hawaii / tourists
6. not to eat the fish
7. cooking it over boiling water / steaming it

III. Writing

C. (16 points: 4 points per sentence)
Answers will vary. Possible answers:
8. Ich habe gehört, dass die Fajitas sehr gut sind.
9. Aber iss ja das Steak nicht!
10. Was bekommen Sie?
11. Ich hätte gern die Fajitas.

ANSWERS Quiz 12-3A

A. (20 points; 1 point per item)
1. -
2. es
3. -
4. es
5. e
6. e
7. en
8. en
9. em
10. em
11. en
12. e
13. e
14. e
15. e
16. en
17. en
18. e
19. e
20. e

B. (5 points; 1 point per item)
21. besser
22. älter
23. teurer
24. neuer
25. mehr

C. (10 points: 1 point per item)
26. e
27. e
28. en
29. en
30. en
31. en
32. es
33. e
34. e
35. e

ANSWERS Quiz 12-3B

I. Listening

A. (10 points: 2 points per item)
1. salopp (*casual*) / elegant
2. at a hotel restaurant
3. a pleated black skirt and new blouse
4. jacket and tie
5. The food is supposed to be very good.

II. Reading

B. (8 points: 2 points per item)
6. synthetics
7. uniforms   pessimists
8. pretty, individualistic   optimists clothing
9. comfortable

III. Writing

C. (12 points: 4 points per sentence)
Answers will vary.

Scripts for Chapter Test Kapitel 12

I. Listening

A.

FRED   Weißt du, was ich gern machen würde? Nach Mexiko fahren!

MAX   Kein schlechter Vorschlag. Wie denkst du dir das? Sollen wir in die Hauptstadt fliegen — nach Ciudad Mexico? Oder nach Acapulco?

FRED   Nein, nein. Wir fahren mit dem Auto — mit meinem. Dann können wir überallhin fahren, sogar bis nach Yucatan. Die Kultur in Yucatan würde mich ganz besonders interessieren. Ich habe gehört, dort kann man superbillig in einer Hütte direkt am Strand wohnen und sich ein wenig mit den Mexikanern anfreunden. Vielleicht kann man auch im Meer fischen.

MAX   Wäre das nicht fürchterlich heiß, jetzt im Sommer? Und man hat mir gesagt, dass es dort Ungeziefer gibt und giftige Schlangen, und so was.

FRED   Ach wo! Du hast doch nicht vor Insekten Angst, oder? Und wir würden natürlich eine Sonnenbrille aufsetzen und einen breiten Hut und uns ganz dick mit Sonnencreme einschmieren.

MAX   Und was essen wir? Ich habe gehört, man soll dort kein frisches Obst essen und überhaupt kein Leitungswasser trinken.

FRED   Das schadet nichts. Leitungswasser trinkst du sowieso nicht sehr gern. Cola gibt es doch bestimmt auch.

MAX   Ja, Cola gibt es überall auf der Welt. Und die alte Kultur würde mich doch interessieren. Gab es dort nicht vor den Spaniern schon diese Pyramiden? Warte mal, ich hole meinen Reiseführer. Chichen Itza heißt doch diese historische Stadt, nicht wahr? Aber ich glaube nicht, dass sie an der Küste liegt.

FRED   Max, die Kultur meine ich doch gar nicht! Die Geschichte und die Vorgeschichte sind mir ja egal. Das müssen wir in der Schule lernen! Jetzt sind aber Ferien!

B.

PAT   Was soll ich denn alles mitnehmen? Reicht dieser Koffer? Ich muss viel mitnehmen, nicht wahr?

LUISE   Der Koffer ist zu groß, Pat. Wo willst du den im Zugabteil abstellen? Er passt gar nicht in die Gepäckablage über den Sitzplätzen.

PAT   Ich dachte, wir würden die Koffer hier aufgeben und in den Gepäckwagen bringen lassen.

LUISE   Dann müsstet ihr an jedem Bahnhof eure Koffer aufgeben und am nächsten Bahnhof abholen. Das dauert zu lange. Deine Klassenkameraden machen das bestimmt nicht. Außerdem, wenn du den großen Koffer schleppen würdest, würdest du Schwierigkeiten haben, ihn in den Bus hineinzukriegen, wenn ihr zur Jugendherberge fahrt. Oder du müsstest ihn tragen, wenn ihr zu Fuß geht.

PAT   Was soll ich bloß machen?

LUISE   Ich würde einfach eine Reisetasche nehmen. Am besten eine Schultertasche.

PAT   Aber wo packe ich alle die Sachen hin? Ich brauche ein Kleid, die guten Schuhe, diese weite Hose, die beiden Pullover, den Trainingsanzug, den Regenschirm, die ...

LUISE   Wozu brauchst du das Zeug denn? Ihr fahrt doch nur für acht Tage. Ich würde einen Schlafanzug mitnehmen, zwei oder drei T-Shirts, eine Jeanshose und natürlich Unterwäsche, eine Haarbürste ... und die Zahnbürste!

PAT   Was würdest du anziehen? Für die Reise, meine ich.

LUISE   Ganz einfach: Jeans, ein T-Shirt, Turnschuhe und eine praktische Jacke mit Kapuze, falls es regnet. Und vergiss nicht, einen Pausenbrotbehälter mitzunehmen!

PAT   Einen Pausenbrotbehälter!?

LUISE   Na ja. Wahrscheinlich nehmt ihr jeden Tag von der Jugendherberge belegte Brote mit. Wenn du keinen gut schließenden Pausenbrotbehälter hast, dann riechen deine Klamotten lange nach Wurst und Käse!

Answers to Chapter Test Kapitel 12

I. Listening Maximum Score: 30 points

A. (15 points: 3 points per item)   **B.** (15 points: 1 ½ points per item)

1. c	6. a
2. d	7. a
3. a	8. b
4. b	9. a
5. c	10. b
	11. a
	12. b
	13. b
	14. a
	15. a

II. Reading Maximum Score: 30 points

C. (15 points: 3 points per item)   **D.** (15 points: 3 points per item)

16. b	21. c
17. c	22. a
18. e	23. d
19. a	24. b
20. a	25. b

III. Culture Maximum Score: 10 points

E. (10 points: 1 point per item)

26. a
27. b
28. b
29. b
30. a
31. b
32. a
33. b
34. a
35. a

IV. Writing Maximum Score: 30 points

F. (15 points: 3 points per sentence)
Answers will vary.

G. (15 points: 3 points per sentence)
Answers will vary.

I. Listening

A. Anna and Tina are sisters. Read the following statements before you listen to their conversation. After you listen, mark the statements **a)** true or **b)** false. (10 points)

_____ 1. Elke Meier is having a birthday party.

_____ 2. Tina had already decided to wear her jeans with lots of zippers on them.

_____ 3. She'd like to wear her "sloppy" shirt with the jeans.

_____ 4. Her camisole top is out of style.

_____ 5. Anna thinks Tina should wear her shirt that looks like an American flag.

_____ 6. Tina likes that idea because she has worn the shirt to school a lot.

_____ 7. Tina will have to spend at least half the money she earned in order to buy a present to take to the party.

_____ 8. Tina has a record of taking good care of any clothes she borrows from Anna.

_____ 9. Tina can't buy anything new to wear because she didn't get paid.

_____ 10. Tina wasn't planning to try to borrow anything from Anna this week.

B. You are about to hear several people giving directions from the **Hauptbahnhof** to different locations in the Dresden **Altstadt**. Follow the directions on the map and determine to which destination each set of directions leads. (10 points)

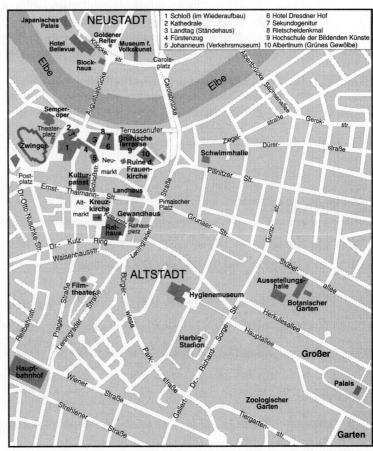

City map of "Dresden" aus *Baedeker Allianz Reiseführer Dresden.* Fourth Edition. Reprinted by permission of *Baedeker.*

_____ 11. a. Rathaus
            b. Kulturpalast
            c. Semperoper
            d. Ruine der
                Frauenkirche

_____ 12. a. Kreuzkirche
            b. Gewandhaus
            c. Schloss
            d. Neumarkt

_____ 13. a. Botanischer
                Garten
            b. Hygienemuseum
            c. Palais
            d. Schwimmhalle

_____ 14. **a.** Schwimmhalle   **c.** Rathaus
     b. Albertinum   **d.** Hochschule für Musik

_____ 15. **a.** Semperoper   **c.** Kulturpalast
     b. Zwinger   **d.** Kreuzkirche

C. Kathy is an American exchange student who has been living in Germany. Listen to her conversation with some of her friends at a party, and then complete each statement by choosing the best answer from among the alternatives given. (10 points)

_____ 16. The person hosting this party is
     a. Magda.   **c.** Henno.
     b. Kathy.   **d.** Kurt.

_____ 17. From Magda's remarks, it is clear that she
     a. will accept some more food.
     b. doesn't really care for American food.
     c. liked the roasted chicken.
     d. thinks American mustard is too spicy.

_____ 18. From Kathy's remarks, we can conclude that
     a. she's embarrassed about her German.
     b. she wishes she could get American food in Germany.
     c. she's not interested in cooking.
     d. she's been going to a German school all year.

_____ 19. From the conversation, we can conclude that
     a. Henno has passed his graduation exams (**Abitur**).
     b. it's Henno's birthday today.
     c. Henno needs to go home early and study.
     d. Henno and Kurt are in the same class in school.

_____ 20. Kathy's friends think that she
     a. should work harder on her German accent.
     b. has become "typically German" about accepting compliments.
     c. is too free and easy with her compliments.
     d. was always shy about being complimented.

II. Reading

Maximum Score: 30 points

A. Monika is on an exchange visit to Japan. Read the following excerpt from one of her letters home to Germany, and then complete the statements that follow. (10 points)

> *Jetzt will ich dir vom ersten Sonntagsfrühstück erzählen. Das war auch ganz lustig, du! Natürlich hat es Reis gegeben. Reis ist ja für die Japaner wie für uns das Brot — sie essen den nämlich morgens, abends und zwischendurch.*
>
> *Dazu hat es ein Ei gegeben. Ich habe natürlich gedacht, das Ei wäre gekocht. Meine Gastgeberin hat mich gerade noch davon abhalten können, es zu köpfen! Es war nämlich roh. Die anderen haben das Ei über dem Reis aufgeschlagen und darunter*

gemischt. Zum Glück hat es aber auch eine Suppe gegeben — eine klare Brühe. Da habe ich mein Ei runtergemischt. Die Brühe war eigentlich aus Fisch und einem Sojaprodukt — Miso nennen sie das — und hat mir ziemlich versalzen geschmeckt.

Es gab keine Wurst, stattdessen hatten wir zum Reis ein Stückchen gebratenen Fisch, so ähnlich wie Salzhering, aber mit Sojasoße gewürzt. Käse ist anscheinend nicht so beliebt, oder nur eine Weichkäsesorte, die wie unreifer Camembert schmeckt. Zum Trinken hatten wir anstatt Kaffee den japanischen Tee — also den grünen Tee, den man ohne Zucker und Milch trinkt.

Als die Familie mich gefragt hat, ob mir das Frühstück geschmeckt hat, habe ich natürlich glatt gelogen und gesagt, es wäre „oishii, oishii!" (sehr lecker!). Dann hat mir der Vater auf Deutsch erklärt, das hätten sie nun extra für mich gekocht. Normalerweise werden wir „modern" frühstücken: mit einem Butterbrötchen, einem gekochten Ei, etwas Obst und Bohnenkaffee mit Milch. Darüber bin ich sehr froh!

_____ 21. Monika says that rice is
    a. one of her very favorite foods.
    b. served once a day in Japan.
    c. better when it's mixed with a raw egg.
    d. the Japanese "daily bread."

_____ 22. Monika's breakfast included all of the following EXCEPT
    a. rice.
    b. bacon.
    c. fish.
    d. eggs.

_____ 23. The host family served Monika a raw egg because
    a. that was what they usually ate on Sunday mornings.
    b. they wanted to play a little joke on her.
    c. they wanted her to experience a traditional Japanese breakfast.
    d. they were very old fashioned people.

_____ 24. When Monika said that the breakfast was delicious, she was
    a. telling the truth.
    b. trying to be polite.
    c. hoping to have the same meal often.
    d. trying to be funny.

_____ 25. We can assume from this letter that Monika
    a. has lived in Japan for several years.
    b. is not really in Japan.
    c. has recently arrived in Japan.
    d. wants to go back to Germany.

FINAL EXAM

B. Look over the questions before reading the passage. Then, with the questions in mind, read the passage carefully and choose the best answers from among the alternatives given. (10 points)

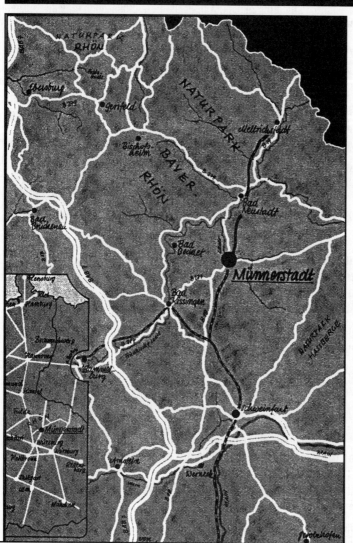

Hand auf's Herz — kennen Sie Münnerstadt? — Nein!? Dann machen Sie es doch wie viele und suchen Sie abseits der bekannten Wege einmal die echte Überraschung. Sie werden Münnerstadt entdecken. Nur wenige Minuten von der A 7 stoßen Sie auf die B 19, eine der alten Handelstraßen Deutschlands. Und plötzlich öffnen sich vor Ihnen die Tore Münnerstadts! Sie fühlen sich zurückversetzt in die Zeiten von Mittelalter und Barock. Sie wandern durch eine andere Welt — ruhiger, gemütlicher, vielleicht menschlicher als anderswo. Hier läßt sich's leben, hier fühlt man sich wohl.

Umgeben von bekannten Kurorten wie Bad Kissingen, Bad Bocklet, Bad Neustadt/Saale und Bad Königshofen — Münnerstadt liegt in einer ausgesprochen „gesunden Ecke". Die B 19 bringt Sie direkt hierher. Von der BAB 7 sind es nur rund 30 Minuten — von Süden über die Ausfahrt „Schweinfurt", von Norden über die Ausfahrt „Bad Kissingen". Die Bundesbahn fährt Sie über Würzburg und Schweinfurt mitten in unsere alte Stadt. Hier beginnt der Naturpark „Bayrische Rhön" und gleich um die Ecke erwartet Sie der Naturpark „Haßberge" — unverfälschte Landschaften von einzigartiger Schönheit und eigenartigem Reiz.

Area map of Münnerstadt and excerpts from brochure, *Münnerstadt Naturpark Bayerische Rhön* by Bruno Eckert, E. Riescher, map by E. Riescher. Reprinted by permission of **Stadt Münnerstadt.**

_____ 26. This passage most likely appeared in a
  a. German high school textbook.
  b. a newspaper.
  c. a travel brochure.
  d. a magazine.

_____ 27. The passage implies that
  a. Münnerstadt is a common stop for tourists in Germany.
  b. many people have not yet discovered Münnerstadt.
  c. Münnerstadt is a well-known industrial center.
  d. Münnerstadt would not be an interesting place to visit.

_____ 28. **Münnerstadt liegt in einer ausgesprochen „gesunden Ecke"** refers to the fact that
  a. there are many doctors and hospitals in the town.
  b. there are many health spas in the area.
  c. the health clinic is on the corner.
  d. people in town rarely get sick.

Holt German 2 Komm mit!, Final Exam

_____ 29. **B 19**, **A7**, and **BAB** 7 are probably
     a. airports.
     b. highway exits.
     c. highways.
     d. famous health spas.

_____ 30. Münnerstadt would probably be a good vacation spot for someone who
     a. wants to relax and enjoy nature.
     b. wants to visit a modern German city.
     c. likes to experience exciting nightlife.
     d. wants to go to the beach.

C. After each of the numbered paragraphs, choose the one answer that summarizes the paragraph or best completes the thought. (10 points)

_____ 31. Erik sagt:
„Mein Vater ist der Meinung, wir sollen aufs Land ziehen, oder wenigstens in einen Vorort. Einerseits stimme ich ihm zu, weil hier die Luft immer so stickig ist und der Verkehr wirklich lebensgefährlich ist. Aber auf der anderen Seite
     a. hat er eigentlich schon Recht."
     b. bin ich dagegen, weil ich auf dem Land wohnen möchte."
     c. ziehe ich die Großstadt vor, weil hier immer was los ist."
     d. würde ich lieber den Großstadtlärm vermeiden."

_____ 32. Ulrike sagt:
„Ich weiß nicht, was für eine Bluse ich kaufen soll. Meine Mutter hat mir gesagt, ich soll ja keine heißen Farben tragen — also kein Knallgelb oder Feuerrot — und ja nichts mit horizontalen Streifen oder Ringelmuster. ‚Zieh dir auch nichts an, was dich breiter macht'. Sie meint
     a. Feuerrot passt gut zu meiner Hautfarbe."
     b. die Bluse mit Ringelmuster ist mir zu weit."
     c. ich sehe doch in Knallgelb sehr gut aus."
     d. horizontale Streifen stehen mir nicht."

_____ 33. Klaus sagt:
„Am liebsten möchte ich die Ferien auf einer Dude Ranch in Arizona verbringen. Da könnte ich reiten und mit dem Lasso Stiere fangen lernen und mit anderen Jungen in einem Bunkhaus wohnen. Ich habe einen Reiseprospekt dafür. Aber meine Eltern sind dagegen, bloß weil ich in Mathe eine Fünf habe und in Latein eine Vier. Deshalb muss ich zu Hause bleiben und Nachhilfeunterricht nehmen."
     a. Klaus wird in diesem Sommer Cowboy spielen.
     b. Klaus würde gern eine Dude Ranch besuchen.
     c. Klaus wäre gern Cowboy.
     d. Klaus hätte gern Nachhilfe in Mathe und Latein.

_____ 34. Martina sagt:
„Was ich gern machen würde? Wenn ich ganz viel Geld hätte, würde ich die Ferien in Cannes am Mittelmeer verbringen. Da würde ich in einem Hotel mit Pool und Wellenbad und Sauna und Diskothek wohnen. Bekannte von meiner Schwester waren mal da, und sie sagten, sie haben ganz viele Filmstars dort gesehen."
     a. Martina bezweifelt, dass viele Filmstars Cannes besuchen.
     b. Martina ist sicher, dass viele Filmstars in Cannes wohnen.
     c. Martina hat gehört, dass viele Filmstars Cannes besuchen.
     d. Martina ist nicht sicher, ob sie in diesem Sommer Cannes besucht.

FINAL EXAM

_____ 35. Rosa sagt:

„Mir ist es eigentlich egal, was die Politiker sagen. Ich würde natürlich lieber in einem Einfamilienhaus wohnen als in diesem schäbigen Wohnblock. Und wer hätte es nicht gern, wenn die Umwelt schön sauber wäre? Aber ich schaue keine politischen Diskussionen an, weil

   a. ich mich nicht dafür interessiere, wenn die Leute bloß reden und nichts tun."
   b. ich mich darauf freue, wenn sie über ihre Zukunftspläne sprechen."
   c. ich keine Ahnung habe, worüber die Leute sprechen sollen."
   d. ich nicht sicher bin, ob die Leute über etwas sprechen, was mich interessiert."

III. Culture

Maximum Score: 10 points

A. Choose the best answer from among the alternatives given. (10 points)

_____ 36. Common complaints that Germans voice about their cities include all of the following EXCEPT
   a. stickige Luft
   b. viel Verkehr
   c. Lärm
   d. öffentliche Verkehrsmittel

_____ 37. The population density of Germany is
   a. about twice that of the United States.
   b. more than eight times that of the United States.
   c. about the same as the state of Oregon.
   d. mostly concentrated in and around Berlin.

_____ 38. One German "fashion" that you probably can't buy in your local department store is
   a. Tracht
   b. Smoking
   c. Lackschuhe
   d. Sakko

_____ 39. The majority of vacationing Germans travel by
   a. airplane.
   b. bus.
   c. train.
   d. automobile.

_____ 40. Getting a driver's license in Germany costs about
   a. five dollars if you take a driving class at school.
   b. about 1,500 euros.
   c. fifty to one hundred dollars.
   d. about 150 euros.

_____ 41. Public television in Germany is paid for by
   a. charitable grants and local fund-raising drives from viewers.
   b. the federal government.
   c. license fees levied on all TV sets in homes, etc.
   d. advertising sponsors alone.

_____ 42. If you go to a restaurant that advertises **gutbürgerliche Küche**, you can expect
   a. an elegant decor and a long wine list.
   b. home-style cooking.
   c. German-style fast food.
   d. cafeteria style self-service.

_____ 43 If you take an excursion from Berlin to Potsdam, you probably intend to see
   a. den Berliner Dom
   b. das Schloss Sanssouci
   c. die Reste der Mauer
   d. das Pergamonmuseum

_____ 44. If you go to a German **Lokal,** it's NOT acceptable to
   a. seat yourself at the **Stammtisch** unless you are a regular there.
   b. take your dog in with you.
   c. ask if you can join other people at their table.
   d. wear cutoffs or a running suit.

_____ 45. If you go to a **Biergarten** in Germany, it is usually acceptable to
   a. bring your own food and beverage.
   b. bring your own cola.
   c. act rowdy.
   d. bring your own sandwiches if you buy a cola.

IV. Writing
Maximum Score: 30 points

A. Someone asks you the location of each of the following places in Dresden. Using the map of Dresden from Listening Activity B, give at least two types of information that will orient the person to each location. (10 points)

BEISPIEL   **Das Albertinum liegt am Neumarkt, nicht weit von der Carolabrücke, neben der Hochschule.**

1. das Museum für Volkskunst

_____

_____

2. das Rathaus

_____

_____

3. das Johanneum (Verkehrsmuseum)

_____

_____

4. das Schloss

_____

_____

5. die Semperoper

_____

_____

FINAL EXAM

B. Your pen pal is coming to visit for two weeks so you have planned some activities, including a short trip to an interesting place near your town. Write to your friend and tell him or her what you could do and make suggestions as to what he or she should bring to wear. Also mention one or two things he or she should be sure to bring, as well as anything he or she definitely should not bring along. (10 points)

_____

_____

_____

_____

_____

_____

_____

_____

C. You are writing to your pen pal about your summer plans. First tell what you definitely will do this summer. Then dream a little. If you had no limits on money or time, where would you go and what would you do? What would interest you there? (10 points)

_____

_____

_____

_____

_____

_____

_____

_____

FINAL EXAM

Name _____ Klasse _____ Datum _____

Final Exam Score Sheet

Circle the letter that matches the most appropriate response.

I. Listening
Maximum Score: 30 points

A. (10 points)   **B.** (10 points)   **C.** (10 points)

1. a b	11. a b c d	16. a b c d
2. a b	12. a b c d	17. a b c d
3. a b	13. a b c d	18. a b c d
4. a b	14. a b c d	19. a b c d
5. a b	15. a b c d	20. a b c d
6. a b		
7. a b	SCORE [＿＿＿]	SCORE [＿＿＿]
8. a b		
9. a b		
10. a b		

SCORE [＿＿＿]

II. Reading
Maximum Score: 30 points

A. (10 points)   **B.** (10 points)   **C.** (10 points)

21. a b c d	26. a b c d	31. a b c d e
22. a b c d	27. a b c d	32. a b c d e
23. a b c d	28. a b c d	33. a b c d e
24. a b c d	29. a b c d	34. a b c d e
25. a b c d	30. a b c d	35. a b c d e

SCORE [＿＿＿]   SCORE [＿＿＿]   SCORE [＿＿＿]

FINAL EXAM

III. Culture

Maximum Score: 10 points

A. (10 points)

36. a b c d

37. a b c d

38. a b c d

39. a b c d

40. a b c d

41. a b c d

42. a b c d

43. a b c d

44. a b c d

45. a b c d

SCORE [   ]

IV. Writing

Maximum Score: 30 points

A. (10 points)

1. _____
   _____

2. _____
   _____

3. _____
   _____

4. _____
   _____

5. _____
   _____

SCORE [   ]

B. (10 points)

_____

_____

_____

_____

_____

_____

_____

_____

_____

_____

SCORE [ ]

C. (10 points)

_____

_____

_____

_____

_____

_____

_____

_____

_____

_____

SCORE [ ]

TOTAL SCORE [ ]

FINAL EXAM

Listening Scripts for Final Exam

I. Listening

A.

TINA Du, Anna, ich bin Samstagabend zu einer Fete eingeladen, bei Elke.

ANNA Elke Meier? Prima! Die gibt doch tolle Partys, nicht wahr? Was wirst du anziehen?

TINA Das ist es eben. Ich weiß es echt nicht.

ANNA Also, zieh doch die neue Jeans mit den vielen Reißverschlüssen an!

TINA Ja, aber was dazu? Das weite Hemd mit dem Ringelmuster bestimmt nicht — viel zu salopp. Dann habe ich noch das weiße Trägerhemd, aber das passt schlecht zu dieser Jeans.

ANNA Madonna ist sowieso nicht mehr in Mode. Zieh dir doch das rot-weiß gestreifte Hemd mit den Sternchen an — dein USA-Hemd, mein ich.

TINA Aber dieses Hemd habe ich leider schon öfters zur Schule getragen.

ANNA Weißt du, was ich machen würde? Du hast doch vorgestern von deiner Nachhilfeschülerin 30 Euro bekommen, nicht wahr? Ich würde mir was Neues kaufen.

TINA Kann ich nicht. Ich muss ein Geschenk mit auf die Fete nehmen. Elke hat Geburtstag. Dafür werde ich mindestens 15 Euro ausgeben müssen. Kannst du mir nicht etwas zum Anziehen leihen, Anna? Bitte!

ANNA Ach ne! Also, Schwesterchen, von mir kriegst du gar keine Klamotten mehr zum Anziehen. Das letzte Mal, als du meine seidene Bluse in der Diskothek anhattest, hast du Cola darauf geschüttet. Die Reinigung hat das nicht mehr rausgekriegt. Wie das Loch reingekommen ist, weiß ich noch immer nicht. Nein, nein!

TINA Aber Anna, dein Hemd mit dem Giraffenaufdruck würde doch ganz prima zu meiner neuen Hose passen!

B.

11. So weit ist es ja nicht. Also, gehen Sie hier über die Wiener Straße. Da sehen Sie schräg gegenüber von uns die Pragerstraße. Das ist eine Fußgängerzone. Gehen Sie die Pragerstraße immer weiter geradeaus, über die Waisenhausstraße und den Külz-Ring bis zum Altmarkt. Sie gehen dann über den Marktplatz geradeaus, und auf der anderen Seite des Marktplatzes in die Schlossstraße. Gehen Sie in die Schlossstraße hinein, und da werden Sie die schon sehen. Die steht mitten auf dem Neumarktplatz.

12. Also, sehen Sie da drüben die Pragerstraße? Sie gehen die Straße entlang, bis Sie zum Altmarkt kommen. Auf der rechten Seite werden Sie dort die Kreuzkirche sehen. Gehen Sie an der Kirche vorbei und gleich danach biegen Sie nach rechts in die Kreuzstraße ein. Das werden Sie bald links sehen, an der Ecke, gegenüber vom Rathaus.

13. Gehen Sie zuerst die Wiener Straße rechts runter. Dann biegen Sie nach links in die Gellertstraße ein und gehen weiter geradeaus auf der Dr.-Richard-Sorger-Straße, bis Sie zur Hauptallee kommen. Da gehen Sie nach rechts und dann geradeaus. Da direkt vor Ihnen ist der Eingang.

14. Gehen Sie vom Hauptbahnhof in der Wiener Straße nach links in die Leningrader Straße. Die gehen Sie immer geradeaus bis Sie zur Pillnitzer Straße kommen. Sie biegen dann rechts in die Pillnitzer Straße ein. Gleich auf der linken Seite ist sie.

15. Gehen Sie die Wiener Straße links hinunter. Dann biegen Sie nach rechts in die Reitbahnstraße ein. Sie gehen dann immer geradeaus und weiter geradeaus auf der Dr.-Otto-Nuschke-Straße, bis Sie zum Postplatz kommen. Vom Postplatz aus sehen Sie den schon direkt vor Ihnen.

FINAL EXAM

c.

KATHY Bitte, bedient euch, doch! Magda, noch ein bisschen Brathendl? Brustfleisch und Flügel sind leider alle, aber „Drumsticks" gibt's noch in Mengen.

MAGDA Danke, Kathy. Das hat aber geschmeckt. Und wie! Ich habe mich wirklich satt gegessen. Aber sag doch mal, wie machst du eigentlich diese „Baked Beans"?

KATHY Tja, die werden im Ofen gebacken, ganz ganz langsam, mit Melasse. Das ist so ein Nebenprodukt von Zucker. Und der Geheimtipp: ein wenig Senf daruntermischen.

HENNO Nun, euer amerikanischer Senf ist ein bisschen schärfer als der bei uns, glaube ich jedenfalls.

MAGDA Schmeckt aber echt herzhaft. Findest du nicht, Henno?

HENNO Ja, stimmt. Übrigens sprichst du ausgezeichnet deutsch, Kathy.

KATHY Meinst du?

HENNO Doch. Doch.

KATHY Na, es geht schon. Viel schlechter als vor 10 Monaten, als ich zu Magda in die Klasse gekommen bin, dürfte es ja eigentlich nicht sein.

MAGDA Na, siehst du, Kathy. Du bist schon so lange hier, dass du keine Komplimente mehr akzeptieren kannst. Früher hast du immer nur danke gesagt und süß gelächelt.

KATHY Lächeln kann ich immer noch. Ja, und nun wollen wir endlich dem Henno zum bestandenen Abitur gratulieren. Auf dein Wohl, Henno!

MAGDA Zum Wohl!

KURT Prost, Henno! Gratuliere!

Answers to Final Exam

I. Listening Maximum Score: 30 points

A. (10 points: 1 point per item)
1. a
2. a
3. b
4. a
5. a
6. b
7. a
8. b
9. b
10. b

B. (10 points: 2 points per item)
11. d
12. b
13. c
14. a
15. b

C. (10 points: 2 points per item)
16. b
17. c
18. d
19. a
20. b

II. Reading Maximum Score: 30 points

A. (10 points: 2 points per item)
21. d
22. b
23. c
24. b
25. c

B. (10 points: 2 points per item)
26. c
27. b
28. b
29. c
30. a

C. (10 points: 2 points per item)
31. c
32. d
33. b
34. c
35. a

III. Culture Maximum Score: 10 points

A. (10 points: 1 point per item)
36. d
37. b
38. a
39. d
40. b
41. c
42. b
43. b
44. a
45. d

IV. Writing Maximum Score: 30 points

A. (10 points: 2 points per item) Answers will vary.
B. (10 points) Answers will vary.
C. (10 points) Answers will vary.

To the Teacher

Speaking Tests

The primary goal of **Komm mit!** is to help students develop proficiency in German. These speaking tests have been designed to help assess students' proficiency in listening to and speaking German. The speaking tests, which measure how well students use the language in contexts that approximate real-life situations, reflect the interview/role-playing format of the Situation Cards in the *Activities for Communication* ancillary. You can choose whether to set up interviews with each student, role-play the short situations with individual students, or have pairs of students role-play the situations spontaneously as you observe.

Administering a speaking test requires approximately three to five minutes with each student or pair of students. You might administer a speaking test to one student or pair while the others are working on the reading and writing sections of a Chapter Test. Make sure that you and the student(s) are seated far enough from the others so that they will not be disturbed. Instruct the student(s) to speak in a soft but audible voice. If such an arrangement is not possible, meet with students at mutually agreed-upon times outside class.

The Speaking Test Evaluation Form on page 342 will help you assess each student's performance. At the end of each test, take a moment to note your impression of the student's performance on the evaluation form. The following guidelines offer one possibility for assessing a student's global score, based on this evaluation.

18-20 pts: The student accomplishes the assigned task successfully, speaks clearly and accurately, and brings additional linguistic material to the basic situation; for example, the student uses new functions or structures that beginning language learners seldom use spontaneously.

16-17 pts: The student accomplishes the assigned task successfully with a few errors. The student is able to communicate effectively in spite of these errors and offers meaningful responses.

14-15 pts: The student accomplishes the task with difficulty. He or she demonstrates minimum oral competence, hesitates frequently, and shows little creativity, offering only minimal, predictable responses.

12-13 pts: The student is unable to accomplish the task or fails to demonstrate acceptable mastery of functions, vocabulary, and grammatical concepts.

0-11 pts: Communication is almost nonexistent. The student does not understand the aural cues and is unable to accomplish the task. Errors are so extreme that communication is impossible.

SPEAKING TESTS

Name _____ Class _____ Date _____

Speaking Test Evaluation Form

Chapter _____ ☐ Interview ☐ Role-playing ☐ Other format

Targeted Function(s) _____

_____

_____

Context (Topic) _____

COMPREHENSION (ability to understand aural cues and respond appropriately)	(POOR) 1 2 3 4 (EXCELLENT)	
COMPREHENSIBILITY (ability to communicate ideas and be understood)	(POOR) 1 2 3 4 (EXCELLENT)	
ACCURACY (ability to use structures and vocabulary correctly)	(POOR) 1 2 3 4 (EXCELLENT)	
FLUENCY (ability to communicate clearly and smoothly)	(POOR) 1 2 3 4 (EXCELLENT)	
EFFORT (inclusion of details beyond the minimum predictable response)	(POOR) 1 2 3 4 (EXCELLENT)	

TOTAL POINTS ☐

NOTES:

_____

_____

_____

_____

_____

_____

SPEAKING TESTS

Holt German 2 Komm mit!, Speaking Tests

Bei den Baumanns

Speaking Test

Targeted Functions: asking for and giving information about yourself and others; describing yourself and others; expressing likes and dislikes; identifying people and places; giving and responding to compliments; expressing wishes when buying things; making plans; ordering food and beverages; talking about how something tastes

A. Interview

Provide the student with a photo of a person. Tell the student that he or she just witnessed this person snatching a purse in a park. You are the police officer in charge of taking the deposition. Have the student respond to the following questions in German.
1. Wie groß war der Mann so ungefähr?
2. Beschreiben Sie bitte seine Augen und seine Haare.
3. Wie alt war er ungefähr?
4. Sagen Sie bitte, ob er sportlich aussah.
5. Was hatte er an? Wie sahen seine Klamotten aus?

B. Role-playing

Have pairs of students act out the following situation, or you can act it out with individual students.

You just landed at the Zurich airport to visit your Swiss pen pal. Unfortunately she forgot to pick you up. You call her house and talk to her sister or brother, who agrees to pick you up. Since you two have never seen each other, you need to describe yourself and have him or her describe himself or herself to you.

Bastis Plan

Speaking Test

Targeted Functions: expressing obligations; extending and responding to an invitation; offering help and telling what to do; asking and telling what to do; telling that you need something else; telling where you were and what you bought; discussing gift ideas; expressing likes and dislikes; expressing likes, preferences, and favorites; saying you do or don't want more

A. Interview

You just met a student on his or her way home from the mall. You both just bought presents for your families. Have the student respond to the following questions.
1. Hallo (Linda), wo warst du denn?
2. Was hast du in der Mall (im Einkaufszentrum) gekauft?
3. Was hast du (deiner Mutter und deinem Vater) gekauft?
4. Und was schenkst du (deiner Schwester)?

B. Role-playing

Have pairs of students act out the following situation, or you can act it out with individual students.

Your best friend's house is a mess, and everything must be cleaned up. Your friend asks you to help with several cleaning chores, but you make excuses to avoid helping. You finally give in and ask what you can do to help. Your friend tells you what chores you can do.

Wo warst du in den Ferien?

Speaking Test

Targeted Functions: reporting past events, talking about activities; reporting past events, talking about places; asking how someone liked something; expressing enthusiasm or disappointment; responding enthusiastically or sympathetically

A. Interview

Tell the student that he or she just returned from a trip to Bavaria. Using the **Bayern** Location Opener on pp. 1-3 of the Level 2 *Pupil's Edition* or the **München** Location Opener on pp. 184-187 of the Level 1 *Pupil's Edition*, have the student answer the following questions in German.

1. Hallo (Donna)! Sag mal, du warst in Bayern? Wo warst du denn?
2. Was hast du alles gemacht?
3. *(Depending on student's answers)* Und wie hat dir (**Schloss Kranzbach**) gefallen? Wie war denn (**Kloster Ettal**)?
4. Erzähl von den bayerischen Spezialitäten, die du gegessen hast!
5. Welche Spezialität hat dir besonders gut geschmeckt?

B. Role-playing

Have pairs of students act out the following situation, or you can act it out with individual students.

It's the first day of class. In the school yard, you meet a friend you haven't seen all summer. Ask about his or her vacation. Your friend wants to find out about your vacation, too, and asks you questions about what you did.

Gesund leben

Speaking Test

Targeted Functions: expressing approval and disapproval; asking for information and responding emphatically or agreeing with reservations; asking and telling what you may or may not do

A. Interview

Tell the student that you work for a teen magazine. You're writing a story on teenagers' health habits and the different activities in which they are or are not allowed to take part. Have the student respond to the following questions in German.

1. Darf ich dich etwas fragen? Wie fühlst du dich heute? Und warum?
2. Sag mal, gibt es etwas, was du nicht essen darfst? Und warum?
3. Und wie steht's mit (Fleisch)?
4. Sagen deine Eltern, dass du bestimmte Sachen nicht tun darfst? Welche Sachen denn?
5. Und warum darfst du diese Sachen nicht tun?

B. Role-playing

Have pairs of students act out the following situation, or you can act it out with individual students.

You're at the doctor's office for your annual physical. The doctor asks you questions about your health and comments favorably or unfavorably on the answers you provide. Every time the doctor makes a negative comment about one of your unhealthy habits, you counter by telling him or her about the healthy things you do.

Holt German 2 Komm mit!, Speaking Tests

Gesund essen

Targeted Functions: expressing regret and downplaying; expressing skepticism and making certain; calling someone's attention to something and responding

A. Interview

Tell the student that you are a nutrition expert. You are going to ask a series of questions in order to prepare his or her nutrition profile.

1. Was hast du heute zum Frühstück gegessen?
2. Was isst du denn lieber zum Frühstück? Und am liebsten?
3. Und wie ist es mit dem Mittagessen? Was hast du denn normalerweise auf deinem Sandwich?
4. *(Construct your next question based on student's responses up to this point.)* Du isst wohl viel (Fleisch), was?

B. Role-playing

Have pairs of students act out the following situation, or you can act it out with individual students.

You and your friend are on a picnic together. You were responsible for bringing the main course; your friend was supposed to bring a side dish and something to drink. As you unpack the picnic, ask your friend about the things he or she has brought, and answer his or her questions to you. Talk about the kinds of things you prefer to have on a picnic. If your friend mentions something you didn't bring, be sure to respond regretfully and offer a substitute.

Gute Besserung!

Targeted Functions: inquiring about someone's health and responding; making suggestions, asking about and expressing pain; asking for and giving advice; expressing hope

A. Interview

Have students respond to the following in German.

1. Guten Tag, (Jane)! Wie fühlst du dich?
2. Tut dir was weh? Was denn?
3. *(Feign an illness or injury.)* Mir ist nicht gut!
4. Ich habe (Bauchschmerzen).
5. Was soll ich bloß machen?

B. Role-playing

Have pairs of students act out the following situation, or you can act it out with individual students.

You and your friend are running at the track when your friend suddenly falls and doesn't seem to be able to get up. You rush to your friend and ask questions about how he or she is feeling and what you can do to help. Your friend answers your questions.

KAPITEL 7

Stadt oder Land?

Speaking Test

Targeted Functions: expressing preference and giving a reason; expressing wishes; agreeing with reservations; justifying your answers

A. Interview

Have students respond to the following in German.

1. Sag mal, wo wohnst du am liebsten? Warum?
2. (*Adjust to student's response.*) Ich stimme dir zwar zu, aber das Leben auf dem Land ist todlangweilig *or* das Leben in einer Großstadt ist viel zu hektisch. Was meinst du dazu?
3. Was möchtest du gern haben, wenn du mal hunderttausend Dollar in der Lotterie gewinnen solltest?
4. Und was wünschst du dir für die Umwelt?
5. Bist du ein Lärmmuffel? Was tust du, um Verkehrslärm zu mindern?

B. Role-playing

Have pairs of students act out the following situation, or you can act it out with individual students.

You and your friend would like to go on vacation together, but you can't agree on a destination. You like large cities and she or he is a nature lover. Discuss the pros and cons of a vacation in the city and in the country.

KAPITEL 8

Mode? Ja oder nein?

Speaking Test

Targeted Functions: describing clothes; expressing interest, disinterest, and indifference; making and accepting compliments; persuading and dissuading

A. Interview

Tell the student that you are writing an article on fashion among teenagers. Have the student respond to the following questions in German.

1. Interessierst du dich für Mode? Und warum (nicht)?
2. Deine (Jeans) steht dir aber gut!
3. (*Show student a picture of a model or a movie star.*) Beschreib bitte die Klamotten, die diese Frau (dieser Mann) anhat und sag mir, wie gut sie dir gefallen.
4. Sag mir mal, was heute „in" ist. Was ist denn modisch?

B. Role-playing

Have pairs of students act out the following situation, or you can act it out with individual students. You might want to provide students with a catalog for reference.

You and your friend are shopping for clothes you plan to wear to a party. You each try to persuade the other to buy certain items and also to discourage each other from buying particular items.

SPEAKING TESTS

Holt German 2 Komm mit!, Speaking Tests

Wohin in die Ferien?

Targeted Functions: expressing indecision; asking for and making suggestions; expressing doubt, conviction, and resignation; asking for and giving directions

A. Interview
Tell the student that you are a tourist and you have stopped the student to ask for directions to specific places. Provide the student with a map and show where on the map both of you are standing.
1. Entschuldigung! Wo ist bitte (die Evangelische Kirche)?
2. Und wie komme ich bitte zur (Hauptstraße)?
3. Wissen Sie vielleicht, wie ich (zum Ulrichsbrunnen) komme?
4. Verzeihung! Ich möchte gern (schwimmen gehen). Was soll ich machen? Wohin soll ich fahren?
5. Ich bezweifle, dass ich das (Stadttor) finden kann. Was soll ich machen?

B. Role-playing
Have pairs of students act out the following situation, or you can act it out with individual students.

You and your friend are planning a vacation. You're both athletic, but you have different tastes in sports. Discuss possible destinations for your vacation and talk about the different features these vacation spots might or might not offer.

Viele Interessen!

Targeted Functions: asking about and expressing interest; asking for and giving permission; asking for information and expressing an assumption; expressing surprise, agreement, and disagreement; talking about plans

A. Interview
Have the student respond to the following questions in German.
1. Schaust du Fernsehen? Für welche Programme interessierst du dich?
2. Weißt du, ob heute Abend etwas Besonderes im Fernsehen läuft?
3. Und jetzt in der Schule. Wofür interessierst du dich in der Schule?
4. Sag mal, (Lydia), was wirst du nächsten Monat (*or depending on the season* zu Weihnachten, in den Ferien, zu Ostern) machen?
5. (*Looking at an object nearby, say*) (Lydia), kann ich bitte mal (das Heft) haben?

B. Role-playing
Have pairs of students act out the following situation, or you can act it out with individual students.

You and your cousin want to watch television. Discuss your interests in programs, ask each other for permission to do certain things, and talk about some of the features of your television.

SPEAKING TESTS

Mit Oma ins Restaurant

Targeted Functions: asking for, making, and responding to suggestions; expressing hearsay; ordering in a restaurant; expressing good wishes

A. Interview
Provide the student with the entertainment section of a local newspaper or a German paper if possible. Have him or her respond to the following in German.
1. Was sollen wir am Wochenende machen?
   (*Vary the following questions based on the information in the newspaper.*)
2. Würdest du gern (ins Theater) gehen?
3. Wie wäre es mit („Romeo und Julia")?
4. Was hast du über (dieses Stück) schon gehört? Soll es gut sein?

B. Role-playing
Have pairs of students act out the following situation, or you can act it out with individual students.

> You and your friend would like to eat out. Discuss with him or her the different kinds of restaurants to which you could go. Each of you should also talk about what you heard about the food or entertainment offered at each of the restaurants mentioned.

Die Reinickendorfer Clique

Targeted Functions: reporting past events; asking for, making, and responding to suggestions; ordering food; expressing hearsay and regret; persuading and dissuading; asking for and giving advice; expressing preference; expressing interest, disinterest, and indifference

A. Interview
Have the student respond to the following in German.
1. Ist Mode für dich wichtig? Wofür interessierst du dich?
2. (*Show the student a catalog or some actual pieces of clothing.*) Welche (Hose) findest du schöner, diese (rote Hose) oder die (gestreifte)?
3. Ich geh am Samstag zu einer Fete. Was soll ich anziehen?
4. Nach der Fete gehe ich mit ein paar Freunden essen. Wohin sollen wir gehen? Was schlägst du vor?
5. Hast du schon bei (*restaurant*) gegessen? Was hast du darüber gehört?

B. Role-playing
Have pairs of students act out the following situation, or you can act it out with individual students.

> You meet a friend who just came back from vacation. Ask several questions to find out about what he or she did on vacation, and then suggest that the two of you go to an ethnic restaurant. Your friend can respond positively or negatively to your suggestion.

Holt German 2 Komm mit!, Speaking Tests